Praise for

50 Philosophy Classics

"This book explains and discusses briefly, but with remarkable lucidity, some of the ideas of fifty philosophical thinkers from ancient times to the present day. Complex views on a whole range of important and enduring issues are made accessible to the general reader. A sympathetic account is given of each thinker and his or her thoughts, conveying the insights and capturing some of the excitement of seeing the world and human life from novel, distinctive, or unusual perspectives. The book is both enjoyable and instructive."

C.L. Ten, Professor of Philosophy, National University of Singapore

"*50 Philosophy Classics* is an impressively wide-ranging compendium of nutshell clarity. It strikes just the right balance between accurate explication, insightful contextual analysis, and breezy illustrative anecdote."

Dr. Phil Oliver, Department of Philosophy, Middle Tennessee State University, USA

50 Philosophy Classics

Your shortcut to the most important ideas on being, truth, and meaning

THE GREATEST BOOKS DISTILLED

by Tom Butler-Bowdon

The *50 Classics* series has sold over 500,000 copies

50 Economics Classics, 2nd ed 978-1-39980-099-0 (2022)

50 Philosophy Classics, 2nd ed 978-1-39980-097-6

50 Politics Classics, 2nd ed 978-1-39980-098-3 (2022)

50 Psychology Classics, 2nd ed 978-1-85788-674-0

50 Self-Help Classics, 2nd ed 978-1-47365-828-8

50 Success Classics, 2nd ed 978-1-47365-835-6

50 Spirituality Classics 978-1-47365-838-7

50 Business Classics 978-1-85788-675-7

50 Philosophy Classics

Your shortcut to the most important ideas on being, truth, and meaning

Tom Butler-Bowdon

NICHOLAS BREALEY
PUBLISHING
London • Boston

First published in 2013 by Nicholas Brealey Publishing
An imprint of John Murray Press
An Hachette company

This updated edition first published in 2022

1

British Library Cataloguing-in-Publication Data
A catalogue record for this book is available from the British Library.

ISBN 978 1 399 80097 6
UK eBook ISBN 978 1 399 80436 3
US eBook ISBN 978 1 399 80434 9

Typeset by KnowledgeWorks Global Ltd

Printed and bound in Great Britain by Clays Ltd, Elcograf S.p.A.

John Murray Press policy is to use papers that are natural, renewable and
recyclable products and made from wood grown in sustainable forests. The logging
and manufacturing processes are expected to conform to the environmental
regulations of the country of origin.

Nicholas Brealey Publishing
John Murray Press
Carmelite House
50 Victoria Embankment
London, EC4Y 0DZ, UK
Tel: 020 3122 6000

Nicholas Brealey Publishing
Hachette Book Group
Market Place Center, 53 State Street
Boston, MA 02109, USA
Tel: (617) 523 3801

www.nicholasbrealey.com
www.butler-bowdon.com

Contents

CONTENTS

Preface

SECOND EDITION

Much of the original edition of this book was written in the wood-panelled splendour of Oxford's Bodleian Library. I had access to every possible volume of philosophy, including many older editions. Some of the philosophers I was writing about, from John Locke to A.J. Ayer to Iris Murdoch, had studied or taught in rooms nearby.

The word 'rareified' may come to mind in imagining this scene, and indeed when intensively researching and writing about philosophy, one feels slightly removed from normal life. Yet philosophy should not be seen as an optional extra or a luxury. Exploring it, understanding it, and using it can improve lives, individual and societal.

How the book came about: A decade ago, I had written several books on the literature of personal development and psychology, but was keen to expand my mind by reading the work of history's really great minds. I knew writing this book would not be an easy task; I baulked at the enormity of it. Yet by tackling one title, one philosopher at a time, slowly the book took shape. When published, it found an audience, and continues to do so. I'm grateful for the many readers who have reached out with comments or questions.

Most philosophy introductions are arranged by theme or era. *50 Philosophy Classics* is perhaps idiosyncratic in that it is organized by alphabetical order of the philosophers covered. That means you are free to make your own connections between books and thinkers, whether they are ancient or modern. At any rate, the Introduction does offer some thematic organization.

This revised second edition includes a number of new chapters. They include commentaries on books I wish there had been space for in the original book: Plotinus' *Enneads*, Aquinas' *Summa Theologica*, Isaiah Berlin's *The Hedgehog and the Fox*, and Mary Midgley's *The Myths We Live By*. Though wildly different, just that list alone should give a sense of the diversity of philosophy: respectively ancient, early medieval, modern (20th century), and contemporary (2003 is contemporary in this genre). But even with these huge differences in time, there are threads. Plotinus, Aquinas, and Berlin (channeling Tolstoy), for instance, all point to a universal intelligence that lies beneath everyday reality. Whether we can do anything with that knowledge is another matter, but it's certainly philosophy's domain to try to articulate the ineffable.

This edition also includes new chapters on Judith Butler's *Gender Trouble* (1990) Peter Sloterdijk's *You Must Change Your Life* (2013) and Michael Sandel's *The Tyranny of Merit* (2020). Butler took the feminist philosophy of Simone de Beauvoir as her starting point for a revolutionary new take on the intersection between sex and gender. It caused ructions in academia, but the impact on popular language and thinking about gender in society at large has been even greater. Sloterdijk's book caused a revolution for me personally; having intensively studied the field of personal improvement, what seemed very lacking was a philosophical framework to understand it – that is, why humans are a self-improving species, constantly engaged in practices to transcend themselves. His book certainly provides this, and he's rightly regarded as one of Europe's great contemporary philosophers. Sandel's work as a political philosopher has had a big impact, not least because he is willing to leap the walls of academe and communicate with the wider public. It seems to me that his counterintuitive book on merit explains many of the political and social trends, including dark ones, in Western polities of the last 20 years. Yet Sandel draws on a tradition of political philosophy that goes back over two millennia.

Butler's influences include Lacan, Foucault, and Kristeva; Sloterdijk's main ones are Nietzsche, Heidegger, and Spengler; with Sandel it's Aristotle, Kant, Locke, J.S. Mill, and John Rawls. Each happily admit their debt to earlier philosophers, and their copious references help you realize just how close and interconnected is the tissue of influence in philosophy. The deeper in you go, the more you realize just how large and dense this map of knowledge is.

You may want to read *50 Philosophy Classics* alongside two of my other books, *50 Politics Classics* and *50 Economics Classics*. The publishers and I nicknamed this trilogy "PPE." It's of course a reference to Oxford University's famous Philosophy, Politics, Economics degree, first taught in 1921. PPE was an alternative to a pure Classics curriculum, and was meant to equip students for the modern world (specifically the Civil Service) while sharpening conceptual skills. That it was a great success – alumni include national leaders such as Harold Wilson, David Cameron, Aung San Suu Kyi, Benazir Bhutto, and Bob Hawke, and more recently Malala Yousafzai – suggests that philosophy is a kind of x-factor that enables students to get a uniquely large perspective compared to only studying functional disciplines. Philosophy is a *meta*-discipline, against which all other subjects can be seen and understood. It is hard to really understand the political or economic world, for instance, without studying political philosophy. One needs to go back to first principles about why humans create societies in the first place, the concepts of justice they are based on, and the rights of the individual next to the group. Philosophy does this, and much more.

Not many people get the chance to systematically read a number of great works of philosophy within a relatively short time frame. It was my great good fortune that I was given the opportunity, and then to be able to communicate the most intriguing ideas to the public. Of the books I've written, this one has been the most valuable in terms of opening my eyes to new universes of thinking and seeing the world. I keep coming back to what I learned as the foundation for further research into things such as the history and philosophy of personal development.

No introduction to philosophy can be truly objective, and this one does not claim to be – indeed you may find some of the choices and commentary idiosyncratic. But I still think you will gain something. What stops many people from approaching philosophy is knowing where to start. It seems such a daunting, high-minded subject. This book is only an entry point, but it gets your foot in the door. I hope it takes you to some amazing places.

Tom Butler-Bowdon

Introduction

*"Philosophy is at once the most sublime and the most
trivial of human pursuits. It works in the minutest
crannies and it opens out the widest vistas.
It 'bakes no bread,' as has been said, but it can inspire our souls
with courage; and repugnant as its manners, its doubting and
challenging, its quibbling and dialectics, often are to common people,
no one of us can get along without the far-flashing beams of light it
sends over the world's perspectives."*
William James, Pragmatism

The word philosophy comes from the Greek *philo* (love) and *sophia*
(wisdom). Both as a discipline and as a personal outlook, philosophy is
about the desire to think, exist, act, and see in better ways – to get at the
truth of things.

The *Oxford English Dictionary* defines philosophy as "the use of reason and
argument in seeking truth and knowledge of reality, especially of the causes and
nature of things and of the principles governing existence, the material universe,
perception of physical phenomena and human behaviour." In other words,
philosophy is high-level thinking to establish what is true or real, given the limits
of human thought and senses, and the implications of this for how we act.

While philosophy has multiple strands, its focus on what we can really
know is perhaps its most salient feature. The discipline's constant questioning
of assumptions has annoyed many, even its own practitioners – "Philosophers
have raised a dust and then complain they cannot see," George Berkeley
said – yet in our age, with its seemingly increasing extremes and uncertainty,
philosophy's focus on what can be known comes into its own. Indeed, as
Nassim Nicholas Taleb points out in *The Black Swan*, it is what we do not
know that matters, because it is always the unforeseen that changes our world,
both personal and public.

Perhaps the greatest divide in philosophy is between those who believe
that all our information must come from the senses (the empirical, materialist
view) and those who believe that truth can be arrived at through abstract
reasoning (the rationalists and idealists). The first camp has a long lineage,
from the second-century skeptic Sextus Empiricus to the Englishman Francis

Bacon and Scottish Enlightenment thinker David Hume, and to the twentieth-century "logical positivists," including A.J. Ayer and philosopher of science Karl Popper. The second camp counts among its number Plato (his theory of nonphysical "Forms" that undergird the universe), Descartes (his famous separation of mind and matter), and Kant (who resurrected the idea of "moral law" in modern philosophy). The purpose of this book is not to tell you who is "right," but to lay out some of the ideas and theories of note to help you make up your own mind.

As William James observed in *Pragmatism*, philosophers like to believe that they are erecting impartial and accurate systems to explain human action and the universe, when in fact philosophies are expressions of personal biases and outlooks. Philosophy is made by philosophers – imperfect people offering their version of the truth. Yet this is what makes it interesting, and this book, as well as describing some of the key philosophical theories, also tries to give a sense of the people who devised them. To what extent was their thinking simply a projection of their own minds, or did they get to the heart of something universal?

Since I have already written books on the classic writings in psychology, spirituality, and personal development, the most valid question for me was what philosophy provides that these fields do not. After all, because it has an experimental methodology, many believe that psychology is a more trust-worthy discipline when it comes to human questions. However, as Wittgenstein noted in *Philosophical Investigations*, scientific method can sometimes hide a lack of conceptual depth. What is reality? What does it mean to be a human? What is the meaning of life? Philosophy is the only real "meta" discipline, Nietzsche claimed, made to consider the totality of things. While it might be said that theology and spirituality are designed for such questions, they lack the neutrality that is needed for a real discipline open to all-comers.

This is not to say that philosophy is "scientific." Bertrand Russell noted that it is the business of science to know more facts, while the work of philosophy is to establish valid conceptions and laws through which science can be seen. Rather than science enveloping philosophy (a belief of the physicist Stephen Hawking), it is philosophy that can help put raw data and scientific theories into a larger context. Science is after all a very human project, and if it is the attempt to make our theories fit nature, then it is *human* nature with which we first have to contend. To know what we are looking at, we must be aware of the lens through which we view it; that is, how we see the world. We know, for instance, that the old Newtonian perspective on the universe, with its focus on matter, no longer copes with the strange, fluid reality that quantum physics suggests. Philosophy is well equipped to look at these uncertainties because of its focus on objectivity and consciousness itself. The twentieth-century particle physicist David Bohm had to turn to philosophy to explain the movement of electrons under his microscope. It was not possible to construe the world in terms of mind looking at matter, he concluded; rather, consciousness is at least as important an element in the working of the universe as is matter itself. In this book I look at these and other fascinating matters in more depth.

In addition to the primary meaning given above, the *Oxford English Dictionary* defines philosophy as "a personal rule of life."

We all have such a philosophy and it shapes everything we do. Our larger outlook on the world is usually the most interesting and important thing about us, expressing "our more or less dumb sense of what life honestly and deeply means," as William James wrote in *Pragmatism*. Far from being the preserve of lofty professors, our philosophy is practical; we could barely operate without one. As G.K. Chesterton wrote:

> *"for a landlady considering a lodger, it is important to know his income, but still more important to know his philosophy ... for a general about to fight an enemy, it is important to know the enemy's numbers, but still more important to know the enemy's philosophy ... the question is not whether the theory of the cosmos affects matters, but whether, in the long run, anything else affects them."*

There is, of course, a difference between a personal philosophy and philosophy as a discipline. This book seeks to bridge the two. It is not about what a particular philosophy says or means in isolation, but what it may mean to me or you – whether it can increase the quality of our lives, guide our actions in the world, or shed light on our place in the universe.

Whether it is Aristotle or Epicurus providing recipes for a fulfilled and happy life or Plato outlining the ideal society, the ideas of these ancient thinkers remain powerful, if only because in over 2,000 years humans have not changed much. Philosophy is resurgent because the big questions never go away, and it provides ready-made concepts for addressing them. The brilliance of philosophy is that despite its lack of objectivity, it still has the power to send "far-flashing beams of light" over the world, allowing us to see things anew.

Not only does philosophy give us a framework for seeing all other knowledge, on a more personal and exciting level it offers us fresh and often liberating ways of thinking, being, acting, and being.

THINKING
The limits of our knowledge, the sense of self

Philosophy is first about how to think and, given the human propensity to get things wrong, this often means questioning the bases of our knowledge. Descartes went to some lengths to show how easily the mind could be misled by data from the senses, and from this wondered how anything could be said truly to exist. Yet from this position of extreme doubt he made his breakthrough: surely, if he had the ability to be deceived in his thinking, there had to be an "I" that was experiencing the deception. He wrote:

> *"I thereby concluded that I was a substance, of which the whole essence or nature consists in thinking, and which, in order to exist, needs no place and depends on no material thing."*

Even if we are constantly deceived about what we perceive to be fact, it cannot be doubted that we perceive. We are, first and foremost, "thinking things." Consciousness is our essence, and what we are conscious of the most is ourselves: what we are thinking, how we are doing, what we will do next, what we know. As Descartes put it, "I am thinking, therefore I am."

David Hume and John Locke believed that the only knowledge we could trust was that derived directly from our senses, and Hume took this a step further by suggesting that human beings are simply a bundle of thoughts, impressions, and feelings, which at any one time provide a sense of being an "I," even if that identity lacks a solid core. Far from possessing an immortal soul, we are more like a constantly moving banquet of experiences and perceptions, and therefore certainty and knowledge remain elusive.

Philosophy is associated with the quest for self-knowledge, but Iris Murdoch is another who has questioned the idea that there is some eternal core to us that we must be on a mission to reveal. She writes in *The Sovereignty of Good*:

> *"'Self-knowledge', in the sense of a minute understanding of one's own machinery, seems to me, except at a fairly simple level, usually a delusion ... Self is as hard to see justly as other things, and when clear vision has been achieved, self is a correspondingly smaller and less interesting object."*

On the other hand, Murdoch says, this lack of self-solidity should not stop us making efforts to improve ourselves. It is natural and right for us to strive to be perfect, even if we are beset by deficiencies of perception and lack of courage.

In his *Essays*, Michel de Montaigne provided a forensic examination of the self using his own prejudices and weaknesses as the subject matter, and came to the conclusion that the self is a mystery: human knowledge is limited to such an extent that we barely know anything about ourselves, let alone the world at large. We are continually thinking, but rather than the rational beings we suppose ourselves to be, we are a mass of prejudices, quirks, and vanities.

Human fallibility is a rich vein to tap. Nassim Nicholas Taleb also takes up this theme, noting that we believe we understand more of what's going on in the world than we actually do; we often wrongly ascribe meaning to events after they've happened, creating a story; and we overvalue facts, statistics, and categories, which make us feel comfortable that we can predict the future. Our shock at unexpected events shows just how illusory is this feeling that we are in control. And yet, we wouldn't attempt half the things we do if we had a more accurate picture of what we can achieve in a certain timeframe. Seen this way, error is not a defect of the human condition, but part of its eventual glory.

On that same positive note, even arch-empiricist Karl Popper (*The Logic of Scientific Discovery*), who also mistrusted the senses and proposed an extremely difficult standard for the acceptance of any scientific truth, argued that it is humankind's role and privilege to theorize about the laws that may govern the universe. We may be physiologically set up to get things wrong much of the time, but nevertheless our ability to think in a vaguely logical way – to use an older term, reason – makes us unique in the animal world.

BEING
Chances for happiness and a meaningful life, free will, and autonomy

Philosophers since ancient times have suggested that happiness results from moving away from the self, either throwing ourselves into causes or work important to us, or loosening the bands of the ego through appreciating nature, through love, or via spiritual practice.

For Epicurus, virtue made for a pleasant and happy life, because doing the right thing naturally puts our mind at rest. Instead of being anguished about the consequences of our bad actions, we are liberated to enjoy a simple life of friends, philosophy, nature, and small comforts.

Aristotle believed that happiness comes from expressing what we have rationally decided is good for us over the longer term, such as service to the community. Everything in nature is built with an end or purpose in mind, and what is unique to humans is the ability to act according to our reason and preselected virtues. A happy person is one who is stable through their cultivation of virtue, who makes the vagaries of fortune irrelevant. "Activities in accord with virtue control happiness," Aristotle said. Happiness is therefore not pleasure, but a by-product of a meaningful life, and meaning tends to come from striving and self-discipline.

Bertrand Russell noted almost the same in his very personal *The Conquest of Happiness*. Effort, even more than actual success, he wrote, is an essential ingredient of happiness; a person who is able to gratify all whims without effort feels that attainment of desires does not make for happiness. A focus on the self is a cause of unhappiness, while joy comes from directing our interests outward, throwing ourselves into life.

Leibniz was parodied by Voltaire for suggesting that the world we live in is "the best of all possible worlds," but his real point was more subtle. The best possible world is not the one specifically designed for human happiness. Human beings are driven by self-interest and are not aware of the good result of everything that happens. We see matters in terms of cause and effect, but our appreciation of the relationship between them is naturally limited. Only a supreme being has the overview of how everything knits together, Leibniz argued, and our role is to trust in this benevolence of intention. The world we live in is the best possible world, he famously said, even if it appears to contain a great deal of evil, because "an imperfection in the part may be required for a greater perfection in the whole."

But what if you believe, as the existentialists did, that the universe has no inherent purpose or meaning? Sartre's answer was to live "authentically," choosing your own destiny instead of blindly accepting society's rules or the moral "laws" of the day. He wrote: "Man is condemned to be free; because once thrown into the world, he is responsible for everything he does." From such an unpromising premise, Sartre developed a philosophy of freedom that did not depend on any God, attracting a whole generation keen to live in their own way.

This outlook assumes that we are autonomous beings with free will – but are we? Spinoza, Schopenhauer, and Montaigne, among others, argued that we are the subject of causes and larger forces of which we can be only dimly aware.

Heidegger argued that it is impossible for us not to find our existence meaningful. I love, I act, I have an impact – this is the nature of my being. Beyond this, there is the astonishing fact of having consciousness. Why do I have it to this advanced level, when a sheep or a rock does not? A human being is "thrown" into the world, Heidegger said, into a particular place, time, and situation not of their choosing, and life is about making sense of this "fall" into space and time. We feel some responsibility to do something with our lives, and fortunately we come equipped with the capacities for speech and action, which give us the opportunity to reveal something of ourselves. A good life is one in which we seize what possibilities we have and make something out of them. Given our rich raw materials of consciousness and environment, life is inherently meaningful.

Hannah Arendt noted that while nature may be an inexorable process of living and dying, humanity was given a way out of this through the ability to act. "Men, though they must die, are not born in order to die but in order to begin," she wrote in *The Human Condition*. Other animals can only behave according to their programmed survival instincts and impulses, but human beings can go beyond our selfish biological needs to bring something new into being whose value may be recognized in a social and public way. Our deeds are never quite predictable, and every birth carries with it the possibility of a changed world. In short, we *matter*.

Peter Sloterdijk sees humanity as a "practicing" species. *Homo artista* is constantly engaged in activities – artistic, athletic, religious – better itself or rise higher. An alien visiting Earth would find an "acrobatic" race, reaching for the impossible and sometimes achieving it.

ACTING
Power and its use, liberty and justice, fairness and ethics

"Act only according to that maxim by which you can at the same time will that it should become a universal law."

Immanuel Kant's "categorical imperative" says that individual actions are to be judged according to whether we would be pleased if everyone in society took the same action. People should never be seen as means to an end. Although this principle is espoused by the world's religions, Kant was determined to show that it made rational and philosophical sense as well. Moral law was as unchanging as the stars at night, he believed, and by going against it we are destined to be frustrated and unhappy. By doing what is right, we create for ourselves a world of order and peace.

The Roman orator Cicero believed that every individual is a spark or splinter of God, and so treating another human being badly is like doing the same to ourselves. To him, this is a simple fact of universal law. We are social animals, born for the sake of each other, and the aim of life is simple: "to contribute to the general good by an interchange of acts of kindness, by giving and receiving, and thus by our skill, our industry, and our talents to cement human society more closely together, man to man." Cicero aimed to explode the idea that you must sometimes sacrifice doing "what is right" for the sake of doing what is expedient. Doing what is right, he wrote in *On Duties*, is always what is expedient.

Plato believed that doing the right thing is its own reward, since it brings the three parts of our soul (reason, spirit, and desire) into harmony. Acting justly is not an optional extra, but the axis around which human existence must turn; life is meaningless if it lacks well-intentioned action. And while justice is an absolute necessity for the individual, it is also the central plank of a good state, which he outlines in *The Republic*.

A few centuries earlier in China, Confucius said much the same, noting that although we are born human, we become a person through fulfilling responsible roles in society in a selfless way. The wise person loves virtue more than anything, and will always seek the best outcome for everyone without self-calculation. We are, after all, just one link in a chain of being that stretches into the past and future.

In *The Life You Can Save*, contemporary philosopher Peter Singer quotes Epicurus: "It is impossible to live the pleasant life without also living sensibly, nobly and justly." The good life is not merely good health, property, new cars, and holidays, but thinking and acting on what can be done to make the world more just. Singer's rationale for personal giving to end world poverty is a reminder of how powerful philosophy can be for the real world.

This utilitarian outlook can be traced back to Jeremy Bentham in the eighteenth century. Bentham spent a lifetime promoting his principle of "the greatest happiness of the greatest number." His wish was to legislate happiness into being, a radical idea because in his time Britain's laws were more aimed to protect established interests rather than to bring about the greatest benefit for all. In this Bentham faced an uphill battle, yet he was passionate in his belief that utilitarianism was the best hope for a fair and civilized society.

In his landmark *A Theory of Justice*, John Rawls asks us to imagine that everyone in a society has lost their memory about their place and status, and then to configure a new society based on giving maximum opportunity for everyone to flourish. Given that in the lottery of life we could be born a pauper as much as a king, would we not go out of our way to ensure that everyone at least had an equal opportunity to succeed? Where there is inequality of wealth or status, it should have arisen only where there has been full access to compete for such resources or prizes in the first place. No sacrifices need to be made to some "greater good" as in utilitarianism, and people will accept inequalities of wealth and status so long as they know that they or their children have an equal chance at achieving these aims themselves. Rawls's philosophy is in the same tradition as Rousseau, who believed that a free society raises up and ennobles its citizens, but also entails responsibilities and a willingness to give up some personal liberty for the needs of the whole. Rawls, in turn, has influenced the political philosophy of Michael Sandel. His *The Tyranny of Merit* makes a strong case that widening inequality is the direct result of an idea we hold dear: meritocracy. A just society does not make "the lottery of birth" (i.e., inborn talents) the basis of success.

John Stuart Mill's timeless rationale for individual freedom, *On Liberty*, contained his famous "nonharm" criterion for ensuring freedom: "The only purpose for which power can be rightfully exercised over any member of a civilized community, against his will, is to prevent harm to others." A government should not impose a law just because it is considered to be for people's "own good." Rather, unless a citizen's action is shown to be demonstrably bad for others, it should be allowed. Mill noted the tendency for government power to increase and individual freedoms to be eroded, unless this is monitored and held in check. Yet this fact, and its warning of government creep, did not mean that governments had no legitimacy at all.

What, then, is the correct balance between personal freedom and the need for state control? Mill described this as "the question of the future," and indeed we still grapple with it now. As Plato argued in *The Republic*, we should be happy to live with some restricted freedoms and accept our place in society, given the alternatives of exile or life beyond laws. The problem, as Machiavelli pointed out with brutal honesty in *The Prince*, is that the average citizen simply does not appreciate what it takes to keep a powerful state going, and can continue to live a moral life while the rulers have to take "dirty" decisions. Long seen as an inspiration for tyrants, *The Prince* in fact lays out a reasoned defense of the exertion of power: it is not for the self-aggrandizement of the ruler, but rather for the strength of the state – and a strong state is desirable because it allows people to flourish and prosper. With this just end in mind, unpleasant means can sometimes be justified.

Noam Chomsky, a perennial thorn in the side of Western liberal compla-cency, takes a similarly dark view of power. Most contemporary states, he believes, are set up to serve the interests of power, and the real enemy of those in power is their own population; most wars are designed to take attention away from the domestic situation. Although Chomsky's focus has been on the United States, his message is that the corrupting nature of power is universal. And yet, he notes causes for optimism. It is less acceptable now to treat people as objects or means to an end ("Slavery was considered a fine thing not long ago," he writes), and even if power structures only pay lip-service to freedom, self-determination, and human rights, at least these are acknowledged as ideals.

Perhaps the last word on morality and power should go to Iris Murdoch, who argues in *The Sovereignty of Good* that if we seek the good first, everything else worthwhile will come to us naturally. In contrast, seek only to have muscular will, and that is all, in the end, that we will have. Just as Kant suggested, good intentions are everything.

SEEING
Plato's cave and truth, philosophy as a language problem, living in a media world

Plato's allegory of the cave is one of the most famous passages in philosophy. It continues to resonate because of its startling suggestion that most of us go through life chasing shadows and the appearance of things, when all along there exist the eternal "forms" of Truth, Justice, Beauty, and the Good, waiting to be recognized. Kant, too, believed that, as beings existing in space and time and with the limitations of our senses, we are cut off from perceiving things as they really are ("things in themselves"). Yet there is an elemental, metaphysical truth behind the world of perceptions, and through reason we can at least make some approach to it.

Modern philosophers have lined up to dismiss such notions, pointing out that we are animals with a brain that perceives and organizes phenomena in certain ways. Knowledge is based only on what comes through our senses, not on metaphysical insight, and science is a matter of increasing our objectivity. Hegel, however, argued that objective analysis is an illusion, because things only exist in the context of the observer's perception of them; consciousness is as much a part of science as the world of objects that it purports to analyze. For Hegel, the real story of science is not the "discovery of the universe," but rather the discovery of our own mind – consciousness itself. History, science, and philosophy are simply expressions of how consciousness has awakened over time.

Hegel's grand, holistic idea of awakening "Spirit" or consciousness in human affairs fell out of philosophical fashion because world wars and depressions seemed to counter the notion that history had a positive direction. Indeed, as philosopher of science Thomas Kuhn showed in *The Structure of Scientific Revolutions*, and as Michel Foucault also noted, knowledge does not proceed in a neat line upward, with one discovery building on another; rather, each age has a completely different lens through which it views the world, and something is perceived to be real only if the lens allows it to be seen.

Whoever is right here, any assessment of our ability to comprehend the world accurately must involve language. In *Philosophical Investigations*, Wittgenstein admitted that he had been wrong in the view expressed in his earlier *Tractatus* that language is a means of describing the world. Words do not simply name things, they often convey elaborate meaning, and many different meanings from the same word. Language is not a formal logic that marks the limits of our world, but a social game in which the order of play is loose and evolves as we go along. Philosophical problems only arise, he said, when philosophers see the naming of some idea or concept as all-important, while in fact contextual meaning is what matters. Philosophy, Wittgenstein famously said, is a constant battle against the "bewitchment" of the discipline by language itself. This was a dig at the analytical tradition of philosophy (whose adherents included Bertrand Russell and A.J. Ayer), which saw the misuse of language as a welcome mat for so much meaningless metaphysics, whereas its good use could give us a more accurate picture of reality.

In *Naming and Necessity*, the brilliant Saul Kripke showed the faults of this conception, noting that the meaning of something is found not in the descriptions given of it, but in its essential properties. A person, for instance, is simply who they are, and no amount of language accuracy is going to add, take away, or prove that identity. Gold is not defined by our descriptions of it, such as "yellow, shiny metal," but rather by its essential property, the atomic element 79.

From Plato to Kant, Hegel to Wittgenstein, an idea recurs through the history of philosophy: the world is not simply how we perceive or describe it. Whether we use the term forms, things-in-themselves, or essential properties, there is an underlying reality that may not be obvious to the senses. David Bohm was a leading theoretical physicist turned philosopher, and in *Wholeness and the Implicate Order* he made a compelling case for the existence of two orders of reality: the implicate and the explicate. While the latter is the "real world" that we can perceive with our senses, it is simply the unfolding of a deeper, "implicate" reality that holds every possibility. Both are part of a larger "holomovement," a flowing whole of reality. This is very similar to the wholeness of the universe of which Heraclitus spoke. It is only humans who break things into parts and categories.

***

Philosophy's historical obsession with the questions "What is real?" and "What is true?" is seen by some commentators as a red herring. Jean Baudrillard declared that, in the media-saturated world we now inhabit, "reality" has no meaning. In a hyperreal universe, something is real only if it can be reproduced endlessly, and what is unshareable electronically does not exist. A person today is not a project in selfhood, pursuing what is "true," but more like a machine that consumes and reproduces ideas and images.

Baudrillard was influenced by Marshall McLuhan, who argued that the mass media and communications technology were not neutral inventions but in fact change the way we are. Before the advent of the alphabet, humankind's main sensory organ was the ear. After it, the eye became dominant. The alphabet made us think like a sentence is constructed: in a linear way, and with the sequential connection of facts or concepts. The new media environment is multidimensional, and media information now comes to us so thick and fast that we no longer have the ability to categorize it properly and deal with it in our minds. Children growing up today do not only have their parents and teachers to influence them, they are exposed to the whole world. As McLuhan famously said:

> *"Ours is a brand new world of allatonceness. 'Time' has ceased, 'space' has vanished. We now live in a global village ... a simultaneous happening."*

In this new media world, is Plato's cave allegory still meaningful? Have we lost all chance to perceive the real and true, and does it matter? Such questions will take philosophy into the future, but one thing is for sure: we cannot continue to see ourselves as separate from technology. As "transhumanist" thinkers suggest, we are no longer in a world in which people simply use technology; machines are part of us, and will become ever more extensions of our bodies – through them we will perceive ourselves and the world.

Final word

Hegel took an unusually expansive and generous view of philosophy. As he notes in the famous Preface to *Phenomenology of Spirit*, conventional philosophers see their subject as a field of competing positions in which only one system can be said to "win." They take the perspective of a battlefield of ideologies. Hegel instead adopted a bird's-eye view of the discipline: each competing philosophy had its place, and over time their jostling allowed for "the progressive unfolding of truth." Putting this in botanical terms, he wrote that the buds are forgotten when they burst forth into blossom, and the blossom in turn gives way to fruit, which reveals the truth or purpose of the tree. Hegel's aim was to free philosophy from its one-sidedness and to show the truth of the whole. It was better to see the variety and richness of culture and philosophy as one great project.

Theologian and philosopher Thomas Aquinas wrote in *On the Heavens*:

> *"the study of philosophy has as its purpose to know not what people have thought, but rather the truth about the way things are."*

That is our goal, but knowing what people have thought can still help us. If you don't have a firm view of life, in these pages you will find plenty of powerful concepts through which to view it, or, better still, to challenge your existing worldview. It is natural for us to want certainty, but if there exists any kind of absolute knowledge, it will not be altered or moved by our questioning. Therefore, you have nothing to lose by studying the great works of philosophy, and everything to gain.

What is in the book and why

The list of 50 titles does not claim to be definitive, only to give a sense of some of the key writings in Western philosophy, ancient and modern, with a hint of the East as well. While I would love to have included philosophers from every part of the world and every era, this book is at least a taste of what is a vast literature. At the rear of the book you will find a list of 50 More Classics, most of which could have been in the main text if there had been no space limit.

The focus is less on the usual categorization of philosophical schools, periods, "ologies," and "isms" that is the norm in introductory or academic texts. This is a layperson's guide to philosophy. You are not being trained in anything, only – it is hoped – enlightened. Having said that, like any field philosophy has its own terms and language, so there is also a glossary of common terms to help you at the end of the book.

Philosophy as a formal section of academia has had a relatively short history. Epicurus started his school in the garden of a house in Athens, and today there are philosophy clubs around the world that meet in pubs and homes. Philosophy is a living thing, and its questions will continue to be at the center of human existence. To that end, along with many of the undisputedly great names of philosophy, the list of 50 includes some contemporary works that, although not true classics as yet perhaps, give real insights.

In terms of structure, the alphabetical, nonchronological ordering may seem counterintuitive, and yet by putting books together like this there is less chance of categories, including those of time, being forced on you; you can make your own connections between ideas, writings, eras, and people. Pick out and read the commentaries that look most interesting; or, you may find that reading the book from start to finish will give you more of a sense of a journey, with unexpected discoveries along the way.

Bonus

A bundle of bonus chapters is available free to readers. Spanning thinkers past and present, the chapters cover key works by Heraclitus, Henri Bergson, Julian Baggini, Sam Harris, Daniel Kahneman, Kathryn Schulz, and Slavoj Žižek. Go to www.butler-bowdon.com/50-philosophy-classics.html

Summa Theologica

"Therefore as God is the first universal cause, not of one genus only, but of all being in general, it is impossible for anything to occur outside the order of the Divine government."

"If therefore we consider the order of things depending on the first cause, God cannot do anything against this order; for, if He did so, He would act against His foreknowledge, or His will, or His goodness. But if we consider the order of things depending on any secondary cause, thus God can do something outside such order; for He is not subject to the order of secondary causes; but, on the contrary, this order is subject to Him, as proceeding from Him, not by a natural necessity, but by the choice of His own will; for He could have created another order of things."

"According to the plan of Divine Providence, we find that in all things the movable and variable are moved and regulated by the immovable and invariable."

In a nutshell

If the universe works according to cause and effect, logic dictates there must have been an initial cause, something which created the potential for everything else.

In a similar vein

René Descartes *Meditations* (p 94)
Søren Kierkegaard *Fear and Trembling* (p 154)
Gottfried Leibniz *Theodicy* (p 170)
Blaise Pascal *Pensées* (p 224)

CHAPTER 1

Thomas Aquinas

Why a work of theology in a book of philosophy classics?

In the early Middle Ages, nearly all philosophers were theologians or clerics. Theology *was* philosophy, taking as its remit all the key questions of meaning and knowledge. It embraced human behaviour, long before psychology. Indeed, Aquinas' *Summa Theologica* ('Synopsis of Theology') is much more than a defense of the Christian faith. It is a vision of how the world came into existence and what it is for, providing a sense of reason and certainty that, while God made the world, humankind's role in its fulfilment is paramount.

In his Prologue, Aquinas describes the *Summa* as a work of Christian theology *for beginners*, even though it runs across several volumes and hundreds of thousands of words. He was concerned that existing explanations of the "sacred science" might only confuse people, and so set out to address this with (in his view) a never-before-seen rigour, and the *Summa* was his "all bells and whistles" expression of his position. The structure follows a classical pattern of presentation of an argument, or "objection," then its demolition (supported by scripture, other philosophers, and reason). Despite the image of the work as a theological fortress, thanks to this method the book is actually not difficult to read, and this is how Aquinas intended it.

Aquinas' intellectual influences are fascinating, and broader than you may think. St Augustine is much quoted in the *Summa*, and he was also very influenced by French theologian Peter Lombard. However, it is Aristotle ("the philosopher") who is crucial to Aquinas' arguments; the *Summa* is a brilliant synthesis of Aristotelian philosophy and Christian theology. More surprising to the modern reader is that it also draws on the Islamic philosophers Ibn Rushd (Averroes), Al-Ghazali (Algazel) and İbn Sina (Avicenna), and the Jewish thinker Maimonides. For his reliance on Aristotle and other non-Christian influences, Aquinas was later criticized by the Church. Indeed, you could even argue he was more open-minded than many of today's Christians, accepting that truth was truth, wherever one found it.

The *Summa* took a decade to write, and was still not finished on Aquinas' death. It is hard in a summary of this length to do justice to the work. We focus on Part One, which covers the nature of God, souls, angels and divine governance.

Is philosophy enough?

Aquinas begins by posing the question whether philosophy on its own, without theology, can be sufficient for us. He considers the argument that we should stick to what is observed, known, and based on reason, because everything else is beyond our understanding.

His answer is that "it was necessary for the salvation of man that certain truths which exceed human reason should be made known to him by divine revelation." Some of these truths can discovered through reason, but only a few people are equipped to do this. The average person divines truth through revelation. Moreover, there are limits to what we can know through reason; a point is reached where philosophy stops and theology takes over. As Ecclesiastes 3:25 says: "For many things are shown to thee above the understanding of man."

Humans naturally desire happiness, Aquinas notes, but we are not always good in knowing what happiness consists of. We might believe that happiness comes in the form of riches, or pleasures, and are unable to see the true basis of happiness. Aquinas was influenced by Aristotle in seeing happiness as man's greatest want, yet he took this further, saying that all the things of this world are proxies for happiness; real happiness is found in closeness to God.

How do we know? The case for God

Aquinas raises the objection that God's existence cannot be demonstrated or verified, that rather it is an article of faith. His response is that God's existence is not an article of faith, but rather the *preamble* to the article. Our faith, or lack of it, has no bearing or effect on whether God exists or not.

Even if we cannot grasp the existence of a Supreme Being, this should not stop us assuming that one does exist – in the same way that we can accept a mathematical proof without knowing how to arrive at it ourselves.

Aquinas addresses the view that everything we see in the world can be accounted for by principles other than God. Further, all our voluntary actions can be attributed to will or reason, not to some divine plan. Indeed, we can go along quite easily without needing to suppose that God exists. This leads him to a famous response, his "five reasons for the existence of God":

1. Everything in the world is in motion, and has been caused to move by something else. All motion is the reduction of the potential to the actual, but this can't occur without there being something in a primary state of actuality to begin with. We can draw a chain of cause and effect as long as we like, but this can't go on until infinity. There had to have been a "first mover" that put things into play in the first place: God.

2. Nothing can cause itself to come into being. And if you say that something hasn't been caused, neither can you talk of an effect, so the thing you are talking of can't *ever* have existed. But the fact that things do exist, must mean that they are the result of an original cause.

3. Assume that nothing ever existed. By the laws of cause and effect, this would mean that nothing could exist now. But things do exist, and although the existence of all things is possible, there must have been something whose existence *was* necessary, to bring everything else into being. This we understand to be God.

4. There are gradations in everything that exists, including people. Some are good, true and noble, others less so. But each entity in the universe can be seen against a "maximum." For instance, the degree of hotness of a thing is measured against the maximum kind of heat: fire. In relation to ethics, there must be something that is the best, the truest and the most noble. Every kind of thing in a class must have its ultimate, and that ultimate is the cause of the class. In human terms, whatever is good or true in us is caused by what is good, true and perfect in absolute terms: God.

5. Non-intelligent objects act in a manner that is predictable and efficient, but this could not happen unless there is something of intelligence behind their motion, just as a shooting arrow is found always to have been shot by an archer. By this logic, the world itself must be directed by some intelligence – God.

What about evil?

Aquinas acknowledges the common view that if God existed, and he is all powerful, how could there be evil in the world?

He answers that part of the infinite goodness of God is that he allows evil to exist, in order to produce good out of it. The nature of humans is changeability and imperfection, qualities produced by human reason or will. But Aquinas notes that what is mutable and imperfect must originally have come out of something that was unchanging and perfect. Just because we individually are sometimes bad, it does not mean that God, and the world taken as a whole, is not good.

Aquinas notes that because we cannot know the essence of God, but only his outworking, it makes more sense for us to identify what God is not, rather than what he is. If he is not matter, or motion, or all the things we see in the universe, then we must speak of him in terms of his "simplicity": his changelessness, timelessness, infinity, perfection and unity. It is *we* that are complicated. And while all things can be divided into, firstly, their essence, and secondly, their actual existence, God is the only thing that is whole, and therefore totally simple.

Grace

What exactly is the relationship between God and Man? God has so made the world that everything, despite appearances, inclines towards the good. Each person is a combination of soul and body, and their soul is unique and indivisible. Their will and their intellect are expressions of certain inclinations of their soul, and they seek happiness through achieving certain ends, which are freely chosen. Humans, as a unity of soul and body, and being part of the physical world, naturally focus on things around them, and personal goals, rather than spiritual "universals."

Yet humans still wish to be faithful towards God, and acting in faith (an essentially irrational act) a person can then see faith in terms of reason; by believing, we see what is actually true. The key to this movement is love, which energizes belief and makes it stronger.

Our efforts are divinely boosted through "grace," moments in which God gives us glimpses of ultimate perfection. Through our exercise of the virtues and good habits in everyday life, we substitute our own wills for God's, and through this effort find ourselves coming back to God as the one and only source of real happiness. This is what Aquinas calls the "beatific vision."

Final comments

Though the five arguments for God have had plenty of challenges (most recently in Richard Dawkins' *The God Delusion*) they still make a rational case, and taken out of their context could have been written today.

However, we are reminded that this is a work written in the 1200s when Aquinas then takes us on a ride into the philosophical complexities of the angel realm. This is not to say that angels or demons don't exist (how could we know?), only that in the thirteenth century their reality was assumed. The early medieval worldview gave a lot of weight to spiritual realities (as they were perceived) in relation to matter. In our scientific age, the weighting is the opposite; matter is all that matters. But who is to say that in another few hundred years our super-materialist view of the universe will also not produce wry smiles?

This leads to a question: if Aquinas were alive now, would this most incisive of early medieval minds still believe in God? Or would he rule out a spiritual realm as nonsense? It is tempting to assume the latter, but then we remember his point that philosophy and science are creations of man. They can tell us what the world is, but not *why* it is. The *Summa* tells us that the universe is an outflow of divine love, and that through an ethical, faithful life we can "return to the fold." Only theology, or a very open and sophisticated kind of philosophy, can help us understand such a movement.

Thomas Aquinas

Born around 1224 into an aristocratic Naples family, Aquinas was schooled at the Benedictine abbey of Monte Cassino before attending the University of Naples.

When he joined the newish Dominican order, instead of the Benedictines, his family were infuriated. After the order relocated him to Paris, family members abducted him and brought him back home, then tried to have him seduced by a prostitute. He resisted, and at the age of 20 finally made it to Paris. By his late twenties Aquinas had completed an advanced theological degree.

In 1259, Aquinas wrote the Summa Contra Gentiles, *before taking up a post in Rome to establish a new Dominican college. Here he began writing the* Summa Theologica. *Part Two of the work was completed during a second university posting in Paris (1268–72).*

In 1273, Aquinas reported a mystical experience while saying mass, which left him weak. He never finished Part Three of the Summa, *he told a friend, because his written work now seemed like nothing compared to his vision. He died the following March, in 1274.*

Aquinas' prolific output includes commentaries on John Lombard, Boethius and Aristotle, many syntheses of theological issues and biblical analyses, and hymns.

1958

The Human Condition

"With word and deed we insert ourselves into the human world, and this insertion is like a second birth, in which we confirm and take upon ourselves the naked fact of our original physical appearance. This insertion ... springs from the beginning which came into the world when we were born and to which we respond by beginning something new on our own initiative."

"The task and potential greatness of mortals lie in their ability to produce things – works and deeds and words – which would deserve to be and, at least to a degree, are at home in everlastingness."

In a nutshell

The nature of being human is to do the unexpected, and every birth carries with it the possibility of a changed world.

In a similar vein

Peter Sloterdijk *You Must Change Your Life* (p 292)
Martin Heidegger *Being and Time* (p 130)

CHAPTER 2

Hannah Arendt

G erman-born Hannah Arendt was one of America's leading twentieth-century intellectuals, rising to prominence with her study of Hitler and Stalin, *The Origins of Totalitarianism* (1951), then achieving fame with *Eichmann in Jerusalem* (1962), a study of the trial of Nazi Adolf Eichmann that included her concept of "the banality of evil."

The Human Condition is the best expression of her larger philosophy. Though it is scholarly (she was an expert in classical Rome and Greece) and often difficult, it is genuinely original. And while it can be studied as a work of political philosophy, it also provides a very inspiring theory of human potential.

The miracle of birth and action
Nature is essentially cyclical, Arendt says, a never-ending and inexorable process of living and dying that "only spells doom" to mortal beings. However, humans were given a way out of this through the ability to *act*. Free action interferes with the law of inexorable death by beginning something new. "Men, though they must die, are not born in order to die but in order to begin."

This is Arendt's concept of "natality," inspired by St. Augustine's famous statement, "That a beginning was made, man was created." Arendt writes:

"It is in the nature of beginning that something new is started which cannot be expected from whatever may have happened before ... The new always happens against the overwhelming odds of statistical laws and their probability, which for all practical, everyday purposes amounts to certainty; the new therefore always appears in the guise of a miracle. The fact that man is capable of action means that the unexpected can be expected from him, that he is able to perform what is infinitely improbable. And this again is possible only because each man is unique, so that with each birth something uniquely new comes into the world."

Being born is a miracle in itself, but the real glory is in the way we confirm our identity through our words and deeds. While animals can only behave according to their programmed survival instincts and impulses, human beings can *act*, going beyond our selfish biological needs to bring something new into being whose value may be recognized in a social and public way. (Like Socrates drinking hemlock by his choice, or someone who gives their life for another, we can even act against our very survival instinct.) And because of this ability to make truly free decisions, our deeds are never quite predictable. Action, Arendt says, "seen from the viewpoint of the automatic processes which seem to determine the course of the world, looks like a miracle." Our lives are about "the infinite improbability which occurs regularly." In her other writings she suggests that the essence of fascist regimes is in their denial of this natality, or individual possibility, and this is what makes them so abhorrent.

Forgiveness and promise keeping

Arendt recalls Jesus of Nazareth's emphasis on action, particularly the act of forgiving, as an important point in history, since this discovery allowed us, not only God, the power to nullify past actions. This power Jesus put almost on the level of physical miracles, given its ability to transform worldly situations. Arendt writes:

> *"Only through this constant mutual release from what they do can men remain free agents, only by constant willingness to change their minds and start again can they be trusted with so great a power as that to begin something new."*

Whereas the wish for vengeance is automatic and thus a predictable action, the act of forgiving, because it seems to go against natural reactions, can never be predicted. Forgiveness has the character of real, thought-out action, and in this respect is more human than the animalistic reaction of revenge, because it frees both the forgiver and the forgiven. Action of this type is the only thing that prevents human lives from hurtling from birth to death without real meaning.

Arendt agrees with Nietzsche that what also marks out humans from other animals is the ability to make promises and keep them. Our basic unreliability is the price we pay for our freedom, but we have devised ways of keeping promises real, from social custom to legal contracts. The acts of forgiveness and promise keeping redeem humankind and take us to a new level. They are also creative actions that confirm our uniqueness. In the way these actions are expressed, "nobody is ever the same as anyone else who ever lived, lives or will live."

Labor, work, and action

Arendt delineates the three basic human activities of labor, work, and action:

❖ Labor is the activity of living, growing, and eventual decay that all humans experience; basically, staying alive. "The human condition of labor is life itself," she says.

❖ Work is the unnatural activity that humans perform within a natural world, which can transcend or outlast this world, giving "a measure of permanence and durability upon the futility of mortal life and the fleeting character of human time."

❖ Action is the only activity that does not require things or matter, and therefore is the essence of being human. Action also transcends the natural world, because "men, not Man, live on the earth and inhabit the world." By this Arendt means that human beings are communal, political animals who seek to do things that are recognized by others.

Rediscovering glory

In ancient Greece and Rome, Arendt notes, what mattered was what you did in the public realm. The lives and prospects of poor people and those without political rights (including slaves and women) were essentially carried out in the home; this private domain, whatever its benefits, brought with it no prospect of influence or real action. In contrast, men of means, free of the need to labor to survive and of the daily grind of the household, could be actors on the public stage, taking action to better or advance the whole of society.

In our time, she observes, it is the home that has become the focal point, and we have been reduced to consumers with little stomach for politics. We seek happiness while forsaking our privilege to do things that can change the world and benefit many. The ancient quest for glory seems alien to us, even distasteful, yet in reverting to being mere householders we are giving up our potential to have lives of truly autonomous action (what she calls the *vita activa*):

> "The distinction between man and animal runs right through the human species itself: only the best (aristoi), who constantly prove themselves to be the best, and who 'prefer immortal fame to mortal things,' are really human; the others, content with whatever pleasures nature will yield them, live and die like animals."

Through love is our glory revealed

Humans can know everything there is to know about the natural world, or the world of objects, but will always fall short of knowing themselves ("jumping over our own shadows," as Arendt calls it). *What* we are is our body, she notes, but *who* we are is disclosed in our words and deeds. We come to know who a person is not by being "for" or "against" them, but simply by spending time with them. Over a period of time, who a person is cannot help but be revealed. Thus, people live together not merely for emotional or material support, but in the sheer pleasure of seeing other people reveal their character. What is most interesting to us about an act is not the act itself, but the agent it reveals. The highest revelation of a person we call "glory."

Yet who we are may never be known by us; it is something that can only be seen fully by others:

> *"For love, although it is one of the rarest occurrences in human lives, indeed possesses an unequalled power of self-revelation and an unequalled clarity of vision for the disclosure of who, precisely because it is unconcerned to the point of total unworldliness with what the loved person may be, with his qualities and shortcomings no less than with his achievements, failings and transgressions. Love, by reason of its passion, destroys the in-between which relates us to and separates us from others."*

Our ability to act gives all our lives a new beginning, providing fully justified hope and faith. Why faith? Because if we have the fundamental knowledge that people can act and can change, then it follows that we must have faith not only in them, but in the people we love and in the human race generally.

The beautiful paradox that Arendt leaves with us is that only through love (which by its nature is unworldly, private, and unpolitical) are we energized to have a real effect in public life.

Final comments

The conclusion of biologists and sociologists in the last 30 years that people are shaped by their brain's wiring, their genes, and their environment much more than had been thought would seem to pour cold water on Arendt's theories of action and decision.

And yet, from the viewpoint of history, which is after all the sum of millions of individual decisions, it would be wrong to suggest (as Hegel and Marx did) that the story of humanity involves a certain inevitability. Rather, as one of Arendt's key influences Martin Heidegger was keen to point out, individuals matter. For Arendt, history is a chronicle of the exceeding of expectations. People do amazing things that often even they do not wholly expect.

In the last pages of *The Human Condition*, Arendt admits that the "society of jobholders" that we have become allows people to abandon their individuality and behave as if they were simply a "function," instead of tackling head-on the trouble of living and truly thinking and acting for themselves. They simply become a passive reflection of their environment, an advanced animal instead of a real, aware, deciding person. For Arendt, being great is recognizing that you are not simply an animal with various urges for survival, and not merely a consumer with "tastes" or "preferences." Your birth was a truly new beginning, an opportunity for something to come into being that was not there before.

It can take a while to grasp Arendt's distinctions between labor, work, and action, and you may only understand her thinking fully on a second or third reading. Nevertheless, in its belief in the power of human action and unexpectedness, *The Human Condition* is a genuinely uplifting work.

Hannah Arendt

Born in Hanover, Germany in 1906, Arendt grew up in Konigsberg in a Jewish family. Her father died from syphilitic insanity when she was only 7, but she was close to her mother, an active German Social Democrat. Following high school Arendt studied theology at the University of Marburg, where one of her lecturers was Martin Heidegger. She had an affair with him (he was married), before leaving for the University of Heidelberg. Under her mentor, the philosopher Karl Jaspers, she completed a PhD dissertation there on the concept of love in St. Augustine's thought.

Arendt married in 1930. As the Nazi party rose in influence she was prevented from teaching in German universities and became involved in Zionist politics, from 1933 working for the German Zionist Organization. The Gestapo arrested her but she fled to Paris, working for another organization helping to rescue Jewish children from Austria and Czechoslovakia. Having divorced her first husband in 1940, she married Heinrich Blücher, but only a few months later the couple were interned in German camps in southern France. They escaped and found passage to the United States. Arendt received American citizenship in 1951. During the 1950s she moved in New York intellectual circles that included Mary McCarthy, worked as an editor, and developed The Origins of Totalitarianism.

Arendt became the first female professor of politics at Princeton University and also taught at the University of Chicago, Wesleyan University, and New York's New School for Social Research. She died in 1976. The first two volumes of her autobiographical The Life of the Mind (1978) and her Lectures on Kant's Philosophy (1982) were published posthumously. A good biography is Elisabeth Young-Bruehl's Hannah Arendt: For Love of the World (1982).

Nicomachean Ethics

"[We] become builders by building, and we become harpists by playing the harp. Similarly, then, we become just by doing just actions, temperate by doing temperate actions, brave by doing brave actions."

"And just as Olympic prizes are not for the finest and strongest, but for the contestants – since it is only these who win – the same is true in life; among the fine and good people, only those who act correctly win the prize."

In a nutshell

Happiness comes from expressing what we have rationally decided is good for us over the longer term. Happiness is not pleasure, but a by-product of a meaningful life.

In similar vein

Hannah Arendt *The Human Condition* (p 22)
Epicurus *Letters* (p 106)
Plato *The Republic* (p 230)
Bertrand Russell *The Conquest of Happiness* (p 258)

CHAPTER 3

Aristotle

S o great was his perceived authority on a range of subjects, from physics to psychology to biology, that throughout the Middle Ages Aristotle
was known simply as "the philosopher." Dante called him the "master of
those who know." Aristotle was a crucial influence on Thomas Aquinas and
also Islamic philosophers such as Averroes.

Aristotle's rigor and relentless quest to categorize everything have had a
massive impact on philosophical and scientific thinking over the last 2,000
years, instituting a very rational, left-brain way of seeing that is the essence of
Western civilization.

It is often said that the history of philosophy can be divided between
Platonists and Aristotelians. While Plato believed that everything we perceive
in the physical world has an underlying metaphysical reality and that "truth"
lies behind or beyond the world of appearances, his student Aristotle was
much more of a nuts-and-bolts philosopher, interested in the world as we see
it. After studying under Plato for 20 years, Aristotle came to the view that our
understanding of the world is necessarily based in our five senses; his rigorous
and analytical mind broke things down to their component parts, including
ostensibly vague elements such as happiness and virtue.

The *Nicomachean Ethics* (dedicated to his son, Nicomachus) is the best
expression of Aristotle's moral philosophy. His scientific works are now mainly
of interest to scholars, but the *Nicomachean Ethics* continues to be influential,
providing a recipe for the good life that is still discussed and applied today;
his concept of *eudaimonia* (loosely, "happiness"), for instance, has shaped
contemporary positive psychology. Though the work was compiled from
lecture notes and so seems somewhat incomplete and unpolished, it can be
read without great difficulty.

What is our function?

As distinct from Plato's concept of "form," which indicates the reality underlying things, Aristotle's use of form refers simply to their order or structure.
To understand what an object is (whether it is a chair or a person), you have

to know its function. We do not appreciate a boat, for instance, as pieces of joined-up wood, but as something that can carry us across water. Aristotle's "final cause" says that everything in nature is built with an end or purpose in mind. A tree or a person is programmed to flourish in a certain way, and it uses the conditions available to do so.

However, what could we say is the function of human beings? Not simply growing, as this would make us the same as a plant. Not simply seeing or hearing or smelling, as we have this in common with a horse or an ox. What is unique to us, Aristotle says, is the ability to act according to our reason. A thing's essence is how it is organized, and humans, with their ability to organize their own mind and actions, are unique in nature. A person is ultimately the virtues they have cultivated and the choices they have made, so one who organizes their life according to the highest virtues can become great.

We do not grasp someone's identity through seeing them as a collection of billions of cells, but through what differentiates them. It is in the appreciation of their virtues, or their art, or skills honed over a lifetime, that we can grasp their essence or function. A flautist or a sculptor, Aristotle says, is doing well if they are playing the flute superbly or sculpting with great power. Success depends on the fulfillment of function.

Achieving happiness

The starting point of Aristotle's ethical theory is happiness, because he believes people to be rational creatures who make decisions that will lead to their ultimate good. Though *eudaimonia* is often translated as "happiness," it can also be read as "doing well," "success," or "flourishing."

As rational beings, our greatest happiness comes from choices that we arrive at through reason. We work out what is best for us in the long run, and in following that path happiness comes as a by-product. A life of mere pleasure, since it deprives us of rational, purposeful activity over a lifetime in the quest of a goal, will not make us happy. The most virtuous path is that which gives us the greatest genuine (rather than fleeting) pleasure. The pleasure of reading a light romance or a thriller, for instance, does not provide the great meaning and satisfaction to be gained from reading Tolstoy.

Most people simply seek a life of gratification, but Aristotle thinks them no better than "grazing animals." To have a "complete life," we must combine action with virtue, constantly refining ourselves and developing our skills. Genuine happiness emerges through work on ourselves and our aims over time. "For one swallow does not make a spring, nor does one day," Aristotle says, "nor, similarly, does one day or a short time make us blessed and happy."

He describes time itself as "a good partner in discovery," revealing both our own natures and that of the world.

Friendship is part of a good and complete life, Aristotle says, because it promotes the sharing of reasoning and thinking. Through reasoned, constructive action, we help friends achieve their aims, and in doing so our own rational qualities, or our character, are enlarged. This naturally makes us happy. The same principle applies to the community or city in which we live. By working for its betterment, we naturally strengthen our own character and therefore increase our happiness.

Finally, Aristotle regards study as one of the great sources of happiness, if not the greatest, because it allows us the full expression of our rational nature. In appreciating philosophical or scientific truths and incorporating them in our own knowledge, we are reaching the peak of what it is to be human.

Aristotle's pleasing conclusion is that happiness is not predetermined by fate or the gods, but can be acquired habitually by consciously expressing a virtuous life through work, application, or study. "[We] become builders," he says, "by building, and we become harpists by playing the harp. Similarly, then, we become just by doing just actions, temperate by doing temperate actions, brave by doing brave actions." In other words, we become a successful person through habit.

We should not judge a person's life according to their ups and downs, but by the enduring virtues that they develop and express. This is the real measure of success. A successful and happy person is one who is stable in their cultivation of virtue, who makes the vagaries of fortune irrelevant. It is this stability, nobility, and magnanimity that we admire the most. "Activities in accord with virtue control happiness," Aristotle says.

Action and decision

Plato believed that the mere appreciation of virtue is enough to make a person virtuous. But for Aristotle, a good life must be one of virtue expressed in action: "And just as Olympic prizes are not for the finest and strongest, but for the contestants – since it is only these who win – the same is true in life; among the fine and good people, only those who act correctly win the prize."

He makes a distinction between voluntary and involuntary action. Young children and animals can take voluntary actions, but do not make real *decisions*, because these involve significant reason or thought. Since adults have the faculties of deliberation and decision, using these in a good way (for instance to pursue a goal that requires us to limit natural appetites) will make us feel we are living how we are supposed to – as rational beings focused on creating something worthwhile. We can wish for something, but to attain it we have to decide to take particular actions. Similarly, we can believe certain things, but it is action that forms our character. The "incontinent" person, Aristotle says, acts from appetite, or what is pleasant. In contrast, the "continent" person "does the reverse, by acting on decision, not on appetite."

Aristotle also makes an interesting distinction between action, on the one hand, and production. The end of production is an object, a thing outside ourselves, and requires the use of craft, or skillful manipulation. But acting well is done as its own end and need not result in anything in particular. Whereas production makes a thing, and the skill in production produces better or worse quality, action, depending on its quality, makes a person better or worse. It is therefore purer and more noble.

Though Aristotle's view on the difference between action and production was shaped by his elevated position in society, the idea has contemporary implications. As Hannah Arendt noted in *The Human Condition*, thinking of ourselves as "producers" and "consumers" is peculiarly modern. Yet we don't exist to produce, but to make a contribution to our community and society. This is why the *Nicomachean Ethics*, a book ostensibly about personal virtue, has many sections relating to friendship and the responsibilities of being a citizen.

Final comments

It is fashionable today for governments to be concerned with "gross national happiness" instead of simply economic output. Their advisers look to Aristotle's ideas on the good life and *eudaimonia* to guide policy making that might engineer the greatest happiness for the greatest number. This is a noble effort. Nevertheless, we should be wary about giving prescriptions for individual happiness. As Aristotle taught, every person will have a different route to the good life based on a unique potential that is theirs to fulfill. Rather than seeking happiness as a goal in itself, our challenge is to pursue the life most full of meaning for us – and in doing so, happiness will naturally follow.

Aristotle is often criticized for his remarks in the *Nicomachean Ethics* that circumstantial elements such as money, status, and family are important contributors to happiness. However, his focus on the meaningful life tells us that one does not need to have these things in order to be content or excited about life. If we feel that we are acting to fulfill our highest function, it is difficult *not* to be happy.

Aristotle

Born in the Macedonian city of Stagira (now northern Greece) in 384 BC, Aristotle was the son of a doctor to the king of Macedonia. At 17 he began his study at Plato's academy in Athens and remained at the school until his teacher's death in 347 BC. He then traveled to Turkey and the Greek island of Lesbos, doing his own research into what we now call marine biology, botany, zoology, geography, and geology. Aristotle married Pythias, one of his fellow students at Plato's Academy, but had a son, Nicomachus, by his mistress, the slave Herpyllis.

During Aristotle's lifetime the Macedonian kingdom under Philip and his son Alexander (the Great) was a conquering power, taking over Greek cities and the Kingdom of Persia. Aristotle enjoyed the patronage of Alexander the Great and was his close adviser until the last years of the emperor's reign, before he fell out of favor because of his Macedonian origins. He died on the island of Euboea, aged 62.

Two-thirds of Aristotle's work is lost, but his corpus covers a vast array of subjects, and he was considered the foremost polymath of his generation. Notable works include Metaphysica, *"On Interpretation,"* De Anima *or "On the Soul,"* Ars Rhetorica, *and* Magna Moralia.

Language, Truth and Logic

*"Philosophy, as it is written, is full of questions ...
which seem to be factual but are not."*

*"If now I ... say 'Stealing money is wrong', I produce a sentence
which has no factual meaning – that is, it expresses no proposition
which can be either true or false. It is as if I had written 'Stealing
money!!' – where the shape and thickness of the exclamation marks
show, by a suitable convention, that a special sort of moral disapproval
is the feeling which is expressed. It is clear that there is nothing said
here which can be true or false."*

In a nutshell

Metaphysics, aesthetics, ethics, and theology are all meaningless
subjects, because nothing that is said in them can ever be verified.

In a similar vein

CHAPTER 4

A.J. Ayer

A t the age of 22 and fresh from Oxford University, Alfred Ayer traveled to Austria to meet with the Vienna Circle, a group of physicists, mathematicians, and philosophers (including Moritz Schlick, Rudolf Carnap, Karl Menger, and Kurt Gödel) working under a shared belief in "logical positivism," the view that the only real knowledge is fact based. Strongly influenced by Wittgenstein's analysis of language and meaning, the group sought to reframe knowledge in terms of the principle of verification, and had a massive effect on twentieth-century philosophy and science.

Through *Language, Truth and Logic* and other writings Ayer became one of the main exporters of these ideas to Britain and America. Written when he was only 25, the book became famous for its forthright, even aggressive exposé of the claims of metaphysics, but it also covers ethics, probability, and language.

The verification principle

Ayer's principle of verification states that a sentence is meaningful only if there are certain circumstances in which we, the language users, can agree with its truth, for the truth of a meaningful sentence must correspond with a possible, observable situation. For example, "There are aliens on Mars" is meaningful, because we know what it would take to confirm it: an observation or other sign of aliens on Mars. Note that we're less concerned with whether or not the sentence is true in itself, only whether or not it is meaningful; that is, verifiable.

Yet Ayer allows some leeway by stressing that we need only confirm claims to be *probably* true, rather than *decisively* true, for them to be meaningful. This is because there are many propositions that, even after making a huge number of observations, we can only confirm to be probably correct. The most common example of such a proposition is a universal law, such as that expressed by the sentence "all arsenic is poisonous." We take this to be a meaningful sentence, but because of the well-known problem of induction, it can only be confirmed as probably true given an increasing number of observations. No number of observations could confirm that all arsenic is poisonous, as we cannot extrapolate with more than probable certainty from any particular examples to the general case.

Ayer also puts forward the idea of emotivism, that statements concerning morality are value judgments driven by the emotion or sentiment of the utterer. Because they cannot be verified by any objective moral "facts" or experience, they have no cognitive significance and are meaningless. When someone says, for instance, "Mary is a good person," they are not defining any objective truth or situation, merely expressing their feeling for Mary. Similarly, when we hear the statement "War is wrong," because it is not a proposition that can ever be conclusively proven one way or the other but is opinion, it is of low or no value. Most language says more about the speaker than it does about "reality."

Metaphysics is meaningless

By applying the principle of verification to philosophy, Ayer comes to question the very basis of metaphysics, aesthetics, ethics, and theology. He considers a typical sentence from a metaphysics book at the time, picked out at random from F.H. Bradley's *Appearance and Reality*: "The Absolute enters into, but is itself incapable of, evolution and progress."

Ayer insists that there is no situation in which one would be able to observe that this sentence is true. Moreover, what can it possibly mean for anybody to say that "the Absolute" (whatever that may be) "enters into evolution"? If a sentence is only meaningful if it is, in principle, verifiable, it is unclear under what circumstances (if any) one could observe the truth of Bradley's statement. How could one ever tell that the Absolute was, or was not, evolving? On the assumption that Bradley is using these words with their common meaning, Ayer concludes that we ought to judge the sentence as meaningless.

Ayer is concerned with factual significance. For instance, the factual significance of "It's raining!" is that it is raining – precisely the kind of meaning that metaphysical statements lack. This is to be distinguished from other senses of meaning that a sentence may have, such as emotional significance; poetry, for instance, might lack factual significance, but that is no reason to cast it aside, because the poet does not try to claim that poems are to be taken as true descriptions of reality. Their literal meaning is not what is generally celebrated. Metaphysicians, on the other hand, often insist that phrases about such abstract concepts as "the Absolute" present a faithful description of reality when they are nonsensical. Though an atheist, Ayer rejected the idea that one could even talk about atheism with meaning, because it was just as nonsensical to say "There is no God" as it was to say "God exists," as neither statement could ever be verified.

Ayer's thinking on verifiability and significant statements came out of his belief in "naturalism," or the idea that philosophy should be treated on the same level as natural science; that is, putting every kind of assertion of truth under the closest scrutiny. Though he could not have hoped to dismantle the whole field of metaphysics, he could restrict philosophers to pronouncements that at least made sense.

Final comments

In stressing the limits of human knowledge, Ayer was very much the heir to David Hume, whom he revered. This, combined with the skeptical outlook of the Continental logical positivists, the language-analyzing influence of Wittgenstein, and the certainty of a 25 year old, made *Language, Truth and Logic* a powerful work.

For readers of today's academic philosophy, which typically studies very particular questions in great depth, the broad sweep of the book is refreshing. Its brevity and lack of technical language make it very readable, and though many have noted that it is not totally original, it is still a brilliant entry point to analytical philosophy and logical positivism.

Following the success of the book, Ayer was once asked what came next. In his usual arrogant way, he replied, "Nothing comes next. Philosophy is over."

A.J. Ayer

Ayer was born in 1910. His mother belonged to the Dutch-Jewish family that had started the Citroën car company and his father worked in finance. He was an only child and gained a scholarship to Eton College.

Studying philosophy at Christ Church, Oxford, his tutor was the philosopher of mind Gilbert Ryle. Ayer worked in British military intelligence during the Second World War, and held academic posts at Christ Church and University College, London, as well as being a well-known media figure.

Ayer married four times, including one remarriage, and had many affairs. In a biography (A.J. Ayer: A Life), *Ben Rogers recounts the time Ayer was entertaining some models at a New York party, when there was a commotion in a bedroom. The supermodel Naomi Campbell was screaming that her boyfriend Mike Tyson was assaulting her. Ayer went in to speak to Tyson, who said, "Do you know who I am? I am the heavyweight champion of the world." Ayer politely replied, "And I am the former Wykeham Professor of Logic ... We are both preeminent in our field. I suggest we talk about this like rational men."*

After his retirement, Ayer championed many progressive social causes, including reforming the law on homosexual rights. He was knighted in 1970 and died in 1989.

Other books include The Foundations of Empirical Knowledge *(1940),* The Problem of Knowledge *(1956),* Russell and Moore: The Analytical Heritage *(1971),* Hume *(1980),* Philosophy in the Twentieth Century *(1982), and the autobiographical volumes* Part of My Life *(1977) and* More of My Life *(1984).*

Simulacra and Simulation

"Today abstraction is no longer that of the map, the double, the mirror, or the concept. Simulation is no longer that of a territory, a referential being, or a substance. It is the generation by models of a real without origin or reality: a hyperreal. The territory no longer precedes the map, nor does it survive it."

"No more mirror of being and appearances, of the real and its concept ... the real is produced from miniaturized cells, matrices, and memory banks, models of control – and it can be reproduced an indefinite number of times from these. It no longer needs to be rational, because it no longer measures itself against either an ideal or negative instance."

"We live in a world where there is more and more information, and less and less meaning."

In a nutshell

We no longer live in a world where signs and symbols point to truth; they *are* the truth.

In a similar vein

Noam Chomsky *Understanding Power* (p 76)
Harry Frankfurt *On Bullshit* (p 118)
Marshall McLuhan *The Medium Is the Massage* (p 188)

CHAPTER 5

Jean Baudrillard

J ean Baudrillard died in 2007, and we are still absorbing and processing many of his ideas. The greatest theorist of postmodernity, he was strictly speaking a sociologist, spending 20 years in the sociology department at Nanterre University in Paris; his career spanned the student revolts of 1968, the fall of communism, and the rise of what he called the "hyperreal" order of media-centered capitalism.

Baudrillard's thinking marks a huge and rather subversive break from the traditions of Western philosophy, with its typical focus on questions of the self, free will and knowledge, and even the existentialist's idea of living an "authentic" life. His vision was instead a world in which individuality is a myth, and where people are units reflecting whatever is happening in the media, their only purpose to consume images and signs; in this new universe, something is real only if it can be reproduced endlessly, and what is singular or unshareable does not exist.

Simulacra and Simulation was the book that made Baudrillard fashionable outside France, and it is surprisingly accessible. Though the examples he gives relate to culture and politics in the 1970s, for most readers contemporary instances of his ideas will easily come to mind.

The territory no longer matters

In one of his novels, Jorge Luis Borges told the tale of the mapmakers of a kingdom who created a map so accurate and so comprehensive that it spread like a sheet over the actual territory of the land. Though a nice story, Baudrillard argues that in the contemporary world such enterprises seem quaint, since all that really matters is the map itself; we do not try to pretend that it is simply an abstraction that helps us get to reality – it *is* reality. "But it is no longer a question of either maps or territories," he says. "Something has disappeared: the sovereign difference, between one and the other, that constituted the charm of abstraction."

Thus, the charm of a map lies in the room we give it not to be an accurate representation of reality. Now we make no such allowance; rather, we do what we can to make "reality" conform to our abstractions. We no longer live in a world of the dual: being and appearance, the real and the concept. What is "real" can be endlessly produced from computer programs and, most disturbingly, this new reality no longer has reference to some rational base of truth:

> *"It is no longer a question of imitation, nor duplication, nor even parody. It is a question of substituting the signs of the real for the real..."*

Baudrillard calls this new world the "hyperreal" and one of its interesting qualities is that it obviates the need for the imaginary, since there is no distinction between what is reality and what is imagined. We are left with a world that is a "gigantic simulacrum" (a simulation or likeness), one that is "never exchanged for the real, but exchanged for itself, in an uninterrupted circuit without reference or circumference."

Though it is not an analogy Baudrillard uses, a useful one to think of here is paper money – it is hardly ever exchanged for the gold or silver it is theoretically convertible to; rather, paper money *is* money, not a representation of it. The fact that "in truth" it is simply paper is irrelevant.

In place of the real, we make a fetish of the past

For Baudrillard, the turning point in history was a transition from our acceptance of a world of signs that indicate truth or ideology, and that put a premium on secrecy, to a world that does not bother to make such an attempt. In the era of simulacra and simulation, he says, "there is no longer a God to recognize his own, no longer a Last Judgment to separate the false from the true."

When this happens, nostalgia creeps in and there is a surface hankering for "truth" and "authenticity." There is "Panic-stricken production of the real and of the referential, parallel to and greater than the panic of material production." When everything becomes abstract, the value of the "real" is inflated – but is it really the real that we want, or only the signs of the real? Once we are in the world of simulacra and simulation, it is difficult to step out of it; we barely know the difference between it and reality.

Baudrillard suggests that we are like the Tasaday people, who were found by ethnologists deep in the rainforest in the 1970s. To avoid their being wiped out, they were moved to an area of unreachable virgin forest. This living museum aimed to keep alive their "realness" and allow them to live in their traditional ways, but sealing them off was itself a great act of simulation. Similarly, Western scientists spend a great deal of money conserving Egyptian mummies, not because ancient Egypt means anything to us, but because such objects are a sort of guarantee that old things have particular meaning: "Our entire linear and accumulative culture collapses if we cannot stockpile the past in plain view." Such "museumification" is the mark of a culture that hates secrets and wishes to "own" other cultures by dissecting and categorizing them. They are valuable to us as symbols of the fact that they were superseded – by us.

Baudrillard portrays Disneyland as a classic case of simulacra, because it is presented as an imaginary place only "in order to make us believe that the rest [of our society] is real." Disneyland preserves the fantasy of a separation between truth and fabrication, a fantasy we need in order to keep existing in a fabricated world. Places like this help us avoid the fact that the larger America itself belongs to the realm of simulation.

Politics in a hyperreal world

Baudrillard goes beyond the typical leftist/Marxist view of capitalism as immoral. Rather, capitalism is a "monstrous unprincipled enterprise, nothing more." Capitalism and the capitalist media focus on "the economy," "economic indicators," and "demand" as if these were the core of society, and in doing so, "every ideal distinction between true and false, good and evil" is destroyed "in order to establish a radical law of equivalence and exchange." In capitalism, we are mere consumers. Yet to preserve the illusion that we are free-willed citizens living in a dynamic democracy, capitalism manufactures crises that aim to stop us from seeing that its way of life is only a construct.

Political power as we witness it today – the elections, the obsession with presidential activities, and so on – is a charade, and the growing intensity of coverage is a sign that traditional executive power no longer exists. Power is, rather, in the whole *system*, a fact that the media frenzy around politics seeks to obscure. And as people hate politics more and more, the charade will only grow more intense in order to evoke the feeling that it is real. Baudrillard portrays the Kennedy assassinations as the last real political deaths in the West, since JFK and Bobby were seen to be truly exercising power. They were too real, and so they had to go. Even so, Baudrillard says that in an age of simulation, actual assassinations are no longer required; they can be simulated, as with Watergate and Nixon's political decapitation, which became the template for the modern political death ritual. The more important you are, the greater the chance of your "sacrifice."

The hyperreal media society

In 1971, a television crew lived with a Californian family, the Louds, for seven months, filming their every move. The family fell apart under the gaze of 20 million viewers, which led to the question of how much of a role the show played. The producers marketed it as being "as if the cameras were not there," which Baudrillard describes as a Utopia of "reality" that was of course a brilliant fake, but it exemplified the pleasure that we, the audience, have when something real becomes hyperreal.

The typicalness of the family (upper-middle-class Californians, decorative housewife, three garages, several children) ensured that they would be destroyed, since what a hyperreal culture needs is frequent sacrifices. However, in this modern version, "Because heavenly fire no longer falls on corrupted cities, it is the camera lens that, like a laser, comes to pierce lived reality in order to put it to death." Beaudrillard wonders: does reality television "refer to the truth of this family or to the truth of TV?" Television became the Louds' truth, because in a culture based on simulacra and simulation, "it is TV that is true, it is TV that renders true."

In a fascinating analysis of 1970s cinema, Baudrillard discusses the connection between real events and films. He argues that the nuclear spill at Three Mile Island in the United States had its Hollywood counterpart in *The China Syndrome*; the film event became as important as the real, taking on a truth greater than the artistic expression. This is the sort of violence done to truth in a hyperreal world.

Presaging the rise of the internet and the social media phenomenon, Baudrillard notes that people are now measured by the extent of their involvement in the flow of media messages. "Whoever is underexposed to the media is desocialized or virtually asocial," he says, and the flow of these messages is unquestioned as a good that increases meaning, just as the flow of capital is considered to increase welfare and happiness. One of the standout lines of the book is:

"We live in a world where there is more and more information, and less and less meaning."

He asks: "Are the mass media on the side of power in the manipulation of the masses, or are they on the side of the masses in the liquidation of meaning, in the violence perpetrated on meaning, and in fascination?" Whereas in the old order people worried about the first, surely the second is more disturbing.

Advertising is conventionally seen as superficial in relation to the actual things and products to which it refers, but in Baudrillard's thinking advertising is the core of our civilization. The commodities to which it points are relatively valueless – what matters is our identification with the stories, signs, and imagery that front those commodities; it is *these* that we desire and consume. We go shopping not so much to acquire things, but to keep ourselves within the boundaries of the hyperreal (not to want to consume these signs and symbols is subversive). The notion of a free-willed, rational individual is a total myth; we are best seen as entities fully wrapped up in, and part of, the technology and consumer culture.

Final comments

Baudrillard's compelling argument was that the universe we now inhabit is totally different from the modernist world of "clashes of ideologies." He argued that the terrorist attacks on 9/11 were not a case of the "clash of civilizations," or of Islam against America, but rather the focal point of a world reacting against its own globalization and shift into the hyperreal, a sort of last, horrible shot fired against the encroachment of media and technology into all aspects of our lives, subsuming value systems.

Philosophers have spent centuries arguing about the relative weight between "subject" (I) and "object" (the world), but Baudrillard saw the debate as having long since become insignificant – the object had won hands down. A person today is not a project in selfhood, as many traditions of philosophy and theology have told us, but more like a machine that consumes and reproduces the ideas and images that are current in the media, advertising, and politics. And, most disturbing of all, the replacement of reality with hyperreality is what Baudrillard calls the "perfect crime," because most of us are barely aware that it has ever happened.

Jean Baudrillard
Baudrillard was born in Reims in 1929. His parents were civil servants and his grandparents farmers. He was the first in his family to go to university. From 1966 to 1987 he held positions at Nanterre University, and then taught at the European Graduate School until his death in 2007.

His first book, The Object System (1968), was greatly influenced by Roland Barthes, and in his early phase Baudrillard was considered a post-Marxist. Later works relating to the media drew on the ideas of Marshall McLuhan. Simulacra and Simulation was an inspiration for the film The Matrix, *which offers an idea of what might happen if hyperreality is taken to its logical, all-pervading extent.*

Other books include Consumer Society *(1970),* Critique of the Political Economy of the Sign *(1972),* The Mirror of Production *(1973),* In the Shadow of the Silent Majorities *(1983),* America *(1986),* Forget Foucault *(1987),* The Gulf War Did Not Take Place *(1991), and* The Perfect Crime *(1995).*

1949

The Second Sex

"One is not born a woman: one becomes a woman."

"The individual life history of woman – because she is still bound up in her female functions – depends in much greater degree than that of man upon her physiological destiny; and the curve of her destiny is much more uneven, more discontinuous, than the masculine curve."

In a nutshell

The concept of "Other" helps us understand the position and power of women through history.

In a similar vein

Judith Butler *Gender Trouble* (p 68)
Jean-Paul Sartre *Being and Nothingness* (p 272)

CHAPTER 6

Simone de Beauvoir

At 40, Simone de Beauvoir was the author of several well-received novels, but was better known as Jean Paul-Sartre's long-time companion. All that changed with the release of *Le Deuxième sex*. The book was a best-seller from the start, and de Beauvoir found herself the most controversial woman in France.

Given her relatively privileged position – teaching career, university degree, movement in Parisian intellectual circles – de Beauvoir herself had never felt much of a sense of injustice or inequality. Nevertheless, she began to realize that people saw her as Sartre's inferior merely because she was female. When she sat down to write *The Second Sex*, she was surprised to find herself putting down the most essential fact of her existence: "I am a woman."

The Second Sex is not simply about the role of women in history or society, but about "Woman" as an archetype and philosophical category that is inter-changeable with the idea of "Other." This philosophical base raises the book above other feminist writing and makes it fascinating reading.

The work spans 700 pages and is not easy to summarize. Book One traces the history of women's place in society from the bronze age to medieval times to modernity, including an analysis of the "myth of woman" through five authors: Henry de Montherlant, D.H. Lawrence, Paul Claudel, André Breton, and Stendhal. Book Two traces the situation of woman today, from childhood to sexual awakening, marriage to menopause, including portraits of woman as lover, narcissist, and mystic, before ending on a more upbeat note with a chapter on women's independence.

Woman as Other

The Second Sex is an attempt to answer the basic question "What is Woman?" – that is, as an archetype or category as opposed to women as individuals. Throughout history, men have differentiated and defined women in reference to themselves, rather than as beings in their own right. A person is a man, and no more expla-nation is necessary, while a woman must be described as a person of the female sex. The result, de Beauvoir says, is that woman is "the incidental, the inessential as opposed to the essential. He is the subject, he is Absolute – she is the Other."

The term "Other," she notes, can be applied to any group in society that is not considered the "main" group. In Western civilization, for instance, white men are the "essential," the "Absolute," while any other kind of person, including women, people of color, and Jews, have been – whether consciously or unconsciously – put in the Other basket. When a group in society is made inferior in this way, they *become* inferior through lost opportunities and debasement.

Men do not feel that they have to justify themselves on any objective basis, but get their feeling of superiority from not being women. This results in the clichéd, although true, view that a women has to do twice as much to be seen as the equal of a man. Discrimination against women, de Beauvoir writes, is "a miraculous balm for those afflicted with an inferiority complex, and indeed no one is more arrogant toward women, more aggressive or scornful, than the man who is anxious about his virility." Today we are familiar with such a truth, but imagine the affront that it caused in bourgeois France 60 years ago.

De Beauvoir expresses her amazement that although women make up half of the human race, they can still be discriminated against. She observes that in democracies men like to say that they see women as equal (or democracy would be a lie), but their attitudes on many levels tell a different story.

Is biology destiny?

De Beauvoir goes back to the earliest conceptions of biology to show how science itself served to reduce the power and potency of the female in favor of the male. In conception, for instance, the passivity of the female was contrasted with the "active principle" of male sperm, which was thought to determine all the characteristics of the newborn. Yet in conception, de Beauvoir notes, neither male or female gamete is superior to the other; rather, they both lose their individuality when the egg is fertilized.

The burden of the continuity of life is still a female one, and given the energy and time required for this the female's possibilities are severely restricted, because "the woman is adapted to the needs of the egg rather than to her own requirements." From puberty to menopause, she is at the mercy of a body changing itself according to reproductive needs, and must put up with a monthly reminder of this. In pregnancy in the early stages, vomiting and loss of appetite "signalize the revolt of the organism against the invading species." Many a woman's maladies do not stem from external threats, but from dealing with her own, often problematic reproductive system. Moreover, the more intense emotionality of women is related to irregularities in secretions in the endocrine system, which have an effect on the nervous system. Many of these traits, de Beauvoir points out, "originate in woman's subordination to the species." In contrast, "the male seems infinitely favoured: his sexual life is not in opposition to his existence as a person, and biologically it runs an even course, without crises and generally without mishap." Though women tend to live longer than men, they are ill more often, and overall are less in control of their bodies – their bodies control them. However, menopause can bring liberation, as a woman is no longer determined or judged according to the childbearing function.

While a woman's biological features are therefore the key to understanding her situation in life, de Beauvoir optimistically says, "I deny that they establish for her a fixed and inevitable destiny." Biology is not reason enough for male/female inequality, nor grounds for woman being cast as "Other," and a female's physicality does not condemn her to remain subordinate. Moreover, while animals can be studied as static organisms, it is much harder to make assessments of *people* as male or female human beings, since our sex does not define us in the way it does other animals. In many physical respects a woman is less rugged than a man, so ostensibly her projects and prospects are more limited, but, drawing on Heidegger, Sartre, and Maurice Merleau-Ponty, de Beauvoir notes that "the body is not a thing, it is a situation." When viewed in this way, women's prospects may be different to men's, but no more limited. What is more, many of women's "weaknesses" are such only in the context of male ends. Physical inferiority, for instance, becomes meaningless if there is an absence of violence and wars. If society is different, so the evaluation of physical attributes changes.

Becoming woman

Book Two contains de Beauvoir's famous comment that "one is not born but rather becomes a woman." In childhood there is no difference between the sexes in terms of what they are capable of. Differentiation begins when boys are told of their superiority and how they need to prepare for the difficult, heroic path ahead. While pride in his sex is pointed out to a boy by adults, the girl's sexual anatomy does not receive the same reverence. Urinating also produces a sexual difference: for the boy it is a game, but for the girl a shameful and inconvenient procedure. Even if a girl has no "penis envy," the presence of an organ that can be seen and grasped helps a boy to identify himself and it becomes a kind of alter ego. For the girl it is the doll that becomes the alter ego. There is really no "maternal instinct," de Beauvoir argues, but through play with the doll the girl ascertains that the care of children falls on the mother, and "thus her vocation is powerfully impressed upon her."

Yet when she becomes mature, a girl realizes that it is no privilege to be the mother, as men control the world. This revelation helps her to understand that a father's life has a "mysterious prestige." When sexual awakening occurs, boys are aggressive and grasping, whereas for the girl it is often a case of fraught "waiting" ("She is waiting Man"). Since time immemorial, Woman has looked to the male for fulfillment and escape, so girls learn that to please they must abdicate their power and independence.

Woman's character, de Beauvoir concludes, is molded by her situation. Women are not socially independent but form part of groups governed and defined by men. Any club or social service they set up is still within the framework of the masculine universe. "Many of the faults for which women are reproached – mediocrity, laziness, frivolity, servility," de Beauvoir points out, "simply express the fact that their horizon is closed."

Woman and myth

Since women have rarely seen themselves as protagonists, there are not many female myths like those of Hercules or Prometheus. Women's mythical roles are always secondary; they dream the dreams of Man. Man has created myths around woman and all myths have helped to reiterate that woman is the inessential; he has revolted against the fact that he is born from a woman's womb and will also die. Since birth is tied to death, Woman condemns man to finitude.

Women have also been seen as sorceresses and enchantresses who cast a spell on man. Man both fears and desires Woman. He loves her as she is his, but he fears her as she remains the "Other"; it is this Other whom he wishes to make his. Like man, woman is endowed with spirit and mind, but "she belongs to nature and so appears as a mediatrix between the individual and the cosmos." Christianity spiritualized Woman, assigning to her beauty, warmth, intimacy, and the role of pity and tenderness. She was no longer tangible and her mystery deepened. Woman is man's muse, and also a judge who pronounces on the value of his enterprises. She is a prize to be won, the dream within which all other dreams are enfolded. On the positive side, Woman has always inspired Man to exceed his own limits.

Final comments

What would de Beauvoir make of today's gender landscape? Particularly in richer and freer countries, many women feel that *The Second Sex* is outdated, that equality is real, or at least that the gaps in equality are bridgeable, and that girls have futures every bit as bright as boys. However, in countries where misogyny rules, and sexual inequality is written into laws and expressed in custom, de Beauvoir's book remains a potential bombshell, revealing much about the real motives of men.

The book has been criticized for being too anecdotal and circular, for not being a "proper" work of philosophy, but this in itself can be seen as a subtle attack on the author's gender by left-brained, system-building male philosophers. Indeed, that de Beauvoir is often overlooked as a philosopher only proves her point that it is mostly men who end up writing the history of disciplines – and it is not surprising that they focus first on the contributions of their own sex.

Many of de Beauvoir's assertions have been overtaken by science. We are not blank slates but are born with certain behavioral tendencies whether we are male or female. Conditioning is definitely real, as she pointed out, yet it is not the whole story. The more we know about our bodies and brains, the less biology will be destiny. Gender theorists such as Judith Butler say that de Beauvoir overemphasized sex roles, and that gender is a much more fluid thing than even she imagined. In a time of multiple gender identities, how should we understand the term "woman"? As a matter of biology, or of choice?

These debates aside, if you are female, reading *The Second Sex* will remind you of the progress made for women in the last 70 years. If you are male, it will help you gain a greater understanding of the slightly different universe that women inhabit, even today.

Simone de Beauvoir

De Beauvoir was born in 1908 in Paris. Her father was a legal secretary. Her mother was a devout Catholic and she was sent to a prestigious convent school. In her childhood she was very religious and considered becoming a nun, but at 14 she became an atheist.

Studying philosophy at the Sorbonne, she wrote a thesis on Leibniz. In a national exam that ranked students, she came second only to Jean-Paul Sartre (whom she had already met) and was also the youngest person ever to pass. Her relationship with Sartre influenced her first novel, She Came to Stay, *published in 1943.*

De Beauvoir taught philosophy at the Lycée Pierre-Corneille in Rouen, where her friend the feminist Collette Audry also taught. In 1947 she was sent by the French government to the United States to give university lectures on contemporary French literature. In the same year she wrote her popular essay on French existentialism, "The Ethics of Ambiguity." She traveled widely and wrote several travel diaries about her journeys through China, Italy, and America, which she visited several times.

De Beauvoir lived not far from Sartre in Paris and penned A Farewell to Sartre, *a moving account of his last years. She continued her literary and activist work until her death in 1986.*

Principles of Morals and Legislation

"Nature has placed mankind under the governance of two sovereign masters, pain and pleasure. It is for them alone to point out what we ought to do, as well as determine what we should do."

"The business of government is to promote the happiness of the society, by punishing and rewarding. That part of its business which consists in punishing, is more particularly the subject of penal law. In proportion as an act tends to disturb that happiness ... will be the demand it creates for punishment."

"Pleasures then, and the avoidance of pains, are the ends that the legislator has in view; it behoves him therefore to understand their value."

In a nutshell

A just society is most likely to be achieved by using an objective calculus of maximizing pleasure and minimizing pain.

In a similar vein

John Stuart Mill *On Liberty* (p 200)

Plato *The Republic* (p 230)

John Rawls *A Theory of Justice* (p 246)

Michael Sandel *The Tyranny of Merit* (p 264)

Peter Singer *The Life You Can Save* (p 286)

CHAPTER 7

Jeremy Bentham

J eremy Bentham had a huge influence on nineteenth-century Britain, yet he only became well known in the 1820s, quite late in life. We associate him with reform causes in the Industrial Revolution – including relief for the poor, a proper sewage system for London, extending the voting franchise, and plans for schools, workhouses, and prisons (the famous Panopticon) – but most of his writings came earlier. *The Introduction to the Principles of Morals and Legislation,* for instance, was written in 1780, and was to be an overture to a multivolume work (which was never produced) on reform of the penal code and the principle of utility in civil and constitutional law.

Though most people have heard of Bentham's principle of utility, also known as "the greatest happiness for the greatest number," few have read *Principles of Morals and Legislation.* Bentham admits that most of the work is quite dry, but his defense is that "truths that form the basis of political and moral science are not to be discovered but by investigations as severe as mathematical ones." Utility was an almost mathematical principle, he felt, and he wanted to give a sense of its unerring logic, which did not leave much room for artistic flourish. However, the book is still a fascinating text.

As a child John Stuart Mill often spent time at Bentham's home, and was groomed to take over the elder man's utilitarian ideology. Mill's *Utilitarianism* (1863) evolved and refined Bentham's ideas, and is an easier introduction to the subject. The history of philosophy may hold Mill to be of higher import, but it is hard to imagine what Mill would have achieved had not Bentham come before him.

A new way of governing

Bentham discusses various principles that had been used to guide lawmakers, and dismisses each in turn. If the principle of utility is right, he argues, it is right all the time. All other guiding principles must be wrong and can only be measured against the yardstick of utility.

One such guiding principle is "asceticism." Although practiced in monasteries, Bentham notes that it has never been put to work as an actual principle for government, and for good reason. The mass of people are self-interested, driven by desires rather than stilling desire. Bentham was no atheist, but was very clear about religion having no place in political life. The task of knowing divine will is deeply subjective, and therefore inevitably flawed. In contrast, by adopting the principle of utility we gain a clear idea of what is good for all, and thus are seeing divine will in action. For what would God want, if not increased happiness for the greatest number?

Another guiding principle is "sympathy and antipathy": people are driven to act or judge based on whether or not they like something. This is an anti-principle, as it is founded in nothing universal (like utility), only personal whim. Bentham says that the principle of "right and wrong," while seeming to have more gravitas, is merely an extension of like and dislike. The policy of a government often amounts to an expression of its members' personal preferences. There is no conception of utility, or what is actually best for the greatest number.

While governments may hide behind a secular "moral sense" as a reason for their actions, this disguises their fundamental irrationality. Criminal justice does not rest on rational utility, or what is best for the criminal and society, but on the moral biases of people about which crimes are considered worst. Bentham notes "that the principle of sympathy and antipathy is most apt to err on the side of severity." When a group hates a certain behavior, it will want to punish the doer excessively, way beyond the actual negative effects of the crime, and such punishments will have knock-on negative conse- quences. And yet, "the happiness of the individuals, of whom a community is composed, that is their pleasures and their security, is the end and the sole end which the legislator ought to have in view." The balance to be maintained by legislators is allowing for as much freedom as possible while containing any behavior that would lessen the happiness of others (a theme that John Stuart Mill would further in *On Liberty*).

The greatest happiness principle

Bentham notes that even if people claim they do not support the principle of utility, they apply it to their lives: to order their own actions and consider the next action to take, and to judge other people's actions. We are basically machines for seeking happiness, and we judge others on whether they are likely to increase or decrease our own store of happiness. Along with Adam Smith, Bentham saw human beings as essentially self-interested. What, then, was the proper role of government to his mind?

His purpose in writing the book was to "rear the fabric of felicity by the hands of reason and law" – in other words, to legislate happiness into being.

This was perhaps a utopian project, yet he argues that the utility principle is the only one by which the activities of a state can be rationally ordered. This was a radical idea, because Britain's legislative system was based on common law, or precedent. The idea of legislating from scratch with the aim of achieving the goal of the highest benefit of the highest number was never likely to happen in practice, though Bentham's call to "take reason, not custom for your guide" would in time revitalize and shape legal thinking.

In Bentham's grand project, neither history nor other texts could be used as a basis for making laws, since if one text were held as the "authority" on a matter, it could easily be opposed by another text. Only reason alone (specifically, the utility principle) could be the basis for policy and law; indeed, Bentham observed that we would know that the principle was operating in institutions and laws if their purpose was such that people *ought* to like them, even if individually they did not always do so.

In his methodical way, Bentham provides a classification of 12 pains and 14 pleasures, and various degrees of each, such as intensity, duration, and extent, which legislators, or indeed anyone, can use to judge the happiness or unhappiness effect of any given action. Though such an approach can seem a little technical or mechanical, for Bentham it was a vital foundation on which to build a new kind of law that could not be abused by any particular group in society for its own interest. His aim was to "to cut a new road through the wilds of jurisprudence" – to make laws transparent, not benefiting certain people over others. In a country in which hereditary privileges were enshrined in law this was a significant move, and, not surprisingly, Bentham's ideas took a long time to take hold in Britain, despite their great logic. He became much better known in France, where he was lionized by the revolutionaries and made an honorary citizen of the Republic.

Final comments
Bentham was not keen on the idea of "natural rights," but he believed that everyone in society has a right to at least be protected from physical harm, on the basis that wrongful action cancels or reduces an individual's right to happiness.

Bentham's dictum "everybody to count for one, nobody for more than one" was shorthand for the utilitarian principle of justice, and he was ahead of his time in applying this to all sentient beings. He argues in *Principles of Morals and Legislation* that rights should depend not on the ability to reason, but on the ability to suffer. This distinction was a foundation of the modern animal rights movement, notably in the writings of Peter Singer (*Animal Liberation*, 1973).

For Singer, a contemporary utilitarian, the test of actions, including what we eat or how we spend our money, is how much pain these acts can help avoid (whether for people or animals) and whether those same acts can increase the store of life and happiness.

Critics of the utilitarian principle say that it goes against intuition or human nature. For instance, psychological studies have shown that we do not act based on calculations of how many people our actions will benefit, but on whether an action gives us a positive emotional response. Such biases may be wired into us from millions of years of social bonding and the desire to protect our own, and it is unlikely that a seemingly dry philosophical principle can overcome that. Indeed, utilitarianism may seem quite an impersonal or calculating way of looking at life and the organization of society, and Bentham himself admitted as much, which is why he preferred the phrase "greatest happiness principle." Yet he was passionate in his belief that it was our best hope for a fair and civilized society.

On a purely personal level, asking "What would benefit the most people, in the best way, as far as possible into the future?" is surely a good way to approach life and its decisions. Bentham assumed that most people were self-interested, but all religions, and many kinds of moral philosophy, attest to the benefits of cultivating the direct opposite state: thinking of the good of others first is actually the one thing we can count on to deliver our *own* happiness.

Jeremy Bentham

Born in 1748 in London, the son and grandson of lawyers, Bentham attended Westminster School before, at 12, going to Oxford University. He then trained for a career in law, but never practiced. Instead, he pursued his own interests, and later in life an inheritance allowed him to keep writing and researching without worry.

Bentham wrote voluminously and his papers are still being transcribed. He corresponded with American founding father James Madison, South American revolutionary Simon Bolivar, political economist Adam Smith, and French revolutionary Mirabeau. He favored making homosexuality a private matter instead of a criminal offense, opposed slavery, supported women's equality and the right to divorce, and was a promoter of open government, writing that "Where there is no publicity [i.e., full disclosure] there is no justice." As part of his drive for criminal reform, he spent many years developing the influential "Panopticon" prison concept, though his National Penitentiary was never built.

In 1797, Bentham campaigned with Patrick Colquhoun against theft from merchant ships and corruption on the Thames in London, which led to the establishment of a river police force. He founded the utilitarian newspaper the Westminster Review in 1823, and three years later helped set up the University of London, which later became University College, London. Its ethos was openness to all, irrespective of wealth or religious affiliation (in contrast to the universities at Oxford and Cambridge).

James Mill (John Stuart's father) met Bentham around 1808 and spent summers with Bentham and his circle at Forde Abbey, Bentham's country house in Somerset. Bentham died in 1832 and, true to his principles, left his body to science rather than have it buried. His exterior mummified body was dressed and eventually placed on display at University College, London. It can still be viewed today.

Other books include Fragment on Government *(1776)*, Defence of Usury *(1787)*, Panopticon *(1787)*, Parliamentary Reform Catechism *(1817)*, *and* A Treatise on Judicial Evidence *(1825)*.

The Hedgehog and the Fox

"The rare capacity for seeing this we rightly call a 'sense of reality' – it is a sense of what fits with what, of what cannot exist with what; and it goes by many names: insight, wisdom, practical genius, a sense of the past, an understanding of life and of human character."

"Wisdom is ... not scientific knowledge, but a special sensitiveness to the contours of the circumstances in which we happen to be placed; it is a capacity for living without falling foul of some permanent condition or factor which cannot be either altered, or even fully described or calculated; an ability to be guided by rules of thumb – the 'immemorial wisdom' said to reside in peasants and other 'simple folk' – where rules of science do not, in principle, apply. This inexpressible sense of cosmic orientation is the 'sense of reality', the 'knowledge' of how to live."

In a nutshell

There are two levels of reality: the phenomenal world that we can see around us, and a deeper plane of truth that human beings rarely perceive.

In a similar vein

David Bohm *Wholeness and the Implicate Order* (p 62)
Ralph Waldo Emerson *Fate* (p 100)
Plotinus *The Enneads* (p 236)
Arthur Schopenhauer *The World As Will and Representation* (p 280)
Baruch Spinoza *Ethics* (p 298)

CHAPTER 8

Isaiah Berlin

S ir Isaiah Berlin was both a political philosopher and an historian of ideas, one of the great intellectuals of the twentieth century. Though he wrote many influential essays, *The Hedgehog and the Fox* tends to stay in people's minds, if only for the intriguing title. Subtitled 'Reflections on Tolstoy's view of history', on the surface it seems to be about the distinction between two ways of approaching knowledge: between the big picture thinker who knows "one big thing" (the hedgehog) and the person focused on details who knows "lots of little things" (the fox). In fact, this distinction is little discussed in this famous essay. He makes it only to point to something deeper: a fundamental divide in reality, between the relative or "real" world, and the absolute, which Tolstoy alluded to in his writings.

The folly and conceit of history

It was the fashion in the nineteenth century to view every subject in a scientific way, including history. But Tolstoy considered that, despite advanced research techniques to find out "what happened," this approach was ultimately superficial. History, or why events occurred, could not be boiled down to a science, since there were no dependable laws that could even approach those found in the natural sciences. History could only be the telling of a story framed by the historian's choice of material to research, or a lens to be looked through. Only a tiny part of the real truth could be revealed. What humans have always done is reshape events to create a meaningful story.

Tolstoy observed that "history" is not a grand, directional, "macro" picture of what happened, but simply the aggregated outcome of millions of individuals living according to their own impulses. In *War and Peace*, Tolstoy mercilessly slays the conceit of generals and leaders who believe they are shaping events. He shows the generals meeting at the Council of Drissa to be talking nonsense, since (as Berlin puts it), "no theories can possibly fit the immense variety of possible human behaviour, the vast multiplicity of minute, undiscoverable causes and effects which form that interplay of men and nature which history purports to record." According to this view, Napoleon, with his famous claim to be able to "read" events through sheer intelligence or intuition, was a charlatan. And the greater the claim to such ability, Tolstoy believes, the more damage that can be done. Millions would die for Napoleon's conceit.

For Tolstoy, the fiction of controlling history is to be contrasted with the actual lives of people, the real scenes and emotions and relationships that happen in the present, and for which the supposed "grand direction" means nothing – and rightly so. Yet this level of explication remained trivial, like looking at the flowers of life instead of the roots. It did not provide an answer to his basic question of why things happened the way they did. Along with the "great man" view of historical change, Tolstoy also rejected the notion that ideas or books shaped history; this might have been just the bias of academics who studied it. Neither did he subscribe to the belief in scientific sociology (as Marxism would do) that you could detect "laws" in history. People just choose facts after the event to support their theories.

Tolstoy did not believe in some great mystical causation, but rather the opposite: things happened through a multiplicity of infinitesimal causes, which the human brain could not possible be aware of. Both the study of history and the natural sciences were a poor and limited attempt to capture the reality of things.

Tolstoy's free will myth

Tolstoy's vision of history follows a certain understanding of free will: that it does not exist. Echoing Spinoza, he observes that we only believe we are acting freely because we are ignorant of the real causes of things. For many of his characters, Berlin observes, the most important moments in life are those in which they appreciate the natural unfolding logic of events, and their apparently predetermined role in them.

Tolstoy's main thesis, Berlin comments, "is that there is a natural law whereby the lives of human beings no less than that of nature are determined; but that men, unable to face this inexorable process, seek to represent it as a succession of free choices ..." We are only free in trivial acts, such as reaching for a cup. Whenever others are involved we become part of the unstoppable stream of life and events. We see "power" and "accidents" as what cause other things to happen, but for Tolstoy these are just the tip of an iceberg of causality that we never get to see. And it is lucky that we *don't* see these chains of causation, because "if we felt their weight, we would scarcely act at all."

Berlin asks on behalf of Tolstoy: "Since we are not, in fact, free, but could not live without the conviction that we are, what are we to do?"

Tolstoy's answer is not to believe in the "rational optimism" of science, social engineering, military expertise, and so on, and instead to live according to common sense beliefs which have stood the test of time. His character Kutuzov, a simple Russian hero living by his instincts, is Tolstoy's hero – not the general, scientist or politician who believes they can change the world.

Critics have attacked Tolstoy's downbeat assessment of the possibilities of human action, but as Berlin notes, the best passages in *War and Peace* are those in which thoughts, knowledge, feelings and relationships *matter*. Therefore, Berlin suggests, "Tolstoy's notion of inexorable laws which work themselves out whatever men may think or wish is itself an oppressive myth."

Tolstoy was brilliant at observing the specifics of life while demolishing any notion that there was some unifying reality or principle that held it all together. But Berlin argues that Tolstoy "protested too much" – he longed for such a unifying principle or single purpose to exist. But if even he, giant intellect that he was, could not find it, he was not going to accept anyone else's claim that *they* had.

Predictably irrational

Berlin tells of the strong influence on Tolstoy of French political philosopher and diplomat Joseph de Maistre, who was Tolstoy's bedside reading while writing *War and Peace*.

De Maistre and Tolstoy rejected the liberal belief in progress and the naive view that the world could move towards increasing happiness and prosperity. De Maistre was interested in "the superhuman sources of knowledge – faith, revelation, tradition." Next to the power of insight that these things give into reality, science, criticism and secularism are nothing. Or as Berlin puts it, "The natural enemies of this spirit are cleverness and specialisation."

De Maistre believed that only religion understood "the 'inner' rhythms, the 'deeper' currents of the world, the silent march of things." Tolstoy was less interested in such mystical explanations, and more into the millions of causes which produced history. Yet, at the same time, he didn't believe that the more bits of information you had, the more you would "know."

Tolstoy agreed with de Maistre that reason never explained anything about human behaviour. Rather, Berlin notes, "only the irrational, precisely because it defied explanation and could therefore not be undermined by the critical activities of reason, was able to persist and be strong." De Maistre observed that institutions such as hereditary monarchy and marriage were also irrational, and yet they survived, while reasoned alternatives were often short lived.

Tolstoy didn't deny the worth of science in its own realm, but simply saw it as trivial next to the questions of individual action, morality and politics. These questions could never be answered by science, because, as Berlin interprets it, "the proportion in them of 'submerged', uninspectable life is too high." All Tolstoy's heroes have knowledge or glimpses of this underlying framework of truth, and it is their awareness that makes all rational or scientific explanations of things, events and our lives so hollow in comparison.

So what is real?

When Tolstoy's characters have moments of illumination, it is not an appreciation of "the oneness of all things" or "the laws" that govern our lives – it is a moment of revelation about why things have turned out the way they have, or what will happen next – an understanding of the real relationship between things, and the peace that comes in submitting to it.

What these moments give us is an awareness of the limits of reason, of the separation between the world that can be observed and analyzed and constructed … and the underlying structure of reality which contains all this, including our emotional lives and existence. We can't give this framework any names or categories, because names and categories are part of the observed, experienced world only. In practical terms, this perception of true reality is wisdom. It is an awareness of the "shape" of things or how they are moving, or an insight into a person. These insights don't come from rational analysis or science.

Berlin believes that Tolstoy actually saw himself as a fox, as a man of facts. He would have liked to have been empirical type, analyzing only observable phenomena and staying away from the mystical view. But he couldn't manage this, because the empirical view was so limited. To get to the truth of things he had to dig deeper, yet he didn't quite allow himself or the characters of his novels to express a *unified* view of reality – which would necessarily have gone beyond the factual or physical.

Berlin's conclusion is that Tolstoy would loved to have had the hedgehog's view of the world: that there is a unifying truth that underlies everything. Like Moses, the sight of his promised land makes his whole life meaningful, but he felt he could not enter it. At the same time, he denies that anything else, including science or civilization, can penetrate it either. That would be hubris.

Final comments

Berlin sees the end of Tolstoy's life as being tragic. Because he was so clearly a great man, his ferocious doubt and criticism of what he thought were wrong views (belief in rationality on one hand, mysticism on the other) ended up being his own pursuer; if so much was rubbish, what *did* he believe? Without beliefs, or some sense of the reason behind life, there could obviously be no peace. Nor did Tolstoy's scepticism of free will, which puts him in the gloomy company of Spinoza and Schopenhauer, give him any comfort.

But just because Tolstoy himself couldn't seem to access the deeper level of reality that he pointed to, it does not mean that you or I cannot. Through religion, or in contemplation or meditation, it is possible to see the "flow of life," the real way things are despite our constant thinking, imaginings, desires and aversions. As an empiricist, Tolstoy couldn't justify a metaphysical view of the universe, yet his characters are sometimes able to glimpse a truth, gaining knowledge of the way things will go. Whether you call this wisdom, grace or illumination, the fact that so many have experienced it suggests that it is real.

Isaiah Berlin

Born in Latvia in 1907, Berlin's parents were Russian-speaking Jews who moved the family to London when he was in his teens. He won a place at Oxford and was considered so brilliant that he was made a Fellow of All Souls College by his mid-20s. At 32 he wrote an acclaimed biography of Marx (1939), and during and just after the war served as a British diplomat in Washington and Moscow. At 50 he was made Oxford's Chichele Professor of Social and Political Theory, and was president of Wolfson College from 1966 to 1975.

Other works include Historical Inevitability *(1954),* The Age of Enlightenment *(1956),* Two Concepts of Liberty *(1958 - see* 50 Politics Classics*),* Vico and Herder *(1976) and many notable essays. He was also a translator of Turgenev. For more information see Michael Ignatieff's* Isaiah Berlin: A Life *(1997), published a year after Berlin's death.*

Wholeness and the Implicate Order

"Thus, the classical idea of the separability of the world into distinct but interacting parts is no longer valid or relevant. Rather, we have to regard the universe as an undivided and unbroken whole. Division into particles, or into particles and fields, is only a crude abstraction and approximation. Thus, we come to an order that is radically different from that of Galileo and Newton – the order of undivided wholeness."

"So it will be ultimately misleading and indeed wrong to suppose ... that each human being is an independent actuality who interacts with other human beings and with nature. Rather, all these are projections of a single totality."

In a nutshell

The human way of perceiving separate objects and creating categories is an illusion. Reality is in fact unbroken and undivided, and all phenomena are simply perturbations in this single whole.

In a similar vein

G.W.F. Hegel *Phenomenology of Spirit* (p 112)
Thomas Kuhn *The Structure of Scientific Revolutions* (p 164)
Plotinus *The Enneads* (p 236)
Karl Popper *The Logic of Scientific Discovery* (p 242)

CHAPTER 9

David Bohm

David Bohm was one of the twentieth century's outstanding theoretical physicists, known for the DeBroglie–Bohm theory and the Aharonov–Bohm Effect, both relating to the often strange behavior of electrons. The DeBroglie–Bohm theory posits "hidden variables" in quantum physics that display its nonlocal nature (i.e., particles are linked, acting almost like twins, despite vast distances between them). Bohm worked under Robert Oppenheimer (of Los Alamos atomic bomb fame) and collaborated with Albert Einstein. However, in a life bridging East and West, science and metaphysics, he was also greatly influenced by his friendship with Jiddu Krishnamurti, an Indian sage and writer, and by conversations with the Dalai Lama.

Bohm was particularly fascinated by lab results showing that subatomic particles that are far apart can still communicate in a way that could not be explained by physical signals traveling at the speed of light. Such instantaneous (or nonlocal) communication was one of many things that suggested to him that the universe is not empty space containing particles of matter, but rather that space itself is almost alive with intelligence. Space is best understood as one unbroken whole of which consciousness is a part. It is only the human senses that abstract certain phenomena to give the impression that things are separate and autonomous, and that mind and matter are separate. These views went against the deterministic physics establishment, yet science has still to prove Bohm's ideas wrong.

While most physicists are content to burrow away at their specialization, Bohm was vitally concerned about the implications of his ideas. Much of the world's problems, he thought, came from the perception that every person and thing is separate from another, which makes us want to defend ourselves against a perceived "other" and to see humanity as something separate from nature. Such broader thinking turned Bohm into a philosopher, and his work demonstrates how philosophical thinking comes into its own when science fails to reveal the meaning of research.

Bohm wrote *Wholeness and the Implicate Order* for a general audience, and it makes for compelling reading.

A new view of the universe

Bohm points out that the atomic view of the universe seemed like a very good explanation of reality for a long time. However, relativity theory and quantum physics then showed that the base level of reality was not so simple. Actual particles are elusive, to the extent that it is better to understand matter as a form of energy, not as a composite of tiny things. An atom is not so much a thing on its own, but exists more like a "poorly-defined cloud," Bohm says, very much dependent on its environment, including whoever or whatever is observing it. The atom is more like a simplification or abstraction of reality than reality itself. A particle is best seen as a "world tube," he memorably claims, always in motion to the extent that it is a point of energy, not a thing. Each particle/world tube extends through space and has a field around it that merges with other fields.

This view of the universe is not of empty space containing some matter; rather, everything is a unified field and "nowhere is there a break or a division." This is Bohm's notion of "wholeness." His analogy is a pattern on a carpet: it makes no sense to say that the flowers or figures in the design are separate objects – they are obviously part of the carpet.

The implicate and explicate orders

If the first aspect of Bohm's cosmology is wholeness, the second is his notion of the implicate and explicate orders. The explicate order is essentially everything that we can perceive with our senses, the "real world." In the explicate, things exist in their own area of space (and time), apparently separate to other things. The implicate, in contrast, is outside space and time, and contains the seed of everything that manifests in the real world. It enfolds everything possible. To put it another way, order is enfolded in space and time, and only sometimes will it be expressed in the forms of the explicate order. It is the implicate that is genuinely real and stable; the explicate is a distinguished suborder of this more primary reality.

Bohm gives the example of a drop of ink that is put into a large container of viscous fluid. When the container is spun at high speed, the ink appears to dissolve into the fluid and it gets murkier; but when the spinning is reversed, the ink retraces its circular motion in the fluid and winds itself back to its original position. Thus the order of its movement is enfolded in the liquid, even if at a later point this order seems to have disappeared. Later in the book, Bohm takes up this example again to note that the ink's path in the fluid is its implicate order, and its visibility part of the explicate. The latter becomes possible because of the interaction of light and our eye, brain, and nervous system.

How does this explanation relate to wholeness? The whole, including space, time, consciousness, and both implicate and explicate orders, is part of what Bohm calls the "holomovement," an "unbroken and undivided totality." But how are we to understand the fact that our analyses of the world into autonomous parts do actually work? "Holonomy," or "the law of the whole," still allows for things in the universe to seem autonomous, even if they really are not. Each apparently separate thing or event is actually just an aspect (patterns on a carpet, eddies in a river), not in fact separate and self-ruling.

Mind and matter
What is the relationship of thinking, or consciousness, to reality?

To be practical, humans long ago made a big distinction between the fixity, stability, and "reality" of things, and the impermanence and unreality of the thinking realm. This was a distinction of convenience, not of truth. Bohm's "wholeness" view says that if mind and matter both arise from the universal flux, it does not make sense to see "thought" and "reality" as separate. This has important implications for quantum physics and the ethos of an "objective observer" in science. Scientists think that they are standing apart from what they observe, but if you accept reality as one flowing movement, then object, observer, observing instrument, and experimental results must all be seen as part of the same phenomenon.

It is only our individual thoughts arising from the brain and nervous system (call this the ego) that can foster separateness, confusion, and incorrect assumptions. Nevertheless, it is something to be at least aware of this possibility, to be open to what may simply be our own projections and false categorizations, as distinct from the "what is" of the universal whole. This is why, as Eastern philosophy tells us, it is only when we can really observe our thoughts, or in meditation have a moment of "not-thinking," that we can begin to know what really *is*. Your worldview will dictate your relations in the world. If you perceive reality in terms of separate objects, this will be your experience of it. If you perceive reality as one unbroken whole, naturally this will change the way you relate to other forms of life, and to your own consciousness.

Where intuitive knowledge and creativity come from
Bohm makes a distinction between thought, which is naturally linked to memory, and "intelligent perception," which can be a flash of understanding in which we see that all our thinking had been wrong or "conditioned." These perceptions are genuinely new and seem to come from nowhere. As he notes, the prevailing view is that all perception, however fresh it may seem, arises

in neurons and synapses of the brain. However, if perceptions are genuinely fresh and unconditioned, it is not possible that they come from the banks of memory and experience laid down in the brain. They arise from the universal flux of consciousness, which is beyond or greater than any particular arrangement of particles and atoms in the brain.

It is possible to "know" something through perception, without having a basis for knowing it through memory or mechanical thought; we are simply attuned to the universal flux (indeed, we were never *not* a part of it). The same goes for genuine creativity: no one has ever been able to say where an original idea comes from. Creativity is mysterious because it literally does not come from "us," only as the result of our being an abstraction of a greater flow of intelligence. Bohm's analogy is a radio receiver, which, when switched on, will produce a meaningless buzz on its own. "When thought functions on its own," he writes, "it is mechanical and not intelligent, because it imposes its own generally irrelevant and unsuitable order drawn from memory." It is only when thought is attuned to a frequency – an intelligent order – that it becomes an instrument of order and meaning itself.

Final comments

Despite what we know of quantum physics, Bohm notes that scientists continue to have a mechanistic view of the universe. First it was atoms that made up the universe, then electrons, now it is quarks and protons. Though he was writing before the advent of the Large Hadron Collider and the quest to find the Higgs-Boson or "God particle," he would have seen this as part of the same quest to locate the basic building blocks of the universe. But even relativity theory suggested that the existence of a single stable particle was illusory; Einstein preferred to think of the universe in terms of fields. It is only our dogged attachment to finding "things" that has kept us wanting to see the universe as like a container filled with stuff, when space is more like a field pregnant with potential. As Bohm puts it:

> "What we call empty space contains an immense background of energy, and ... matter as we know it is a small, 'quantized' wavelike excitation on top of this background, rather like a tiny ripple on a vast sea ... space, which has so much energy, is full rather than empty."

Bohm's idea that the universe is one flowing whole has been called "neutral monism" in philosophy. The supremely rational Bertrand Russell subscribed to it, and wrote that "the whole duality of mind and matter ... is a mistake; there is only one kind of *stuff* out of which the world is made, and this stuff is called mental in one arrangement, physical in the other."

In Bohm's view, can we say that individual people really exist? He writes, "it will be ultimately misleading and indeed wrong to suppose ... that each human being is an independent actuality who interacts with other human beings and with nature. Rather, all these are projections of a single totality." We do exist as separate phenomena, but only before we are absorbed back into a larger movement. We were never truly separate; we are more like swirls on a carpet or ripples in a stream.

David Bohm

Born in Pennsylvania in 1917, as a boy Bohm enjoyed tinkering and invent-ing. His parents were immigrants from Hungary and Lithuania, and his father owned a successful furniture store. He attended Pennsylvania State College, then the University of California at Berkeley, where he worked at the Lawrence Radiation Laboratory and was part of a theoretical physics group headed by Robert Oppenheimer. At this time he was also involved in radical politics, including the Youth Communist league and anticonscription issues.

Oppenheimer wanted Bohm to work in the Los Alamos project developing the atomic bomb, but because of his student politics he was not given security clearance. Instead he taught at Berkeley, where he obtained his PhD, although with some difficulty: his research became classified and he was refused access to it. After the war, Bohm took up a position at Princeton University, working alongside Albert Einstein. However, in 1950 he was called before Senator Joe McCarthy's House Un-American Activities Committee with reference to his previous communist ties, and refused to testify against friends and colleagues. He was arrested and Princeton suspended him; even after his acquittal in 1951 he was unable to regain his position. Bohm was offered a professorship in physics at the University of Sao Paulo, and in 1951 published Quantum Theory, *a classic account of the orthodox Copenhagen view of quantum physics.*

Bohm moved to Israel in 1955 and worked at the Technion university in Haifa. Two years later he became a research fellow at the University of Bristol, and there with a student discovered the Aharonov–Bohm Effect, which relates to the strange ability of particles to "sense" magnetic fields. In 1961 he took up his final post, as Professor of Theoretical Physics at London's Birkbeck College, where his close collaborator was Basil Hiley. Bohm became a strong promoter of a form of open discussion to end the world's social problems (known as "Bohm dialogue"). He died in London in 1992.

Other books include Causality and Chance in Modern Physics *(1961),* The Ending of Time *(1985, with Jiddu Krishnamurti),* Changing Consciousness *(1991), and* The Undivided Universe *(1993, with Basil Hiley). Lee Nichol's* The Essential David Bohm *(2002) includes a preface by the Dalai Lama.*

Gender Trouble

*"As I wrote it, I understood myself to be in an embattled and opposi-
tional relation to certain forms of feminism, even as I understood the
text to be part of feminism itself."*

*"Gender is the repeated stylization of the body, a set of repeated
acts within a highly rigid regulatory frame that congeal over time to
produce the appearance of substance, of a natural sort of being."*

*"That gender reality is created through sustained social performances
means that the very notions of an essential sex and a true or abiding
masculinity or femininity are also constituted as part of the strategy
that conceals gender's performative character and the performative possibilities for proliferating gender configurations outside
the restricting frames of masculinist domination and compulsory
heterosexuality."*

In a nutshell

Defining persons by gender categories is an act of political force. If
gender becomes performative rather than fixed, people are liberated.

In a similar vein

Simone de Beauvoir *The Second Sex* (p 44)
Michel Foucault *The Order of Things* (p 112)
Martin Heidegger *Being and Time* (p 272)

CHAPTER 10

Judith Butler

F eminism is one of the great movements of the last 150 years, and it won the battle of ideas against reactionaries long ago. But to some philosophers, feminism itself became part of the establishment; it now aggressively defends its territory. Feminism makes assumptions about what a "woman" is, and assumes all female persons to be part of some monolithic bloc.

An important critic of these assumptions is Judith Butler. Her argument is that the creation of female identity through feminism has come at a cost – the cost of exploring identity itself. Butler witnessed an uncle and gay cousin who were forced to leave home because of their sexuality, and then experienced troubles with her family herself after coming out at the age of 16. In a "violently policed" heterosexual world, gender and sexuality choices are not simple matters of lifestyle, but can lead to loss of jobs, lovers and homes. Butler found her spiritual home in the lesbian and gay community of California's Bay Area. As a philosopher she has been driven to expose society's false limits, "to make life possible, and to rethink the possible as such" so that people do not experience "a death within life."

The surprise argument of her landmark book, *Gender Trouble: Feminism and the Subversion of Identity*, is that "Second Wave" feminism (loosely covering the postwar decades from Simone de Beauvoir to Betty Friedan) has been an accomplice in creating a world of binary gender. Throughout history, men had sought to dominate by portraying the female as "Other." So it was understandable that to be emancipated women had to unite in solidarity. However in doing so, feminists avoided the larger discussion of gender and sexuality, and the possibility of a non-binary landscape in which individuals were persons first, genders second.

Butler's key questions: "how do non-normative sexual practices call into question the stability of gender as a category of analysis? How do certain sexual practices compel the question: what is a woman, what is a man?" And if I "turn gay," why does this provoke terror or anxiety in some people?

In examining in depth the edifice of "phallogocentrism and compulsory heterosexuality," Butler sits in the tradition of Foucault and Nietzsche in providing a "genealogy" of power in relation to sex, gender and desire.

She takes Simone de Beauvoir as a starting point, and draws heavily on the "French theory" of Jacques Derrida, Claude Levi-Strauss, Julia Kristeva and Monique Wittig, and the psychoanalytic tradition of Sigmund Freud and Jacques Lacan.

Despite its notoriously difficult prose and ponderous style, *Gender Trouble* is hugely influential because it challenged long-held and, in its author's words, "oppressive" truths.

The problem with feminism

"One is not born a woman, but rather becomes one" Simone de Beauvoir said in *The Second Sex*. A person is born female, but before long becomes a "girl," a "lady," a "mother" – roles we have not chosen and which often reduce our potential.

Feminism sought political representation and better cultural recognition for women, but the new discourse (of which Butler was a part) questioned the category of "woman" altogether. Butler refers to Foucault's idea that society creates categories in order to limit, prohibit, regulate, control and even "protect" the humans that fall into those categories. The problem is that the subjects of these categories start to see themselves fully in light of the category. This means that it's impossible to appeal to this power system to emancipate "women." Emancipation may only come from questioning the whole system and its categories, including sex and gender.

For feminism to establish the idea of patriarchy, it needed to make feminism universal, i.e., all women are in the same boat. The problem with seeing things in binary gender terms is that it fails to fully account for many other facts that "intersect" with a person's experience, i.e., political, economic, class, race, cultural and ethnic. Any one of these identities may be more significant to our chances and recognition than simply being a woman. Politics, language and law require stable identities and subjects, and by conforming to that feminism becomes part of the problem. Not only does it not represent many kinds of identity, even exclude them, but by putting biological "woman" on a pedestal, feminism unwittingly preserves and buttresses existing gender power relations.

Because gender categories entrench power, in cases where representation is extended, this representation further legitimates existing power structures. "Juridical power inevitably 'produces' what it claims merely to represent" Butler says. Therefore, by avoiding the presumption of gender categories in the first place, you question the state's juridical power. The radical thing is not to pursue "women's rights," it is to go back a step and demand a world that is "pregendered."

Gender as human potential

One is born a sex (female), but becomes a gender (woman), de Beauvoir said. Where Butler breaks from de Beauvoir is in insisting that gender can't or shouldn't follow from sex. Even if the biological sexes remain binary (itself contested, given the fact of intersex people), you can't reduce genders to only two. As Butler puts it, "*man* and *masculine* might just as easily signify female body as a male one, and *woman* and *feminine* a male body as easily as a female one." De Beauvoir assumed we know what a woman is, that sex is fixed, but can we assume that the person who "becomes" the woman is in fact female? Here we have a conflation of the category of women with the ostensibly sexualized features of their bodies.

For Butler, there was only one way out of this: the destruction of the category of sex itself and its seemingly logical attributes. In its place would be a person, a self-determining "*cogito*" or point of consciousness as Descartes imagined it.

This brought Butler into the world of ontology, or the philosophy of being. The question became whether "there is 'a' gender which persons are said to *have*, or ... an essential attribute that a person is said to *be*." Butler's schema came down firmly on the latter. Gender is a succession of *performative acts* undertaken socially, under which there is no "ground" or seamless identity. These acts are not expressive of some deeper underlying immutable self, and indeed there is tension in the possibility that we may fail to perform one day, or perform the wrong way. All this does is expose "abiding [gender] identity as a politically tenuous construction." A new genealogy of genders will reduce them to what they are: a matter of acts, not being or substance.

The purpose of Butler's book was to make "gender trouble" by removing gender from any sense of it being a stable thing, and bring on a "subversive confusion and proliferation" of gender roles. It's only this – not seeing the category of "women" based upon sex (which feminism demands) – that will get rid of gender notions that "support masculine hegemony and heterosexist power." If gender is a "performative accomplishment" played out in the social sphere, Butler argues, this negates the whole idea of a permanent gender identity founded in the physical. I am who I psychologically choose to be. I own my self.

Anthropology of gender

Feminist theorists such as Wittig suggested that the denominations of "men" and "women" are "political categories, and not natural facts." They enslave people, and always on the basis that the male is universal, and the female particular. She urged women to say "I" more, to make them the universal subject.

Butler points to Wittig's thesis that there was once a presocial, pre-patriarchal order that was more unified and equal. "Sex" only became powerful as the result of violent cultural processes which amplified the differences between the sexes, so that society could be based around them. If that were the case, it meant that patriarchy had had a beginning - and could therefore have an end.

Butler says we should be careful of traditional feminist agendas here. By highlighting a time before patriarchy, it risks again classing women as some monolithic group. It also glosses over the many other kinds of gender roles and sexualities that may have existed.

By separating sex and gender, de Beauvoir did not entertain the possibility that: a) sex itself was not so immutable, and could be a social/political creation; b) the gender you "take on" may not be the logical complement to its sex; and c) there may be a multiplicity of genders, taken on by a person at different times and for different reasons. In Butler's view, feminism "presumes, fixes, and constrains the very 'subjects' that it hopes to represent and liberate."

Sex and society

In *The History of Sexuality*, Foucault argued that humans only become "sexed" within a web of power relations that emphasize and regulate differences. "Sex" is an effect of society rather than an origin. Foucault's issue with feminism was that it assumes that "sex" is real and immutable in the first place. This is exactly how feminism becomes part of established power relations, rather than breaking it up.

In the Freud/Lacan/Kristeva tradition, alternative forms of sexuality are not really justified in the context of the public "univocal" language of society – in fact, they become forms of psychosis.

Kristeva noted that poetry and childbirth/maternity allow women a non-psychotic release from the patriarchal culture. Lesbianism is an affront to that, because it denies a woman's connection with her mother via having her own child. In breaking the mother–child bond, it involves a loss of selfhood and is a form of psychosis. Wittig even argued that a lesbian is not a woman. Why? Because a woman only exists as the counterpart to a man in hetero-sexual normativity. A lesbian is outside that, and so can't be a woman or man.

Butler's take on lesbianism is that, precisely because it challenges society's established language, it is a model for a world in which sex and gender are no longer fixed. "Lesbian" could even be considered a third gender. After all, it "radically problematizes both sex and gender," going against our system of compulsory sexuality and divorcing anatomical sex from reproduction.

In Foucault's introduction to the journals of "hermaphrodite" Herculine Barbin, he describes Herculine's experience as "a world of pleasures in which the grins hang about without the cat." In this world, there can be a multiplicity of pleasures and identities, and you are not pinned down to the gravity of subject, i.e., male or female, man or woman. But this is an overoptimistic view of Barbin's predicament, Butler says. Forced by authorities to have a clear gender and live as a man, in the end she was defeated by the law and its gender fixity, and committed suicide.

Butler also delves into molecular cell biology, a discipline which historically has assumed binary differences, and finds it hard to account for cases where things are not so clear. The language of biology is not in fact neutral, and should be seen as part of its larger cultural context. For instance, biology takes external genitalia to be the definitive "sign" of sex, but in males where genitalia is underdeveloped, should we be assuming that they are "men?" Or that females with ovaries but more testosterone can neatly be classified as "women?" "The category of sex belongs to a system of compulsory heterosexuality," Butler says, "that clearly operates through a system of compulsory sexual reproduction."

Butler also disputes the "radical disjunction" between heterosexuality and homosexuality. There are aspects of the homosexual within conventional hetero relations, and of course within gay relationships, people are always appropriating conventional gender roles, e.g. "she" for gay men, or lesbian women who like "male" or "butch" women (as opposed to "girl" or "femme" types). This fact clearly "robs compulsory heterosexuality of its claims of naturalness and originality," Butler says. Indeed, whenever you hear someone appealing to get back to the "naturalness" of gender roles, it is inherently political.

Drag is amusing precisely because we see that the original sex and gender designations which are being parodied were a bit forced and fake to begin with; they are just roles for fitting in. Drag denaturalizes sex and gender, making the ground they sit upon quite shaky. Butler says: "In imitating gender, drag implicitly reveals the imitative structure of gender itself – as well as its contingency." In this sense, drag is the "real, not the parody.

"The body is not a 'being,'" Butler says, "but a variable boundary, a surface whose permeability is politically regulated." This echoes Foucault's idea that the body is the thing on which culture is inscribed. The point about drag and gendered bodies is that they are "styles of the flesh." We live in a social theatre in which the body itself becomes performative.

Final comments

Philosophers know that existing language categories create our reality, which is why they are so obsessed with being more explicit and/or creative about our terms and categories, even denying all of them and making new ones. Butler's contribution here is to rethink the established personal pronouns we take for granted, so that gender is in control of the person, not society. Although Butler does not really touch on trans rights, this book is a great place to understand the current controversies around traditional feminists versus trans activists.

It would be easy to see *Gender Trouble* as part of a politically correct agenda, particularly if new gender terminology were to become enforced in an Orwellian way. But there is another, more optimistic way to see Butler's ideas: as human potential beyond sex or gender.

The contingent, probabilistic, in-flux nature of gender is fully in line with the findings of quantum physics about how the world actually is, compared to the fixity of how we thought it was. It is also consistent with many Eastern teachings about the myth of a solid self. In Buddhism, we are the sum of our actions and habits rather than having a changeless core like a soul.

Early feminist philosophers such as de Beauvoir assumed there is always an "I," but Butler's argument is that "there need not be a 'doer behind the deed,' but that the 'doer' is variably constructed in and through the deed." The implication is that feminism pigeonholes and constrains the very people it hoped to liberate. There are many kinds of identity and gender that exist already that are just not allowed to be recognized, and which feminism finds awkward to categorize and encompass. By engaging with the "unnatural," Butler says, you might attain a denaturalization of gender, which would be a good thing: "a new configuration of politic would surely emerge from the ruins of the old."

Judith Butler

Born in 1956 in Cleveland, Ohio, Butler was raised in a Jewish household. She attended Hebrew school and also special classes in Jewish ethics, which sparked her interest in philosophy.

Butler was at Bennington College in Vermont before transferring to Yale University, graduating in 1978 and gaining a PhD in philosophy in 1984. Teaching positions included Wesleyan University, George Washington University, and Johns Hopkins University, and in 1993 Butler moved to the University of California at Berkeley. She is currently a Professor in the Department of

Comparative Literature and the Program of Critical Theory, and holds the Hannah Arendt Chair in philosophy at the private European Graduate School.

In the 90s Butler was on the board of the International Gay and Lesbian Human Rights Commission, and has been outspoken on gay and lesbian rights and marriage. She has supported the antiwar and Occupy movements, and supports sanctions against the state of Israel. Butler is legally non-binary in the state of California, which in 2017 passed an act letting citizens use this designation in official documents. Butler's partner is the political theorist Wendy Brown, and they have a son.

Other books include Bodies That Matter *(1993),* Excitable Speech *(1997),* Undoing Gender *(2004),* Giving an Account of Oneself *(2005), and* The Force of Nonviolence *(2020).* Gender Trouble *has been translated into 27 languages.*

Butler won the Adorno Prize in 2012, and in 2019 was elected a Fellow of the American Academy of Arts of Sciences.

2002

Understanding Power

"The operational criterion for what counted as a war crime at Nuremberg was a criminal act that the West didn't do: in other words, it was considered a legitimate defense if you could show that the Americans and the British did the same thing ... And this is all stated straight out – like if you read the book by Telford Taylor, the American prosecutor at the trials, this is the way he describes it; he's very positive about the whole thing. If the West had done it, it wasn't a crime; it was only a crime if the Germans had done it and we hadn't."

"Despite what you always hear, U.S. interventionism has nothing to do with resisting the spread of 'Communism,' it's independence we've always been opposed to everywhere – and for quite a good reason. If a country begins to pay attention to its own population, it's not going to be paying adequate attention to the overriding needs of U.S. investors. Well, those are unacceptable priorities, so that government's just going to have to go."

In a nutshell

In democracies, power silences dissent through the abuse of language.

In a similar vein

CHAPTER 11

Noam Chomsky

N oam Chomsky is perhaps the most famous contemporary philosopher, but strictly speaking he is a linguist. He made his name with *Syntactic Structures* (1957), which refuted the idea that our minds are a blank slate, instead showing that we are neurologically wired for language (which is why we pick it up so quickly). It is his thinking on politics, power, and the media, though, which puts him at the top of lists of the world's leading intellectuals.

What is an intellectual? Dictionary definitions suggest "a person given to pursuits that require exercise of the intellect," but in a wider social sense it means one who does not blindly go along with society's script, one who questions everything. Chomsky's classic *Manufacturing Consent* (1988) shattered the myth of an impartial media, showing the press to be very much part of establishment agendas. *Understanding Power*, which proceeds in question-and-answer format and is based on transcripts from seminars and talks he gave from 1989 to 1999, offers a more comprehensive picture of his thinking. The book's editors, Peter Mitchell and John Schoeffel, note, "What distinguishes [his] political thinking is not any one novel insight or single overarching idea. In fact, Chomsky's political stance is rooted in concepts that have been understood for centuries. Rather, Chomsky's great contribution is his mastery of a huge wealth of factual information, and his uncanny skill at unmasking, in case after case, the workings and deceptions of powerful institutions in today's world." Indeed, the book has a supporting website with hundreds of pages of footnotes and links to real government documents. Counter to his reputation as a conspiracy theorist, Chomsky's aim is always to get people to think for themselves.

Understanding Power is eye-opening. As an indication of how much ground the book covers, the issues summarized below are only from the first part.

Political language
Chomsky begins with a discussion of how language is used and abused in order to hide unjust actions.

He notes the distinction between the dictionary meaning of words and their meaning as deployed in "ideological warfare." For example, "terrorism" is something that only other people do. Another abused word is "defense." "I have never heard of a state that admits it's carrying out an aggressive act," Chomsky remarks, "they're always engaged in 'defense.'" The media never question this: for instance, no mainstream publication challenged the idea that the United States was "defending" South Vietnam, when in fact it was attacking it. "Defense" becomes an Orwellian term whose meaning is its exact opposite. "The terms of political discourse," he says, "are designed so as to prevent thought."

Chomsky argues that America's wish to portray itself as supporting democracy around the world is an illusion; in fact, it only supports democracies it *likes*. For example, because under the Sandinistas business did not have a big role in the Nicaraguan state, in US eyes it was not a true democracy, so was ripe for dismantling. He contrasts this with El Salvador and Guatemala, governments that were run by the military for the benefit of the local oligarchies (landowners, rich businessmen, and the professional class) whose interests were tied up with those of the United States:

> *"It doesn't matter if they blow up the independent press, and kill off the political opposition, and slaughter tens of thousands of people, and never run anything remotely like a free election, all of that is totally irrelevant. They're 'democracies,' because the right people are running them; if the right people aren't running them, then they're not 'democracies.'"*

The real power

Chomsky does not simply criticize government, noting:

> *"In our society, real power does not happen to lie in the political system, it lies in the private economy: that's where the decisions are made about what's produced, how much is produced, what's consumed, where investment takes place, who has jobs, who controls the resources, and so on and so forth."*

As long as this is the case there will be no real democracy, because capital is in the hands of the few, not the many, and it is money, not political power per se, that is the center of our societies. Today, our economies *are* our societies, so they are run on the basis of "let's keep the rich happy."

Chomsky sees himself as very much part of the classical liberal tradition, which he reminds us was precapitalist, and was focused on "the right of people to control their own work, and the need for free creative work under your own control – for human freedom and creativity." By this reasoning, wage labor under today's capitalism would have been seen as immoral. If you do not control your own work, you are a wage *slave*.

Economies are never framed in terms of what is best for people who actually work, Chomsky says, but for capital itself. This does not mean that he wants nationalization of industries, as this would simply put power in the hands of a state bureaucracy. Instead, he favors actual worker-owned enterprises and control of capital within a market system. Only when this happens will democracy extend to economic power; until it does, "political power [by the people] is always going to remain a very limited phenomenon."

Chomsky was years ahead of the "Occupy" movement when he noted that "about half the population thinks that the government is just run by 'a few big interests looking out for themselves' … people either know or can quickly be convinced that they are not involved in policy-making, that policy is being made by powerful interests which don't have much to do with them."

Discussing the environment, Chomsky notes the contradiction between the desire of people to preserve and enhance life, and the profit motive of corporations: "the CEO of General Electric … his job is to raise profit and market share, not to make sure that the environment survives, or that his workers lead decent lives. And those goals are simply in conflict."

Yet he does see cause for optimism: despite the media's whitewashing of reality and the corporate takeover of politics, people are actually still very skeptical of elites and established commercial and power interests. Disillusionment is not something of the left, he points out. It can be channeled by any cause or group willing to mobilize, which could include evangelists, environmentalists, and, for more recent examples, the occupiers and the Tea Party movement.

States of dependence

Despite the rhetoric of extending freedom around the world, Chomsky argues that the real purpose of American foreign policy is to keep as many states as possible dependent on it. Chomsky was saying this over 20 years ago, but the same could be said today of China and its efforts to "buy" countries like Nepal on its periphery, and of many resource-rich African nations. Large powers resist the independence of smaller powers because they may begin paying more attention to the welfare of their own people, instead of instituting policies that serve the big country's interests. US foreign policy is designed to suit US investors, he says, so if any foreign government brings in measures that actually put their people first, "that government's just going to have to go."

While America insists that developing countries open their markets, Chomsky points out that "there is not a single economy in history that developed without extensive state intervention, like high protectionist tariffs and subsidies and so on. In fact, all the things we *prevent* the Third World from doing have been the *prerequisites* for development everywhere else."

It's all domestic

Chomsky argues that all foreign policy moves are to serve domestic ends. But what are the authorities defending? He gives the example of the Bolsheviks' rise to power in Russia. No one was seriously saying that the Bolsheviks would mount an attack on the United States. Rather, the fear was that Bolshevik ideas would infect US politics. Just after the Russian Revolution, America's Secretary of State Robert Lansing warned President Wilson that the Bolsheviks are "issuing an appeal to the proletariat of all nations, to the illiterate and mentally deficient, who by their very numbers are supposed to take control of all governments." In other words, the elites envisioned the American people actually thinking for themselves and rising up, when they should be kept in their place. The response was to send troops into Russia and launch the "Red Scare" at home to discredit Bolshevism as un-American.

The "war against terrorism" of more recent times might be seen as another manifestation of this, in which civil freedoms are curtailed in order to fight a (perhaps overplayed) threat.

Chomsky points out the contrast between huge defense budgets and emaciated spending on education and health. The reason for this, he says, is that social spending "increases the danger of democracy." If more money is spent on hospitals and schools, it obviously affects people in their local area and they want to get involved in the decisions; in contrast, money spent on a stealth bomber is uncontroversial because it has no direct effect on people's lives, and the average person knows nothing about military aviation. "And since one of the main purposes of social policy," Chomsky observes, "is to keep the population passive, people with power are going to want to eliminate anything that tends to encourage the population to get involved in planning – because popular involvement threatens the monopoly of power by business, and it also stimulates popular organizations, and mobilizes people, and probably would lead to redistribution of profits, and so on."

The costs of imperialism are paid by the people, in taxes, but the profits from imperialism go to the rich. Therefore, the average person simply does not benefit from imperialist foreign policy, but pays through the nose for it.

Final comments

It is hard to view politics and the media in the same way after reading Chomsky, yet it would be wrong to consider this book as an attack on the United States alone. The corrupting nature of power is universal, and wherever you live local examples will spring to mind. To understand power is not simply to know what a particular country or corporation or institution has done, but what it will tend to do if it is not checked and exposed. But given his relentless attack on the American state, surely if it were all-powerful Chomsky himself would have been silenced long ago? His answer is that he is a white male, and white males are seen as sacrosanct in the modern West. To kill one is a big deal, and so would be counterproductive to established interests.

It is often the sign of brilliance when a person tells you how much they do not know, and Chomsky is keen to point out how little science does actually explain the world, particularly when it comes to incredibly complex factors like human action and motivation. Given his dark view of power, he is surprisingly not a pessimist about our future. He does not go along with the sociobiologists who claim that humans are somehow wired for selfishness, instead observing that "if you look at the results of human nature, you see everything: ... you see enormous self-sacrifice, you see tremendous courage, you see integrity, you see destructiveness."

There is always the potential for any gains that have been made to be reversed, but on the whole Chomsky sees progress. It is less acceptable now to treat people as objects or means to an end ("Slavery was considered a fine thing not long ago") and even if power structures only pay lip-service to freedom, self-determination, and human rights, at least these are acknowledged ideals.

Noam Chomsky

Chomsky was born in Philadelphia in 1928. His father had emigrated from Russia and was an eminent Hebrew scholar. At 10 Chomsky wrote an article on the threat of fascism after the Spanish Civil War, and from 12 or 13 he identified with anarchist politics. He entered the University of Pennsylvania in 1945, coming into contact with Zelig Harris, a prominent linguist. In 1947 he decided to major in linguistics, and 1949 married the linguist Carol Schatz.

From 1951 to 1955 Chomsky was a Junior Fellow at Harvard, where he completed his PhD, later published as The Logical Structure of Linguistic Theory. *He received a faculty position at Massachusetts Institute of Technology in 1955 and has been teaching there ever since. In 1965 he organized a citizens' committee to publicize tax refusal in protest over the war in Vietnam, which brought him to public recognition. Four years later he published his first book on politics,* American Power and the New Mandarins *(1969).*

Other books include The Political Economy of Human Rights *(1979, with Edward S. Herman),* Deterring Democracy *(1991),* Powers and Prospects *(1996), and* Failed States *(2006). A documentary featuring Chomsky,* Requiem For The American Dream, *was released in 2016.*

On Duties

"For what, in the name of heaven, is more to be desired than wisdom? What is more to be prized? What is better for a man, what more worthy of his nature? Those who seek after it are called philosophers; and philosophy is nothing else, if one will translate the word into our idiom, than 'the love of wisdom.' Wisdom ... is 'the knowledge of things human and divine and of the causes by which those things are controlled.' And if the man lives who would belittle the study of philosophy, I quite fail to see what in the world he would see fit to praise."

"While the whole field of philosophy is fertile and productive and no portion of it barren and waste, still no part is richer or more fruitful than that which deals with moral duties; for from these are derived the rules for leading a consistent and moral life."

In a nutshell

What is right and what is expedient can never be separate things.

In a similar vein

Confucius *Analects* (p 88)
Immanuel Kant *Critique of Pure Reason* (p 148)
Niccolò Machiavelli *The Prince* (p 182)
Plato *The Republic* (p 230)

CHAPTER 12

Cicero

One of the great figures of ancient Rome, Marcus Tullius Cicero's life (106–43 BC) straddled the democratic, noble, more innocent Roman Republic and the rapacious, autocratic Roman Empire. His story is worth repeating in brief.

From a wealthy, but not aristocratic, landowning family south of Rome, Cicero's father was determined that he and his brother Quintus would make a mark in Rome. After a top-flight education, Cicero's first job was as an assistant to high-ranked generals on the battlefield, but he did not care for war and was happy to return to Rome to carve out a career as a barrister. His skill made him one of Rome's rising stars. However, he was also eager to learn Greek philosophy and law. He spent a couple of years traveling in Greece and Asia, where he heard Epicureans such as Zeno and Phaedrus speak.

At 31 Cicero was given his first post as quaestor (financial officer) in Sicily, where his integrity so impressed the local citizens that he was asked to represent Sicily in a successful prosecution against its greedy governor, Verres. At 37 he was given an aedileship, which put him in charge of organizing games and entertainment in Rome, and at 40 he was made a praetor, or senior magistrate. The peak of his career came at 43, when he was made consul (the equivalent of today's prime minister or president) of Rome – a great achievement for a *homo novus* ("new man") who was not from one of the old senatorial families.

Cicero had come of age in a Rome that still operated through the noble institutions of the Republic, but its purity was becoming muddier by the day because of civil war and the rise of dictators like Julius Caesar. As consul, Cicero saw himself as a defender of the true Rome. This outlook was tested in the first year of his reign by the Cataline conspiracy, in which a disgruntled senator (Lucius Sergius Catilina), barred from being consul due to electoral corruption, conspired to overthrow the government. Cicero got wind of this and declared martial law. He had the conspirators captured and then executed without trial. Cicero painted the event as an attack on the Republic, and himself as its savior. However, his decisive action would later come back to haunt him, when a senatorial enemy, Publius Clodius, had a law enacted for the prosecution of anyone who had citizens executed without trial.

To avoid trial, Cicero was for a time cast into exile and channeled his energies into writing, retiring to his house at Tusculum, near Rome. In less than two years he produced most of his famous writings, including *Discussions at Tusculum, On Friendship*, and *On Duties*.

A philosophy of duty

On Duties (*De Officiis*), Cicero's most influential work, is a long, three-part letter addressed to his son Marcus. While Cicero probably intended it to be read widely, the letter format makes it relatively informal.

It is partly a defense of philosophy itself, with Cicero trying to show his son why it should be relevant to him. In a civilization that honored political success above all else, philosophy was considered a little suspect (even "a Greek thing"). This is one reason Cicero plays up his political career and is very modest about his contributions to philosophy. At the same time, he is passionate about conveying the splendor of Greek philosophy to the Roman public; the aim of *On Duties* is to show how philosophy gives a proper foundation to the most practical questions of moral and social obligation. "For who would presume to call himself a philosopher," he asks, "if he did not inculcate any lessons of duty?"

Cicero believed that the universe was run according to a divine plan, and that each human being was a spark or splinter off God. Therefore, treating another person badly was doing the same to ourselves. He observes the absurdity of one who says that they will not rob or cheat a member of their own family, but puts the rest of society in another "basket." This denial of obligations, ties, or common interests to those they don't know well is the ruin of society, he says. Similarly, those who have strong regard for their fellow citizens, but not foreigners, "would destroy the universal brotherhood of mankind" and any sense of kindness or justice along with it. He points to Plato, who said that "we are not born for ourselves alone, but our country claims a share of our being, and our friends a share." We are social animals, born for the sake of each other. The aim of life is simple, Cicero says:

> "to contribute to the general good by an interchange of acts of kindness, by giving and receiving, and thus by our skill, our industry, and our talents to cement human society more closely together, man to man."

When working out our heaviest obligations, Cicero suggests this order: country and parents first; second our children and family, "who look to us alone for support and can have no other protection"; and finally our countrymen, with whom we must live on good terms and are united in common cause.

What is right and what is expedient

Cicero aims to explode the idea that you must sometimes sacrifice doing what is right for the sake of doing what is expedient. The Stoic view, which he adopted, is that "if anything is morally right, it is expedient, and if anything is not morally right, it is not expedient ... that duty which those same Stoics call 'right' is perfect and absolute and 'satisfies all the numbers.'"

People who are focused only on profit and getting ahead will routinely make a division between the good action and the expedient action, but Cicero says that they are deluded. Doing what is right, aligned as it is with universal moral law, cannot "leave you out of pocket." Everyone who has tried to cheat another and then found themselves lacking in funds knows the truth of this. If someone says "That is the right course, but this one brings advantage," Cicero observes, "he will not hesitate in his mistaken judgment to divorce two conceptions that Nature has made one." The result is an opening of the door "to all sorts of dishonesty, wrong-doing, and crime." Just as two wrongs can't make a right, no matter how good you are at covering it up, "so what is not morally right cannot be made expedient, for Nature refuses and resists."

He warns that even slight transgressions of natural justice can have big consequences. There are few better examples of this than the politician or business fiddling their expense claims, yet the small amounts gained lead them – when found out – to lose their job and status. Surely, he notes, there is no advantage to be gained that is worth ruining the reputation of a "good man," and moreover that person's sense of themselves as just and honorable: "For what difference does it make whether a man is actually transformed into a beast or whether, keeping the outward appearance of a man, he has the savage nature of a beast within?" These statements are obviously reminiscent of biblical statements such as "What profiteth a man to gain the whole world, but lose his soul?" and made Cicero attractive to the early Christians.

The Stoic view of life

On Duties makes multiple references to Panaetius, a Greek Stoic philosopher who lived from c. 185 to c. 110 BC and whose work is now lost. Cicero eloquently expresses the Stoic view of life on a range of matters, outlined here.

The dangers of success

"[W]hen fortune smiles and the stream of life flows according to our wishes, let us diligently avoid all arrogance, haughtiness, and pride. For it is as much a sign of weakness to give way to one's feelings in success as it is in adversity."

Moderation and self-control

"[E]very action ought to be free from undue haste or carelessness; neither ought we to do anything for which we cannot assign a reasonable motive; for in these words we have practically a definition of duty." "[P]eople should enjoy calm of soul and be free from every sort of passion. As a result strength of character and self-control will shine forth in all their lustre."

"And if we will only bear in mind the superiority and dignity of our nature, we shall realize how wrong it is to abandon ourselves to excess and to live in luxury and voluptuousness, and how right it is to live in thrift, self-denial, simplicity, and sobriety."

Following your own character and "genius"

"Everybody, however, must resolutely hold fast to his own peculiar gifts ... For we must so act as not to oppose the universal laws of human nature ... and even if other careers should be better and nobler, we may still regulate our own pursuits by the standard of our own nature. For it is of no avail to fight against one's nature or to aim at what is impossible of attainment ... nothing is proper that 'goes against the grain,' as the saying is – that is, if it is in direct opposition to one's natural genius."

"If there is any such thing as propriety at all, it can be nothing more than uniform consistency in the course of our life as a whole and all its individual actions. And this uniform consistency one could not maintain by copying the personal traits of others and eliminating one's own."

On the use of power

Cicero notes Plato's statement that "all knowledge that is divorced from justice be called cunning rather than wisdom." Bold actions that are not inspired by the public good "should have the name of effrontery rather than of courage," he says. The paradox is that the more ambitious a person is, the more tempted they are to do anything to achieve their goals or win fame. If they are honorable, the "trials and dangers" they have to go through to win eminence give them an "I deserve it" mentality, and make them want to cling on to power or become vulnerable to accept things that are not theirs.

Final comments

Cicero is an enigma. On one hand, he is the great defender of the Roman Republic and its ideal of the rule of law; on the other, he sentenced several conspirators to death without trial. Though at the time Rome was operating under martial law, the conspirators were still citizens, and many thought the act unforgivable.

One cannot doubt his influence, though. He was instrumental in bringing Greek philosophy, particularly that of Plato, to the Roman educated classes. His outlook was adapted by Christian philosophers, notably Augustine, whose life was said to have changed after reading Cicero's *Hortensius* (a work now lost), and his ethics and concept of natural law were foundational to medieval Christian philosophy. Philosophers like Erasmus proclaimed Cicero the archetypal humanist, and Enlightenment thinkers Voltaire and Hume praised his skeptical and tolerant view of the world. Cicero's Republican ideals were a large influence on the Founding Fathers of the United States (John Adams revered him) and he was even taken up by the French revolutionaries. Friedrich Engels, however, grumbled that Cicero never cared about extending economic or political rights beyond the wealthy class.

Tough and uncompromising in office, you might have expected Cicero to be a hard man who believed in duty at the expense of personal aspiration. In fact, his humanism was a contrast to brutal dictators like Sulla and Caesar, and he took pains to say that people should if at all possible go into a career that is true to their character. This kind of sentiment reveals that Stoic philosophy, despite its reputation for stony dutifulness, was actually focused on the individual and the unique role one could play in the world.

Cicero

After Caesar's murder, Cicero hoped that the Republic could be reborn and supported Octavian (Augustus) against Marc Antony. When for a time Augustus and Marc Antony agreed to a power-sharing dictatorship under the Second Triumvirate, both sides wanted their enemies eliminated. Cicero's name was added to the death lists and he was hunted down and killed in 43 BC while attempting to leave for Macedonia. On Antony's instructions, Cicero's hands and head were cut off and displayed in the Senate. Antony's wife Fulvia was said to have delighted in pulling Cicero's tongue out of his head and jabbing it with her hairpin.

Cicero's family name comes from the word cicer, "chickpea" in Latin. His brother Quintus Cicero was also made a praetor, and was governor of Asia with Pompey. Cicero had a son and a daughter with Terentia, who came from a wealthy family. He was grief stricken when their daughter Tullia died in her mid-30s.

The British author Robert Harris's books Imperium *(2006) and* Lustrum *(2009) are the first two volumes in a fictionalized trilogy about the life of Cicero, seen through the eyes of his secretary Tiro, a slave whom Cicero made a freedman.*

Analects

"Tsze-chang asked Confucius about perfect virtue. Confucius said, 'To be able to practice five things everywhere under heaven constitutes perfect virtue.' He begged to ask what they were, and was told, 'Gravity, generosity of soul, sincerity, earnestness, and kindness. If you are grave, you will not be treated with disrespect. If you are generous, you will win all. If you are sincere, people will repose trust in you. If you are earnest, you will accomplish much. If you are kind, this will enable you to employ the services of others.'"

"The Master said of Tsze-ch'an that he had four of the characteristics of a superior man – in his conduct of himself, he was humble; in serving his superior, he was respectful; in nourishing the people, he was kind; in ordering the people, he was just."

"Fan Ch'ih asked about benevolence. The Master said, 'It is to love all men.' He asked about knowledge. The Master said, 'It is to know all men.'"

In a nutshell

We are born a human, but we become a person through fulfilling a responsible role in society in a selfless way.

In a similar vein

Aristotle *Nicomachean Ethics* (p 28)
Cicero *On Duties* (p 82)

CHAPTER 13

Confucius

I t can be argued that Confucius is the most influential philosopher in history, given the sheer number of people his ideas have had an impact on and how long the ideas have been around. He was running a school to train political leaders fully two centuries before Plato established his academy, and his philosophy of personal virtue and political order, or "all-pervading unity," was one of the good things to come out of the Warring States or Spring and Autumn period of Chinese history.

Confucian ethics guided China for hundreds of years, but then during Chairman Mao's Cultural Revolution Confucius was declared persona non grata, because his ideas were seen as part of the feudal system that the Communist Party wanted to destroy. In recent times the Chinese state has allowed Confucianism to flourish because it upholds moral virtues, making for a "harmonious society," and provides a valuable alternative to Western-style liberal democracy. Secondary schools now teach Confucian classics and the government funds Confucius Institutes around the world.

Putting great emphasis on family loyalty and public service, Confucian philosophy is largely an ethic of selflessness and fitting in well to one's community. Its "rules of propriety," expressed in age-old institutions and the proper ways of doing things, are in contrast to the changeability of emotion and personal circumstance. As Confucius scholar D.C. Lau has noted, "there is no individual – no 'self' or 'soul' – that remains once the layers of social relations are peeled away. One is one's roles and relationships." Harmony in these relationships is the goal of life, and only when we act properly to our parents, relations, and rulers do we achieve fulfillment. This does not mean everyone has to be the same; room is made for all types in the larger unity, like the different instruments of an orchestra that make one beautiful sound.

"Confucius" is the Latin version of Kongfuzi, and "Analects" simply means a collection of literary extracts, in this case sayings and stories that his disciples put together as a record of the thoughts of the "Master." After his death, Confucius' band of men spread his teachings across China, each emphasizing a particular aspect of the Master's philosophy that reflected their own defects in virtue.

Becoming a person

Ren is the central concept in Confucian ethics. It has different meanings in the *Analects*, one of which is "benevolence," a trait that we have to develop; another way of understanding it is as the process of "becoming a person," a being who has cultivated the full range of virtues. These include reciprocity (*shu*), respect, and constantly thinking of the good of the whole rather than one's self. Some of Confucius' thoughts on this concept:

> *"The Master said, 'The superior man thinks of virtue; the small man thinks of comfort. The superior man thinks of the sanctions of law; the small man thinks of favours which he may receive.'"*

> *"The Master said: 'He who acts with a constant view to his own advantage will be much murmured against.'"*

> *"The Master said, 'The mind of the superior man is conversant with righteousness; the mind of the mean man is conversant with gain.'"*

The wise person loves virtue more than anything, and will always do what is right. Virtue is like a bridle that a man needs to keep his ambition and passions in check. Confucius compares truthfulness, for instance, to the crossbar to which one's oxen are tied, which enables the carriage to move forward. Without it, the horses will run wild and cause chaos.

As the following passage suggests, one must be true to one's "self," but the paradox is that however much we analyze this self, peeling away the layers of ignorance, we are not likely to find any great truth of personality. Rather, we simply become a vessel for the expression of qualities that benefit everyone:

> *"The Master went out, and the other disciples asked, saying, 'What do his words mean?' Tsang said, 'The doctrine of our master is to be true to the principles of our nature and the benevolent exercise of them to others, this and nothing more.'"*

Qualities of the master

The *Analects* is not just a collection of Confucius' sayings, but is a picture of the man and his qualities drawn by his disciples. One says, "The Master was mild, and yet dignified; majestic, and yet not fierce; respectful, and yet easy." Another notes "four things from which the Master was entirely free. He had no foregone conclusions, no arbitrary predeterminations, no obstinacy, and no egoism."

Though Confucius could often admonish his men, it was without malice and only to act as a mirror to their behavior or outlook. He was still very human (he was for a time inconsolable when one of his favorite disciples died aged only 31), but he was also "beyond personal," with a freedom and clarity of mind of which most only dream. Many passages talk of his composure and of the appropriateness and timeliness of all his actions. "The superior man is satisfied and composed," he is quoted as saying, "the mean man is always full of distress." His method of contrasting two qualities was memorable and even witty:

> *"The Master said, 'The superior man is affable, but not adulatory; the mean man is adulatory, but not affable.'"*

> *"The Master said, 'The superior man has a dignified ease without pride. The mean man has pride without a dignified ease.'"*

His followers were always wanting wisdom from him, but one day Confucius simply said, "I would prefer not speaking." One of them retorted, "If you, Master, do not speak, what shall we, your disciples, have to record?" Confucius replied:

> *"Does Heaven speak? The four seasons pursue their courses, and all things are continually being produced, but does Heaven say anything?"*

How to get ahead
In Confucius' time, obtaining government office was the ambition of many young men. A disciple, Tsze-chang, asks Confucius the best way to gain a good position. He replies:

> *"When one gives few occasions for blame in his words, and few occasions for repentance in his conduct, he is in the way to get emolument."*

He later notes:

> *"A man should say, I am not concerned that I have no place, I am concerned how I may fit myself for one. I am not concerned that I am not known, I seek to be worthy to be known."*

How to govern with justice and a long-term view
> *"The Master said, 'He who exercises government by means of his virtue may be compared to the north polar star, which keeps its place and all the stars turn towards it.'"*

As an adviser to governments and a minister himself, Confucius' insight was that it is better to create policies that lead people toward virtue than to enforce tough punishments for anyone who transgresses a law:

> *"The Master said, 'If the people be led by laws, and uniformity sought to be given them by punishments, they will try to avoid the punishment, but have no sense of shame. If they be led by virtue, and uniformity sought to be given them by the rules of propriety, they will have the sense of shame, and moreover will become good.'"*

He had similarities with another government adviser, albeit a military one, the general-for-hire Sun Tzu (author of *The Art of War*). Both put understanding human nature at the heart of their philosophies.

On how to gain respect as a ruler and avoid corruption, Confucius' recipe was simple. A ruler should "advance the upright" and not promote the crooked, then people will submit naturally because they can see justice in action. If the opposite happens and the crooks are in charge, people will only give lip service to the regime. Confucius outlines other features of a good ruler, such as making sure people are paid well and rewarded, but avoiding excessive spending elsewhere; ensuring that work regimes are not too harsh; and being majestic in person, though not fierce.

Finally, Confucius emphasized patience in building a community or state. Instead of rule by personal whim, one should wish for things to happen at their natural pace. Such a long-term view enables the interests of all to be taken into account, including future generations, and acknowledges the progress that has been made in particular areas by ancestors and past administrations. In a time of war and upheaval, this vision of long-term peace, prosperity, and justice in the state was highly appealing to governors.

Constant learning

Confucius was a great scholar, editing collections of poetry and historical texts that chronicled his native Lu state, and he also wrote an important commentary on the *I-Ching* (Book of Changes).

He saw book learning as a means of self-perfection and could be impatient with disciples who were not so intellectual. A line in the *Analects* attributed to Tsze-hsia says: "Mechanics have their shops to dwell in, in order to accomplish their works. The superior man learns, in order to reach to the utmost of his principles." Confucius himself put it more simply and powerfully: "Without knowing the force of words, it is impossible to know men."

Final comments

Confucius emphasized the value of filial piety, particularly deep respect and loyalty to our parents, and there are several mentions in the *Analects* of the importance of the three-year mourning period after a parent's death. In answer to a disciple's question about the meaning of filial piety, Confucius regrets that it has come to mean mere "support," when a dog and a horse are also capable of support. What is crucial is *reverence*. Revering one's parents refines the self, allowing us to see that we are simply one link in a chain of being that stretches into the past and the future.

Yet Confucius was not yoked to tradition for its own sake. The story is told that he saved and kept in his home a slave boy who had escaped from being entombed with his master, which was the custom of the time. Confucius argued in court that the custom was barbaric, a case of filial piety taken to a horrible extreme, and the boy was saved. His message: duty is important, but it is duty to align oneself always with virtue, not to particular customs or traditions. While these necessarily change, qualities such as respect and honesty are timeless.

Confucius

Born in 551 BC in what is now the province of Shandong, the details of Confucius' life have been the subject of hagiographical accounts, but he was likely born in the house of Song, as a descendant of the Shang Dynasty. His father died when he was only two, and despite his noble background he had an impoverished childhood and adolescence.

He worked in a variety of jobs through his twenties to his forties, but his wisdom gathered followers, and as an official he trained young men for service. He was a successful bureaucrat and at 53 he became the minister for justice in the city of Lu. However, after a falling out with its ruler he was exiled, becoming a freelance political adviser for various rulers. In 485 BC he was allowed to return to Lu and there wrote much of his work, including the Book of Songs *and the* Book of Documents.

By the end of his life, Confucius was revered by his patrons and his disciples, who were said to number over 3,000. He died in 479 BC.

Meditations on First Philosophy

"*But immediately afterwards I became aware that, while I decided thus to think that everything was false, it followed necessarily that I who thought must be something; and observing that this truth: I think, therefore I am, was so certain that all the most extravagant assertions of the sceptics were not capable of shaking it, I judged that I could accept it without scruple as the first principle of the philosophy I was seeking.*"

"*And the whole force of the arguments I have used here to prove the existence of God consists in this, that I recognize that it would not be possible for my nature to be as it is, that is to say, that I should have in me the idea of a God, if God did not really exist.*"

In a nutshell

I can doubt that everything I perceive is real, but the fact that I doubt tells me that I think, that I have consciousness. And if I have this, I must exist.

In a similar vein

Thomas Aquinas *Summa Theologica* (p 16)
Immanuel Kant *Critique of Pure Reason* (p 148)
Thomas Kuhn *The Structure of Scientific Revolutions* (p 164)
Gottfried Leibniz *Theodicy* (p 170)
Baruch Spinoza *Ethics* (p 298)

CHAPTER 14

René Descartes

René Descartes was a man of the Enlightenment, who made profound contributions not only to philosophy, but also to science and mathematics; he gave us, for instance, the concept of the Cartesian plane and coordinate geometry, and made advances in astronomy and optics. In his time, religion, philosophy, and science were not considered separate domains, and he used the metaphor of a tree to capture the holistic approach that he took to knowledge:

> "The roots are metaphysics, the trunk is physics, and the branches emerging from the trunk are all the other sciences, which may be reduced to three principal ones, namely medicine, mechanics and morals."

It was while he was enlisted in the Bavarian army, holed up in a house in the winter, that he had a vision for a new kind of philosophy in which all areas of knowledge could be linked to each other. Living on the proceeds of an inheritance from his father, he left the army, secluded himself in Holland (which had much greater freedom of speech than France or England), and in the ensuing years produced a number of major works of science, scientific method, and philosophy.

Descartes was never a teacher or professor, and his writings were addressed to the intelligent layperson. The *Meditations on First Philosophy* was his attempt to find out exactly what could be known. He wrote:

> "Now therefore, my mind is free from all cares, and that I have obtained for myself assured leisure in peaceful solitude, I shall apply myself seriously and freely to the general destruction of all my former opinions."

His radical aim was to "demolish everything completely and start again right from the foundations if I wanted to establish anything at all in the sciences that was stable." The work has the power to shock even today, and remains very readable, being both short and personal.

Though Descartes saw himself as a man of science, he was also concerned to provide a rationale for divine involvement in the world. This is the other, often overlooked aspect of the book: its ingenious accommodation of science and religion.

Is there anything that we can say is real?

Descartes' first two meditations proceed by his famous "method of doubt." He notes that all information gathered through the senses can be called into question. The obvious example is when we have just had a rich experience, then wake up and realize that it was merely a dream. Or when a square tower appears round from a distance, or perspective plays tricks with our perception. These seem like minor examples, but Descartes raises a more important issue: the physical sciences such as astronomy and medicine rely on observation and measurement by our senses, and therefore can't be trusted. He considers disciplines such as geometry and arithmetic, which do not depend on the existence of anything in the world as such; their very abstractness can make them infallible. After all, two plus two equals four whether I am dreaming or not. On the other hand, since humans frequently make arithmetical errors, we have to doubt the correctness of all our mathematical judgments. So knowledge cannot be claimed in this domain either.

Having pointed out just how uncertain and weak the basis of our knowledge is, Descartes finds something that *can* be depended on. He realizes that in order to be misled over some piece of knowledge, even to be deceived about everything that I consider knowledge, there must be an "I" that is deceived:

"I thereby concluded that I was a substance, of which the whole essence or nature consists in thinking, and which, in order to exist, needs no place and depends on no material thing."

The essence of being human is that we are "thinking things." Though every kind of judgment we make about the world may be flawed (indeed, we cannot even be sure that the physical world exists at all), and though if we may be constantly deceived about what we perceive to be fact, it cannot be doubted that we perceive, that we have consciousness. This line of thought leads Descartes to his famous conclusion: "I am thinking, therefore I am." In philosophy this is known as the "cogito," from its Latin rendering *cogito, ergo sum*. As Descartes puts it:

"I have convinced myself that there is nothing in the world – no sky, no earth, no minds, no bodies. Doesn't it follow that I don't exist? No, surely I must exist if it's me who is convinced of something."

Descartes imagines a "great deceiver" always trying to pull the wool over his eyes in terms of what is real. Yet he reasons that, if he is being deceived, he must exist: "he will never make it the case that I am nothing while I think that I am something."

Descartes' other great insight along this line is that, while he could imagine himself in some strange situation existing without a body, he could not imagine being a body without a mind. Therefore, his essence is his mind or consciousness, and the body is quite secondary.

After arguing that his mind exists, Descartes wants to assure himself of the existence of objects external to the mind. Having doubted everything, he tries to build up a basis of knowledge again. The objects of sensory perception – the things we see, smell, and hear – cannot be part of the mind, he concludes, because they force their effects on us involuntarily. It is not my conscious decision to hear a falling object hit the floor; the sound reaches me regardless. Therefore, the sound cannot originate in my mind, but must be outside it. This encourages him to conclude that external corporeal objects do exist.

In contrast to the imaginary deceiver who tries to make him doubt everything, Descartes notes that, in his benevolence, God – who has given us our bodies and our senses – is not a deceiver. God would not make it seem that the sensory data originated from external objects when in fact it did not. For modern philosophers this assumption is shaky. For instance, a person prone to schizophrenic hallucinations might think that they hear a voice talking to them, when in fact it is all in their mind. Still, Descartes' identification of consciousness as the essence of being human, separating us from our bodies, was a philosophical masterstroke.

The risk was that his journey to discover exactly what we could know would lead him to a nihilistic conclusion, though in fact it seemed to deliver a rock of certainty, providing humanity with confidence in our universe. The "dualism" between mind and body allowed for modern science to flourish, because there was a clear gap between the observer (us) and the observed (the world), which includes our own bodies and other animals. Privileged with a reasoning and observing mind, humankind is justified in dominating nature and creating things that can aim to be an expression of perfection. Our consciousness is a smaller version of God's all-seeing, all-knowing nature.

The purpose of doubt and proofs of God

Descartes considers doubt itself, and notes that it is particularly human. Depending on your point of view, we are either afflicted or blessed by doubt, but knowing is clearly better than doubting, therefore to know is a greater "perfection" than to doubt. Given how much we doubt things, therefore, humans must be imperfect. Moreover, imperfect beings cannot produce perfection, either for themselves or for others; there must be something else that is perfect in the first place, which made them and which generates the idea of perfection. Descartes reasons that if he had created himself he would be perfect, but he isn't, so he must have been created by something else. This is obviously God; therefore, he concludes, God must exist.

For Descartes, the thought of God is not simply a crazy idea of humans, but was the most important thought that the creator made sure we would have. Through this thought we would be able to see that we are not perfect, but come from perfection. Indeed, Descartes says, the thought of God is the "Maker's mark" on us.

Not only omnipotent, Descartes' God is benevolent, waiting for humans to reason their way to the truth of divine existence and helping us along in this process, almost expecting that we would come to a point where we doubted everything (not only God, but that the world itself exists). However, God also expects us to reason our way back to some essential truths. He does not lead us up a blind alley. The divine nature is not merely to tell us everything through faith or through reason alone. We have to experiment, ask questions, find out for ourselves.

Descartes came to believe that nonbelief in God would be perverse, yet he also promoted the idea of keeping separate religion and science, which are, if you like, symbolic of mind and matter. Ultimately, all humankind's achievements in science, art, and reason are our way of getting back to ultimate truths, and matter was simply one expression of such truth.

Final comments

Contemporary philosophers like to gloss over or deprecate Descartes' metaphysical side, seeing it as the blemish on an otherwise brilliant conception of the world. Textbooks tend to "forgive" his desire to provide proofs of God, pointing out that this most rational of men could not escape the religious nature of his times. Surely, if he were alive today, he would not even dip his feet into such metaphysical murkiness?

Let's not forget that Descartes' "tree of knowledge" has metaphysics as its very trunk, from which everything else spreads out. His thinking on consciousness, the separation of mind and matter, and his love of natural science are simply branches. Science and a skeptical outlook would do nothing to dismantle divine reality.

However, Descartes was also a supreme rationalist who helped to dismantle the medieval idea that objects were invested with "spirits." His duality between mind and matter dispensed with such superstitions, allowing for the rise of the empirical sciences while at the same time not disowning the notion that the universe was the creation of an intelligent mind. Indeed, Descartes' brilliant balancing act between mind and matter, physics and metaphysics was a remarkable echo of Aquinas, whose writings he had studied in his youth. His dualistic system was also a huge influence on subsequent rationalist philosophers such as Spinoza and Leibniz.

René Descartes

Descartes was born in 1596 in La Haye, France, which was later renamed Descartes in his honor. He received an excellent education at a Jesuit college that taught Aristotelian logic, metaphysics, ethics, and physics, within the embrace of Thomist (as in Aquinas) theology. He studied law at the University of Poitiers, then at 22 went traveling around Europe, working as a military engineer. It was while in the service of the Duke of Bavaria that he had his famous philosophical visions. For the rest of his life he lived quietly, and not much is known about his personal life. In his fifties he was invited to Sweden to be the philosophy tutor of Queen Christina, but the work was more taxing than his normal solitary regime and he died there of pneumonia in 1650.

Descartes' first work was the Treatise of the World, *but he decided not to publish it because it contained the heresy that the earth revolved around the sun, and he did not want to get into the same trouble as Galileo. Other books include* Discourse in Method *(1637),* Principles of Philosophy *(1644), and* Passions of the Soul, *published after his death.*

Fate

"But if there be irresistible dictation, this dictation understands itself. If we must accept Fate, we are not less compelled to affirm liberty, the significance of the individual, the grandeur of duty, the power of character."

"History is the action and reaction of these two, – Nature and Thought; – two boys pushing each other on the curb-stone of the pavement. Everything is pusher or pushed: and matter and mind are in perpetual tilt and balance, so. Whilst the man is weak, the earth takes him up. He plants his brain and affections. By and by he will take up the earth, and have his gardens and vineyards in the beautiful order and productiveness of his thought. Every solid in the universe is ready to become fluid on the approach of the mind, and the power to flux it is the measure of the mind."

"A breath of will blows eternally through the universe of souls in the direction of the Right and Necessary."

In a nutshell

The case for us being simply products of fate is strong, yet paradoxically it is only in accepting it that we can realize our creative power.

In a similar vein

Hannah Arendt *The Human Condition* (p 22)
Isaiah Berlin *The Hedgehog and the Fox* (p 56)
Baruch Spinoza *Ethics* (p 298)

CHAPTER 15

Ralph Waldo Emerson

W hen not quite 40, the great American transcendentalist Ralph Waldo Emerson wrote "Self-Reliance." This acclaimed essay became symbolic of the ethic of American individualism, but it was more complex than generally appreciated. Though he promoted personal responsibility and the duty always to be oneself in the face of social conformity, Emerson's deeper message was that the wish to succeed is not about exerting our will against the world, but in fact working with the grain of the universe.

Almost 20 years later, his essay "Fate" was an attempt to solve this issue of how much we are the result of our own efforts, or the product of unseen forces. It is still a superb meditation on this basic philosophical question.

The case for fate

Emerson begins by admitting that the "irresistible dictation" of life is true: fate is real. And yet, he also affirms the "significance of the individual" and the "power of character" as real forces. How does one reconcile these apparent opposites?

At a personal level, most of us feel that our individuality strikes a balance with the world, that we somehow bridge a gap between necessity and liberty, and that though there be "irresistible dictation, this dictation understands itself." Our lives are essentially the working out of our wills within the spirit and limitations of the age in which we live. "The riddle of the age," Emerson says, "has for each a private solution."

Emerson admits the perception of superficiality in the outlook of the typical American, noting that great nations have not been "boasters and buffoons, but perceivers of the terror of life, and have manned themselves to face it." He mentions the Spartans who happily ran to their deaths in battle, and Turkish, Arab, and Persian peoples who did the same, easily accepting their "preordained fate." Even the old Calvinists, he notes, had a similar dignity, according to which their individuality meant little against the "weight of the

Universe." Emerson implies that it is hubris to believe that our little selves can have any real effect, when, as Chaucer put it, destiny is the "minister-general" that actually decides the course of war and peace, hate and love.

What is more, Emerson writes, nature is not sentimental, "will not mind drowning a man or woman," and will swallow a whole ship "like a grain of dust." Races of animals feed on each other, volcanoes explode, a change in the seabed swamps a town, cholera overcomes a city. Will "providence" save us from any of these things? Even if providence exists, it moves on tracks indiscernible to us and is not a force on which we can count at a personal level; it is pure vanity, he says, to "dress up that terrific benefactor in a clean shirt and white neckcloth of a student in divinity."

Nature is not only no sentimentalist, its forms are tyrannical. Just as a bird's existence is determined by the shape and length of its bill and the extent of its feathers, so humans' gender, race, climate, and talents mold their possibilities: "Every spirit makes its house; but afterwards the house confines the spirit." Our DNA and family heritage create our destiny:

> "Men are what their mothers made them. You may as well ask a loom which weaves huckaback, why it does not make cashmere, as expect poetry from this engineer, or a chemical discovery from that jobber. Ask the digger in the ditch to explain Newton's laws: the fine organs of his brain have been pinched by overwork and squalid poverty from father to son, for a hundred years ... So he has but one future, and that is already predetermined in his lobes ... All the privilege and all the legislation of the world cannot meddle or help to make a poet or a prince of him."

Emerson was well versed in Eastern spiritual literature, particularly the concepts of karma, reincarnation, and the "wheel of life," which all point to nature and the circumstances of our present lives being largely the result of actions and experiences in previous incarnations. Yet in the Western tradition he finds support for this outlook, noting German philosopher Friedrich Schelling's remark that "there is in every man a certain feeling, that he has been what he is from all eternity, and by no means became such in time." Everyone is "party to his present estate." If this is true, what gives us the temerity to see ourselves as blank slates?

Looking back over scientific history, it often seems inevitable that a certain discovery emerged at a particular time. We like to ascribe inventions and insights to an individual, but usually there were two, three, or four people who came to the same conclusions simultaneously. The truth is that progress is impersonal and has its own momentum. Particular people are interchangeable "vehicles," and to think otherwise provokes laughter from the gods.

The weight of fate will, however, seem different to different people. A brutish person, Emerson suggests, will find themselves hemmed in on all sides by an equally brutal destiny, whereas a finer person will seem to experience finer checks on their actions. Yet while our limitations, or our fate, become less heavy the purer our soul, "the ring of necessity is always perched at the top."

The case for personal power

Having put the strongest argument for the weight of fate, Emerson suddenly changes tack. Fate, he begins to say, is itself subject to limitation. For there is another force that moves the world, which he calls "power." If fate is "natural history," power is its nemesis, and humankind is not "ignominious baggage" but a "stupendous antagonism" that throws a spanner into the works of an apparently determined history.

Part of fate, Emerson says, is human freedom, and "So far as man thinks, he is free." To dwell on fate is not wholesome, and among the weak and lazy it becomes easy to blame everything on it. The right way to see fate is to invoke its natural might without lessening our own liberty to act. It can inspire us to steadfastness when otherwise we might be blown about by the winds of emotion or circumstance:

"A man ought to compare advantageously with a river, an oak, or a mountain. He shall have not less the flow, the expansion, and the resistance of these."

As others believe in fate as a force for harm, we should see it as a force for good, knowing ourselves to be "guarded by the cherubim of destiny." Having spoken at length of the unexpected wrath of nature, Emerson suggests that we can "confront fate with fate," for "if the Universe have these savage accidents, our atoms are as savage in resistance." Moreover, we have a creative power that frees us, so that we become not a cog in the machine, but a participant in the universe's unfolding, having epiphanies as to how it operates and yet still finding niches to fill with our own originality. For as we expand to knowledge of the unity of things, it is natural that our value to the world increases; *we* can state "what is" as much as what seems to be written in the book of fate:

"Thought dissolves the material universe, by carrying the mind up into a sphere where all is plastic."

Emerson further observes, "Always one man more than another represents the will of Divine Providence to the period." And with that perception of truth "is joined the desire that it shall prevail." Though the power of nature is significant, a fired-up human will is awesome, potentially galvanizing whole nations or sparking new religions. The hero acts in a way that seems quite oblivious to fate, not even considering that the world could be otherwise.

When you look closely, Emerson suggests, fate is simply causes that we have not completely explained. After all, death from typhoid seemed like "the whim of God" until someone worked out that correct drainage helped to eliminate it; it was the same with scurvy, which killed countless sailors before we realized that it could be stopped by a store of lime juice. Great land masses were intractable until rail tracks were laid. Human ingenuity frequently makes a mockery of seemingly all-powerful "fate."

Emerson's conclusion

At the end of his essay, Emerson comes back to the relationship between people and events. He suggests that "the soul contains the event that shall befall it, for the event is only the actualization of its thoughts ... The event is the print of your form. It fits you like your skin." He goes on to say:

> "A man's fortunes are the fruit of his character ... his growth is declared in his ambition, his companions, and his performance. He looks like a piece of luck, but is a piece of causation."

He likens history to two boys pushing at each other on the pavement. Human beings are either pushed or pushing. One who is weak is pushed by circumstances, while the wise and strong see that apparently immovable objects can be moved, that we can stamp our thoughts on the world. He asks:

> "What is the city in which we sit here, but an aggregate of incongruous materials, which have obeyed the will of some man? The granite was reluctant, but his hands were stronger, and it came."

Final comments

What is the relationship between Emerson's earlier essay, "Self-reliance," and "Fate"? It would be tempting to say that the later work reflects a wiser Emerson who was more attuned to the power of nature and circumstance in people's lives. It is almost as if he is challenging himself to believe his earlier, more forthright essay on the power of the individual.

Yet while it is true that "Self-Reliance" has the certainty of a younger man and "Fate" is more nuanced, the later essay in fact affirms Emerson's basic position on the relationship between person and universe. In the very last part, he talks of something called the "Beautiful Necessity," the greater intelligence or "law of life" that seems to move the universe. This force drives nature and is beyond words. It is neither impersonal nor personal. The wise person sees that there is nothing left to chance, "no contingencies" – everything turns out how it was meant to. But having noted this apparent determinism, and just when one thinks Emerson has finally sided with fate, he says that this beautiful necessity (nature, God, law, intelligence) "solicits the pure in heart to draw on all its omnipotence."

This, finally, is the opening we are given. Although the law of life is unstoppable and has its own reasons, at the same time it wants us to work with it. In doing so we may lose our little selves, but in the process become attuned to something infinitely larger and more powerful. We cease to be simply a subject, and are a powerful co-creator in the world's unfolding.

Ralph Waldo Emerson

Born in 1803 in Boston, Emerson was one of eight children; his father died just before he was 8. He enrolled at Harvard University at age 14, graduating four years later. After some time as a schoolteacher, he attended divinity college at Harvard, became a Unitarian pastor, and married, but his wife Ellen died of tuberculosis. After resigning his post because of theological disputes, he traveled to Europe and met Thomas Carlyle, Samuel Taylor Coleridge, and William Wordsworth.

Returning to America in 1835, Emerson settled in Concord and married again, to Lydia Jackson. The couple had five children. In 1836 he published Nature, *which set out transcendentalist principles; his transcendentalist friends included Henry David Thoreau, Margaret Fuller, Amos Bronson Alcott, and Elizabeth Peabody. In the following two years Emerson delivered controversial addresses at Harvard, the first on American intellectual independence from Europe, the second pleading for independence of belief above all creeds and churches.*

In 1841 and 1844, two series of essays were published, including Self-Reliance, Spiritual Laws, The Over-Soul, Compensation *and* Experience, *and, in the decade 1850–60,* Representative Men, English Traits, *and* The Conduct of Life. *Emerson died in 1882.*

Letters

"We must, therefore, pursue the things that make for happiness, seeing that when happiness is present, we have everything; but when it is absent, we do everything to possess it."

"Death, therefore – the most dreadful of evils – is nothing to us, since while we exist, death is not present, and whenever death is present, we do not exist."

In a nutshell

We can achieve tranquility and happiness by letting go of irrational beliefs and fears and living simply.

In a similar vein

Aristotle *Nicomachean Ethics* (p 28)
David Hume *An Enquiry Concerning Human Understanding* (p 136)
Bertrand Russell *The Conquest of Happiness* (p 258)

CHAPTER 16

Epicurus

When Epicurus began his philosophy school in a house and garden in Athens in 306 BC, his openness to women members as well as men made people think that he was holding orgies; indeed, "Epicureanism" came to mean living for sensual enjoyment. In reality, physical pleasure was just one aspect of his outlook, and when he did praise it, it was only because it meant the absence of pain, which he saw as an evil.

Epicurus' real philosophy was living simply and rationally, and once one's minimal needs were met, enjoying friendship and nature. He did not believe in metaphysical ideas such as Plato's "Forms," instead opting for a materialistic view of the universe; what mattered was what we could perceive through our senses. Because he did not believe in an afterlife, achieving happiness on earth took on real meaning.

Epicurus died in 271 BC, leaving over 300 papyrus rolls of his writings, though only a small amount of his work has survived. His very brief *Principal Doctrines* came to us through Diogenes Laertius' biography of Epicurus in his *Lives of the Eminent Philosophers*, and there is also a collection of aphorisms found in a Vatican manuscript in 1888, along with fragments from archaeological digs. Also surviving are Epicurus' letters to three of his students, Herodotus (not the historian), Pythocles, and Menoeceus. These are representative of his main ideas, and we focus on them here.

The *Letters* dwell at some length on cosmology and nature, and one wonders at first why Epicurus is so interested in such matters. It is easy to forget now that, before science had developed in its own right, questions about the physical nature of the "heavens" were seen as part of philosophy.

The nature of the universe
Writing to Pythocles, Epicurus notes that it is possible to know something about the heavens from our observations; we should not rely on stories and myths to explain how the universe works. There is no "man on the moon," for instance; the faces we seem to see on its surface are merely an arrangement of matter. Equally, changes in weather are not due to the wrath of the gods, but the coincidence of certain conditions in the atmosphere; Epicurus discusses

earthquakes and volcanoes in a similar way. The universe is not run on a moment-to-moment basis by some celestial being, but rather all physical masses were there at the beginning of the world, which continues to be ordered and run according to its own self-evident principles. There is nothing in the universe "that admits of variation of randomness," Epicurus says.

We must be open to knowledge of how the universe really operates, being willing to dispose of our cherished notions if they do not match the facts. Humans get into difficulties, Epicurus says, only when we try to impose our own will or motive on how the universe works. We fear retribution for our actions or loss of consciousness (death), when in fact these mean nothing in the wider scheme of things. The more we know of the universe and its principles, the less we will be inclined to link our own fears and irrational thoughts to that universe, instead appreciating them simply as phenomena inside our heads. He tells Pythocles, "we must not think that there is any other aim of knowledge about the heavens ... than peace of mind and unshakeable confidence, just as it is our aim in all other pursuits." In other words, the more we know, the less fearful we are. Uncovering facts can only ever be a good thing.

In his letter to Herodotus, Epicurus goes into some detail on his theory of the universe's origins and the nature of matter. He suggests that it was created from the opposites of matter and nothingness, and has no limit, "both in the number of bodies and the magnitude of the void." He goes as far as to say that, because there is an infinitude of "atoms" (the ancient Greek term for the smallest particles), there can be an infinitude of worlds. The following lines could have been written by a quantum physicist:

> "The atoms move continuously forever, some ... standing at a long distance from one another, others in turn maintaining their rapid vibration whenever they happen to be checked by their interlacing with others or covered by the interlaced atoms."

However, Epicurus also says that we cannot go on breaking matter down to smaller and smaller parts, otherwise we would reach nonexistence. His other interesting cosmological point is that the universe may have many causes; it is irrational to suggest that there is only a single "story" that explains everything. Rather, rational inquiry is likely to uncover many causes for phenomena. He remarks:

> "whenever we admit one explanation but reject another that agrees equally well with the evidence, it is clear that we fall short in every way of true scientific inquiry and resort instead to myth."

The real sources of happiness

Scientifically, Epicurus seems ahead of his time, but how does his thinking about the universe relate to his views on how to live? His statement "For our life has no need of foolishness and idle opinion, but of an existence free from confusion" can apply equally to science and personal life. In short, happiness is being free from illusions.

All of our choices, Epicurus says in his letter to Menoeceus, should be toward "the health of the body or the calm of the soul, since this is the goal of a happy life." It is natural and good that our actions are in avoidance of pain and fear, and toward pleasure. However, this does not mean that we should merely indulge in any pleasure at any time. The rational person weighs up in their mind the difficulty that may accompany some pleasures, and also knows that some pains are better than some pleasures, because they lead to a greater pleasure at the end:

> "Every pleasure, therefore, because of its natural relationship to us, is good, but not every pleasure is to be chosen."

Discussing food, he remarks that we should be happy with simple fare, not a "luxurious table." If we have the latter every day, we will fear its being taken away from us. In contrast, we will enjoy gourmet foods more if we have them only occasionally.

Epicurus admits that linking pleasure to happiness lays his philosophy open to being seen as reveling in sensuality. His aim is in fact more serious: "freedom from bodily pain and mental anguish." It is not food, drinking, and sex that create a pleasant life, but thinking through all of one's choices, so that we will not do or think things that result in a troubled soul. A virtuous life, for Epicurus, is the same thing as a pleasant life, because doing the right thing naturally puts our mind at rest. Instead of having anguish about the consequences of our bad actions, we are liberated to enjoy a simple life of friends, philosophy, nature, and small comforts.

Epicurus further notes that we should not put our trust in chance or luck, only in prudence, which provides stability. The wise person "thinks that it is preferable to remain prudent and suffer ill fortune than to enjoy good luck while acting foolishly. It is better in human actions that the sound decision fail than that the rash decision turn out well due to luck."

Act in the ways above, Epicurus tells Menoeceus, and "You shall be disturbed neither waking nor sleeping, and you shall live as a god among men."

Final comments

Epicurus did not deny that there were gods, but he also said that they were unconcerned with the trivialities of human lives, and therefore the idea of gods who might want to punish us had to be wrong. Epicurean philosophy seeks to steer people away from irrational fears and superstitions, and to show that happiness is much more likely if one uses reason to make choices. Presaging William James's pragmatic philosophy by 2,000 years, it suggests that if those choices make us happy and allow us to be at peace, then we will know that reason is the best guide to life. The good person is both free from trouble themselves ("not constrained by either anger or by favour," as Epicurus puts it in the *Principle Doctrines*) and does not cause trouble for anyone else. And in another fragment that has come down to us, he counsels:

> *"It is better for you to be free of fear and lying on a bed of straw than to own a couch of gold and lavish table and yet have no peace of mind."*

One source of peace of mind was human connection; fittingly for someone who promoted friendship as life's greatest pleasure, Diogenes Laertius reports that Epicurus had more friends than virtually anyone else of his time.

Epicurus

Born on the Greek island of Samos in 341 BC, Epicurus received an education in philosophy from Pamphilus, a Platonist. At 18 he went to Athens to fulfill his military service, then went to live with his parents, who had moved to Colophon on the Asiatic coast. There another teacher, Nausiphanes, taught Epicurus the ideas of Democritus, including "undisturbedness" as the aim of life.

In 306 BC Epicurus launched a philosophy school in Athens, and the movement that grew up around it became known as the "Garden." Unusually, its students included women and slaves. Epicurus survived on contributions from members, who sought to live according to his dictum "Live unseen," or live quietly without attracting attention. Epicurean communes in ancient Greece and Rome copied the original Garden.

Epicurus' philosophy spread quickly during his lifetime and endured after his death in 270 BC. In Rome, Lucretius helped keep him popular, and Cicero also acknowledged him in his writings. By the Early Middle Ages, Christianity had created a caricature of Epicurus as a gross sensualist, but in the sixteenth century Erasmus and Montaigne, among others, saw him in a new light – as a sensible and rational figure compared to the superstitions and excesses of the Catholic Church. Pierre Gassendi's Eight Books on the Life and Manners of Epicurus *(1647) gave him further credibility.*

There are many good translations of Epicurus. The quotes given here are from Eugene O'Connor's.

The Order of Things

"Historians want to write histories of biology in the eighteenth century; but they do not realize that biology did not exist then, and that the pattern of knowledge that has been familiar to us for a hundred and fifty years is not valid for a previous period. And that, if biology was unknown, there was a very simple reason for it: that life itself did not exist. All that existed was living beings, which were viewed through a grid of knowledge constituted by natural history."

"The sciences are well-made languages."

In a nutshell

Every age has unconscious assumptions about how the world is ordered, making the flavor of knowledge quite different from one era to another.

In a similar vein

Thomas Kuhn *The Structure of Scientific Revolutions* (p 164)
Mary Midgley *The Myths We Live By* (p 194)
Karl Popper *The Logic of Scientific Discovery* (p 242)
Ludwig Wittgenstein *Philosophical Investigations* (p 312)

CHAPTER 17

Michel Foucault

L es Mots et les choses was the book that made Michel Foucault a famous intellectual in France. Subtitled "an archaeology of the human sciences," it attempts to show how knowledge is a cultural product, with different disciplines simply being expressions of the prevailing worldview. When the book was published as *The Order of Things* in America in 1971, literary critic George Steiner wrote:

> *"an honest first reading produces an almost intolerable sense of verbosity, arrogance and obscure platitude. Page after page could be the rhetoric of a somewhat weary sybil indulging in free association. Recourse to the French text shows that this is not a matter of awkward translation."*

The book is indeed very hard to grasp in places, not so much due to the content but to Foucault's style, which takes a page to express an idea that really requires only a line or a paragraph. Luckily, his foreword to the English translation provides a key to the work.

Foucault's basic idea is that each era, or "episteme," is redolent with a "positive unconscious," a way of seeing the world of which it is quite unaware. Our linear minds are used to taking a particular discipline, such as biology or economics, and viewing it as one evolving area of knowledge from its earliest conceptions up to the present day. However, this does not reflect reality. The way people saw the science of life (biology) in the seventeenth century, Foucault says, has more in common with the way they saw wealth and money in that era than it has with biology in the nineteenth century. Each episteme is culturally contained and does not "lead" into another episteme.

Constructing categories

The idea of the book came to Foucault when he was reading a Borges novel and laughed out loud at a reference to a Chinese encyclopedia dividing animals into:

> *"(a) belonging to the Emperor, (b) embalmed, (c) tame, (d) sucking pigs, (e) sirens, (f) fabulous, (g) stray dogs, (h) included in the present*

classification, (i) frenzied, (j) innumerable, (k) drawn with a very fine camelhair brush, (l) et cetera, (m) having just broken the water pitcher, (n) that from a long way off 'look like flies.'"

This bizarre taxonomy led Foucault to the insight that we all possess ways of thinking and seeing that make other ways impossible. But what is it exactly that we find impossible? The weirdness of Borges' list comes from there being no order of linkage between the things listed, no "ground" of knowledge. That leads to the question: What is the ground on which our own categories rest? What is it that we assume to be true or not true, linked or not linked, in *our* culture and time? Foucault suggests that not only do we not perceive anything objectively, our systems of categorization are assumptions, received and accepted unconsciously:

"Order is, at one and the same time, that which is given in things as their inner law, the hidden network that determines the way they confront one another, and also that which has no existence except in the grid created by a glance, an examination, a language; and it is only in the blank spaces of this grid that order manifests itself in depth as though already there, waiting in silence for the moment of its expression."

Foucault wished to replace the idea of a particular science or area of knowledge having a starting point and linear history of discovery, with a view of it as "an epistemological space specific to a particular period," replacing the traditional history of thought whereby "so and so discovered something, and his influences were..." with an analysis that tells us what anyone would have thought or believed in a certain era. On an archaeological dig you are not looking for a particular person, Foucault observes, but want to know how a whole community lived and what it believed. If one is looking at the Swedish naturalist Linnaeus, for instance, it is not enough to outline his discoveries, one must understand the intellectual and cultural "discourse" that allowed them to be expressed and taken note of; that is, the "unspoken order" of the times. The fundamental codes of a culture – those governing its language, its schemas of perception, its exchanges, its techniques, its values, the hierarchy of its practices – "establish for every man, from the very first, the empirical orders with which he will be dealing and within which he will be at home."

Foucault sets out to do this by investigating the threshold between classical knowledge (knowledge prior to the sixteenth century) and the thinking and knowing that come to constitute modernity. He studies art (Velasquez's painting *Las Meninas*) and literature (*Don Quixote*) as a prelude to analyzing three areas: language, economics, and biology.

Creating modernity: Language for its own sake

For Foucault, the key to classical knowing is mental representation. Classical thinkers could disagree about the truth or otherwise of ideas, but they all agreed that ideas were a representation of their objects. From this it followed that language, as a mere representation of truths or objects, could have no real role of its own. Language was the physical representation of ideas, with no meaning except in relation to them:

> *"From an extreme point of view, one might say that language in the Classical era does not exist. But that it functions: its whole existence is located in its representative role, is limited precisely to that role and finally exhausts it. Language has no other locus, no other value, than in representation."*

After Kant's time, Foucault argues, language gained an independent and essential life, beyond the mere representation of ideas. General grammar was no longer enough. Instead there developed philology, or the study of the history of natural languages and its focus on texts themselves, and analytical philosophy, which tried to eliminate the confusions and distortions of language. These two complementary approaches of modern thought came to underlie the division of analytical and continental philosophy. Freed from direct representation of ideas, language could be treated as an autonomous reality, with no system of resemblances binding it to the world. A gulf opened up between content and form, and we moved from a phase of commentary to one of criticism. Language became a truth unto itself.

This new episteme also allowed for the realm of "pure literature," evoked by Mallarmé when he answered Nietzsche's question "Who is speaking?" with the answer "Language itself." Literature is neither resemblance nor representation, but becomes a force of its own. Writing on *Don Quixote*, Foucault says:

> *"in it language breaks off its old kinship with things and enters into that lonely sovereignty from which it will reappear, in its separated state, only as literature; because it marks the point where resemblance enters an age which is, from the point of view of resemblance, one of madness and imagination."*

If you are to write any kind of history that involves opinions, beliefs, prejudices, and superstitions, Foucault says, "what is written on these subjects is always of less value as evidence than are the words themselves." To find out what people really thought in any given era, it is not the content of what they said but how they said it, and making what assumptions, that gives us insights. We think of the sciences as having an objective reality, but Foucault describes them as being simply "well-made languages."

Creating modernity: The "birth of man"

In the development of the modern way of thinking, even more important than language is the figure of "man" itself as an epistemological concept. "Man" did not exist during the classical age (or before), Foucault says. This is not because there was no idea of human beings as a species or of human nature as a psychological, moral, or political notion. Rather, "there was no epistemological consciousness of man as such."

Modernity, however, brought us from the horizontal taxonomy of things to vertical conceptual categorization – abstraction. With this came *humanity* as a concept, just as the "science of life" (essentially a taxonomy of living things) gave way to the more abstract and conceptual science of biology. Yet Foucault argues that "man is an invention of recent date. And one perhaps nearing its end." By this he means that if our current worldview were to crumble, our current exalted picture of ourselves would also, in time, be seen to be severely limited.

Final comments

Foucault's notion of epistemes is not that different to Thomas Kuhn's "paradigms" of scientific thinking, and it is interesting that Kuhn's *The Structure of Scientific Revolutions* was published only four years before *The Order of Things* – perhaps evidence that knowledge comes in the form of particular world-views of which the individual is barely aware. Both books are an antidote to the conceit of current knowledge and the belief in a linear model of knowledge accumulation. In reality, whatever constitutes the ground of knowledge in any field is wont suddenly to open up and swallow everything, with new forms of "knowing" springing up in a completely different place.

It is in the nature of modern French philosophy that many assertions are made without being backed up, and *The Order of Things* is no different. Yet the book is valuable in its "meta" approach to knowledge and its questioning of assumptions and biases. Of his own work Foucault writes, "It would hardly behove me, of all people, to claim that my discourse is independent of conditions and rules of which I am very largely unaware." Indeed, just as we now ridicule the Chinese taxonomy mentioned by Borges, it is likely that people in 100 years' time will laugh at the strange categories and blind associations that we currently call knowledge.

Michel Foucault

Foucault was born in Poitiers, France in 1926. His doctor father wanted him to study medicine, but at school he was more interested in literature and history. He left Poitiers in 1945 to study at the Lycée Henri-IV in Paris, and was admitted to the École Normale Supérieure a year later. Though an excellent student, he was socially awkward, and struggled with his homosexuality. During this time he became friends with Louis Althusser (a Marxist philosopher). Foucault eventually received degrees in philosophy, psychology, and psychiatry.

In 1950 he became an assistant lecturer at the University of Lille. After a time he left France to teach at the University of Uppsala in Sweden, followed by directorships of the French Institutes at Warsaw University and the University of Hamburg. He began to take an interest in history, particularly the changing views of psychiatric practice, which resulted in the very well-received Madness and Civilization. *In 1963 he published* Birth of the Clinic.

When his partner Daniel Defert was posted to Tunisia for military service, in 1965 Foucault moved to a position at the University of Tunis. After The Order of Things *was published to great acclaim in 1966, he was hailed as one of the great thinkers of his time, along with Jacques Lacan, Claude Lévi-Strauss, and Roland Barthes. The same year he published* The Archaeology of Knowledge *and took up the post of head of philosophy at the University of Clermont-Ferrand. In 1970, he was elected Professor of the History of Systems of Thought at the Collège de France. His increasing political involvement and interest in social action were reflected in 1975's* Discipline and Punish, *which examines the "technologies" of organization and control.*

The first volume of The History of Sexuality *came out in 1976. Foucault's reputation grew in the 1970s and 1980s and he lectured throughout the world, spending more time at American institutions. He also made two tours of Iran, writing essays on the Iranian revolution for an Italian newspaper. He died in Paris in 1984.*

On Bullshit

"One of the most salient features of our culture is that there is so much bullshit. Everyone knows this. Each of us contributes his share. But we tend to take the situation for granted. Most people are rather confident of their ability to recognize bullshit and to avoid being taken in by it. So the phenomena has not aroused much deliberate concern, nor attracted much sustained inquiry. In consequence, we have no clear understanding of what bullshit is, why there is so much of it, or what functions it serves."

In a nutshell

Bullshit pervades our culture and we need to know how it is different from lying.

In a similar vein

Noam Chomsky *Understanding Power* (p 76)
Michel de Montaigne *Essays* (p 206)
Ludwig Wittgenstein *Philosophical Investigations* (p 312)

CHAPTER 18

Harry Frankfurt

n 2005, this little book of only 67 pages became a surprise bestseller. It seemed to tap into public concern about the "spin" surrounding America and Britain's launch of the second Iraq War, but its message has resonated beyond particular events.

Bullshit surrounds us, says Harry Frankfurt, a Princeton moral philosophy professor, but we don't see it for what it is. This is why we need a theory of it.

Why it is different to lying

Frankfurt asks whether bullshit is simply the same as "humbug." In his book *The Prevalence of Humbug* (1985), Max Black defined humbug as "deceptive misrepresentation, short of lying, especially by pretentious word or deed, of somebody's own thoughts, feelings, and attitudes."

Bullshit is similar to humbug in that it is an attempt to deliberately mislead, and yet stops short of an outright lie. Bullshit can also be pretentious, and a conscious misrepresentation of the way one really sees a situation. Both humbug and bullshit therefore aim to create an impression that I am thinking or believing something, even if I have not come out and actually said it. In this gap, therefore, a mistruth can arise without my actually stating a lie. Humbug's main aim is not to create a different kind of reality through changing the "facts," but rather for the speaker to be seen differently. A grand political speech, for instance, does not aim to say how the world actually is; its purpose is to make the speaker sound like a patriot, or a spiritual person, or a protector of morals. Frankfurt concludes that humbug does not fully grasp the real nature of bullshit. To explain why, he begins by quoting Longfellow: "In the elder days of art/ Builders wrought with greatest care/ Each minute and unseen part,/ For the Gods are everywhere." An old-school craftsman was not out to make an impression, but rather its opposite: to make sure that something was done right, even if no one noticed the detail of the work. In contrast, shoddily made items are bullshit, because time, craftsmanship, and care are totally left out of the process. Everything is about a hoped-for short-term effect that will benefit the producer, and the quality of the good and its durability are irrelevant.

Frankfurt mentions a recollection by Fania Pascal of her friend Wittgenstein, who called her while she was in hospital having her tonsils out. When she told him, post-operation, that she felt like "a dog that had just been run over," he was disgusted, noting that "You don't know how a dog feels when it is run over." Wittgenstein was not standing up for dogs' feelings, but rather the famous linguistic analyst felt that Pascal was not making the proper effort with language. She was neither stating the facts of her own feelings, nor could she know how a dog felt. Though Wittgenstein's reaction was obviously over the top, Frankfurt draws from it to fashion his own definition of bullshit: that it is not simply outright lying, and indeed often stops short of lying, but is rather a *lack of any concern* whether something is true or not.

The difference between liars and bullshit artists

In a "bull session" (a group of guys getting together to chat about women or politics or sport or cars), the purpose is not to uncover or state any great truth, but merely to talk for the pleasure of it: as a verb, "to bullshit" can simply be a way of revealing one's personality (a world away from giving one's final word or commitment on a subject). Problems start, however, when this kind of self-conscious table talk, in which one is not that concerned with truth, becomes one's whole way of being. To operate well in life we need facts, and when someone seems full of "hot air" we are infuriated.

"Telling a lie is an act with a sharp focus," Frankfurt says, an act that can involve an element of craftsmanship, because we have to create our mistruth against what we clearly know are the facts or accepted morality. The liar, therefore, "In order to invent a lie at all ... must think he knows what is true."

In contrast, a person who wants to bullshit their way through life has much more freedom, because they do not have to fabricate lies in light of the truth, but rather are "running a story" that does not even have to be related to truth or untruth. They can be a lot more creative; the appropriate analogy is art, not craft. The bullshit artist does not actually have to misrepresent or change the facts, because they are a master at spinning them in a way that supports or justifies what they are up to. Unlike the liar or the honest person, the bullshitter's eyes are not on the facts at all; facts are important only to the extent that they help them "get away with it." Given this, Frankfurt concludes, "bullshit is the greater enemy of truth than lies are."

Why is there so much bullshit?

Frankfurt admits that one cannot say whether there is more bullshit now than in previous times, only that the volume is now "undeniably great." One reason is that many of us are called on to talk about matters of which we know little; in a democracy we are expected to have opinions on a range of political issues, so we offer them to avoid saying "I don't know." In addition, we live in a more relativistic world in which the belief that we can identify and isolate truth is itself seen as suspect, so the ideal of revealing what is *correct* is being replaced with the ideal of *sincerity*:

> *"Rather than seeking primarily to arrive at accurate representations of the common world, the individual turns toward trying to provide honest representations of himself. Convinced that reality has no inherent nature, which he might hope to identify as the truth about things, he devotes himself to being true to his own nature."*

Though Frankfurt does not mention him, it could be argued that this particular rot set in with Montaigne, who took delight in saying how little he actually knew of the world and so fell back on examining what he did know: himself. Frankfurt points out the flaw in this view: we cannot say that there is a correct or true view of ourselves, but at the same time suggest that nothing for certain can be said of anything else. Rather, the more we know about the world, the more likely we are to begin to reveal something true of ourselves.

Final comments

A lie can shock or startle, but we accept it as being, after all, consistent with human nature. Bullshitting, however, particularly when it extends beyond individuals to organizations and governments, is perverse, a corruption of humanity. Rejection of the "authority of truth" in favor of selling or telling a story can lead to the rise of Hitlers and Pol Pots, whose spin on history is so captivating that it attracts millions of followers. Since *On Bullshit* was written, of course, the bullshitting of populist leaders and their enthusiasm for fake news has further corrupted the public sphere.

Bullshit matters, and in turning it into a theory Frankfurt has made a valuable contribution to philosophy. Of course, others have written about the subject in other ways; Sartre gave us the concept of "authenticity," for instance, but it was buried in a long, difficult book. If more philosophers used common terms and wrote very succinct books such as this one, their impact on the average person would surely increase.

Harry G. Frankfurt

Born in 1929, Frankfurt received his PhD from Johns Hopkins University in 1954. He taught at Yale and Rockefeller Universities before taking up his position at Princeton, where he remained a professor of moral philosophy until 2002. His areas of academic interest have included Cartesian rationality and truth, the free will–determinism issue (particularly its implications for moral responsibility), and caring and love. Other books include The Importance of What We Care About *(1988),* The Reasons of Love *(2004),* On Truth *(2006), and* Taking Ourselves Seriously and Getting It Right *(2006).* On Bullshit *was originally published in the literary journal* Raritan *in 1986.*

Phenomenology of Spirit

"To help bring philosophy closer to the form of Science, to the goal where it can lay aside the title 'love of knowing' and be 'actual knowing' – that is what I have set myself to do."

"History, is a conscious, self-meditating process – Spirit emptied out into Time."

"The true is the whole."

In a nutshell

The real story of human development is not scientific advance, or "discovery of the world," but rather the awareness of consciousness itself and the way it seeks expression through people, politics, art, and institutions.

In a similar vein

David Bohm *Wholeness and the Implicate Order* (p 62)
Immanuel Kant *Critique of Pure Reason* (p 148)
Søren Kierkegaard *Fear and Trembling* (p 154)

CHAPTER 19

G.W.F. Hegel

The *Phenomenology of Spirit* is legendarily impenetrable, and those who have buckled down to read it and attest to its power can still be forgiven for making an imaginary plea to Georg Hegel: "I sort of get what you are saying, but why did you have to make it so hard?" As Hegel scholar Frederick Beiser notes, Hegel's books are "often a trying and exhausting experience, the intellectual equivalent of chewing gravel."

Beiser also comments that our age seems to have lost Hegel's "taste for the Absolute," and after world wars, the Holocaust, and numerous other evils, Hegel's faith in progress seems horribly naïve. On a more mundane level, in the specialized, atomized, pluralistic world in which we live now, notions of "wholeness" and "unity" (two of Hegel's favorites) do not seem to make much sense either.

Yet the sheer scale of Hegel's vision can still enthrall and his views may not be as much at odds with contemporary life as at first appears. That we now put Hegel into a dusty box marked "nineteenth-century German idealism" prevents us from seeing his brilliance as an explainer and supporter of modernity. Going against the Romantic view that technology, freedom, and capitalism were inimical to the soul, Hegel said that in fact the modern world is our greatest achievement – the opportunity for which humankind had long waited, a great expression of "Spirit" or consciousness that could not be held back. The role of the individual in all of this is slightly problematic, but, as we will see, Hegel's solution is positive.

The *Phenomenology of Spirit* is indeed hard to read, but it would be a shame to miss out completely on its insights. Though the book is impossible to summarize, the following should give some taste of Hegel's views.

The grand overview
As Hegel notes in the famous Preface, conventional philosophers see their subject as a field of competing positions in which only one system can be said to "win." They view matters from the perspective of a battlefield of ideologies. Hegel's rather original approach, on the other hand, is to take a bird's eye view of everything: he sees competing philosophies as each having their place, over time allowing for "the progressive unfolding of truth." Putting this in

botanical terms, he observes that the buds are forgotten when they burst forth into blossom, and the blossoms in turn give way to fruit, which reveals the truth or purpose of the tree. Hegel's aim is to free philosophy from its one-sidedness and to show the truth of the whole. It is better to see the variety and richness of culture and philosophy as one great movement.

The book's title can also be translated as "Phenomenology of Mind," and as such it is not about some mystical "spirit," but rather consciousness itself. Phenomenology is the study of things being made manifest or appearing, so in literal terms the title means how consciousness manifests itself in the real world. Every person is the result of thousands of years of development, and Hegel's goal is to say where we have reached as a species. For him, "science" is not simply the study of natural phenomena, but the development of consciousness over time. "History" becomes the process of an ever greater consciousness of ourselves. The whole manifested universe is simply a process of Spirit extending out and then returning to itself in one movement. To properly understand Hegel's project we can also refer back to its working title, which might have made things clearer for readers: "Science of the Experience of Consciousness."

A larger view of science

In opposition to every empiricist or materialist philosopher before and after him, Hegel thought that it was mad to consider that the project of knowledge should be confined to natural and physical phenomena. Rather, by looking fully into the phenomenal world we would eventually grasp the inner truth behind it, gaining knowledge of the Absolute. Those who felt that humanity should stop at the material world, or that this was the only world there was, Hegel saw as either lacking courage or being lazy. Full understanding had to take in everything, whether material or not. This was the work of real, "capital S" Science.

Hegel's "Notion" (*Begriff*) means the essential nature of something, not only the obvious manifestations. He writes:

> *"True thoughts and scientific insight are only to be won through the labour of the Notion. Only the Notion can produce the universality of knowledge which is neither common vagueness nor the inadequacy of ordinary common sense, but a fully developed, perfected cognition."*

In other words, to be truly scientific, you must go beyond the purely physical and identify the unseen logic of something, or the truth of how matters are unfolding. He admits that this view of science is never going to be well received, and indeed one can see why the later analytical philosophers such as A.J. Ayer and Bertrand Russell gave Hegel short shrift.

As a post-Enlightenment thinker, Hegel had to talk in "scientific" terms, but it is a science that Stephen Hawking would not recognize. And yet, Hegel observed that natural science is seductive, because if we simply look at what is in front of us, no detail seems to be omitted. It therefore gives a sense that we are seeing everything. But this is in fact a poor and abstract kind of knowledge, because it provides information or data, but no understanding. Furthermore, "objective" analysis is an illusion, because things only exist in the context of the observer's perception of them. Object and subject are therefore bound up together: the object, the observer, and the act of seeing are all one. Seeing things in this way makes a mockery of "scientific fact," and tells us that consciousness is as much a part of science as the world of objects it purports to analyze. This, for Hegel, is the more realistic way of apprehending the world.

In his lectures on *The Phenomenology of Spirit*, Heidegger drew attention to Hegel's distinction between "absolute" and "relative" reality. Relative knowledge is simply knowledge of things in their relation to other things. Absolute knowledge is of a reality that exists of its own accord, not needing to have a relation to anything else. According to Hegel, science is about discerning absolute reality through our consciousness. This obviously turns on its head the usual definition of science, which is to examine and make sense of the world of actual things. But Hegel says that the world of relative phenomena is the trees, when what we must do is see the wood, or the nonphysical reality behind everything. The true scientist is willing to look at everything (both relative and absolute knowledge) to get at the truth. And luckily, our consciousness has equipped us to do this. Hegel called philosophy *the* science, because it enabled consciousness of absolute knowledge, which comes before all other kinds of knowledge. As he puts it in his Preface, his aim is to bring philosophy from being mere *love of* knowing to being *actual* knowing.

For Hegel, the real story of science is not our "discovery of the universe," but rather the discovery of our own minds, of consciousness itself. Science, history, and philosophy are really just ways of saying how our consciousness has awakened over time. The trajectory of science is to break down everything into smaller and smaller pieces and categories, and once this is done to put it all back together again, returning to an understanding of the whole.

The individual in Hegel's worldview

What is the implication of recognizing that the unfolding of the world is the unfolding of consciousness (Spirit)? One realizes, Hegel says, that one's contribution must necessarily be very small in relation to such a great movement. We must obviously make ourselves achieve what we can, but we can also be sure that the world does not turn on us.

Perhaps surprisingly for such a big-picture thinker, Hegel offers a recipe for personal happiness. A person becomes happy when they see that their individuality is illusory, that the experience of having a body is merely a temporary "agreement … with thinghood." When we come to see that belief in our singularity is a dead end, while appreciation of our unity with everything else is truth, this cannot make us anything other than happy. Suffering is little more than being caught up in our own little world and believing in its reality. However, awareness that we are merely an expression or agent of Spirit in its unity takes us beyond the happiness/unhappiness dichotomy to truth.

Within a culture or nation, Hegel says, people have an obvious individuality and can express it thanks to the "might" of a nation. It gives them a proper context. But in more universal, abstract terms, what seems like ours alone is in fact "the skill and customary practice of all." What we seem to do for ourselves results in the satisfaction of others' needs and the development of the society as a whole (the "individual in his *individual* work … *unconsciously* performs a *universal* work"). Yet in playing our part in something larger, our individuality is also fully expressed. Showing his political conservatism, Hegel notes that the wisest people of antiquity knew that "wisdom and virtue consist in living in accordance with the customs of one nation."

A person naturally seeks their own ends, taking and enjoying things with forceful abandon, grabbing "hold of life much as a ripe fruit is plucked," without thinking of abstract notions of happiness, and even less about laws or customs. Earth is merely a playground for the pleasurable fulfillment of desires. However, we eventually discover that living for ourselves alone does not provide total satisfaction; this end is set aside for an awareness that one is "only a moment, or a *universal.*"

This transition in self-consciousness, from a simple awareness of self as a bundle of desires ("being-for-self ") to appreciation that one is part of a larger universality or consciousness ("being-in-itself ") or at the very least a community of others, is not always a positive experience, because we see ourselves as simply part of necessity. We have lost something (the feeling of individuality) and there does not appear to be anything to replace it. A person can be "smashed to pieces" on the "uncomprehended power of universality." Yet personal consciousness is not in fact dead, but merely ascended to a new level of consciousness, in which one's self is understood to be part of necessity or the working out of universal law. From being an object in the universe, we become part of that universe's operation, or a "heart which ... has within it a law," which is more open to seeing the welfare of humankind.

The pleasures that we once enjoyed give way to the stupendous realization that giving up our particularity was what was always meant to happen, even if, originally, we would never have willingly done it. What has motivated us is the ego, but the ego does not appreciate that in this movement it is writing its own death sentence. We now see that the law of our own heart becomes the law of every heart; "I" am merely part of the larger growth in consciousness. For Hegel, "virtue" simply means the desire to disregard individuality, which causes all number of perversions ("the way of the world"). Yet we are individual to the extent that the drops from a splash of water are individual. After a brief time separate in the air, they return and fall back into their source.

Hegel's view of religion

As Hegel scholar Stephen Houlgate notes, Hegel's main concern was reason. The universe operates only according to reason, and speculative philosophy is equipped for decoding it. Most people either are not able or do not wish to study philosophy, so this is where religion becomes relevant. For Hegel, the idea that we live in a well-reasoned universe has much more impact if it is *felt*, and this is what religion provides. What in philosophical terms one might call the "ground of being" that gives rise to the material world in religion becomes "God." A love of God is therefore simply a love of reason itself. If we feel that God always works in ways that make perfect sense (perhaps not always at the time, but in retrospect), we will accept a cosmology based on reason rather than randomness.

Hegel's equation of reason with God still allows the modern person to say, "Well, I will believe in reason, you can have God." This is one way to view Hegel, yet he would have said in rejoinder something like, "That is fine, but you may not get a full appreciation of the working out of Reason in the world if you only see it in material terms." For the atheist, all religious beliefs are fairytales, but for the Lutheran Hegel, Christianity was not about taking every word of the Bible literally; religious imagery and narrative are simply a way of revealing reason and its workings. The feelings of "faith" and "love" allow us to express reason in a nonintellectual way.

Note that Hegel did not see religion as a "crutch" or a "comfort," which would suggest that it is a psychological illusion; rather, faith and love are a natural human pathway to the core of reality, taking us beyond the apparent truths of the physical world. As Houlgate notes,

"We must remember that Hegel did not consider faith and philosophy to be offering two rival accounts of the world. Rather, he thought that they both tell the same story and reveal the same truth, but that they take hold of that truth in different ways."

The feeling of certainty that we are the object of divine love is simply another way of expressing the notion that Reason is the force running the universe. This has allowed both believers and atheists to claim Hegel as their own, though they are being selective. His point was that the spiritual and the materialist ways of seeing are equally relevant and true, and his philosophy was so large that both are accommodated without contradiction.

Final comments

Each age seems to judge Hegel anew, and it has been fashionable to view his "science" as anything but, because his vision rests on patently unprovable metaphysics. For many, he is of interest mainly because his ideas provoked reactions that resulted in new philosophies. These include existentialism, pragmatism, the analytical tradition, and, of course, Marxism (Marx's "dialectic" was an outgrowth of Hegel's view of history). There was a revival of serious interest in Hegel in the 1980s and 1990s, but his emphasis on teleology (the world having a positive direction) is still viewed with suspicion by most contemporary philosophers. Denouncing Hegel has become something of a sport, yet this antipathy has only kept his name prominent.

Was he so vastly wrong in his basic precepts? One needs to be quite brave today to suggest that history is essentially the growth of consciousness, and that therefore everything happens for a reason.

Many people had their first encounter with Hegel through Francis Fukuyama's bestseller *The End of History and the Last Man* (1992). Written not long after the collapse of communism in Eastern Europe, this book's argument that historical development was reaching its conclusion with a global transition to liberal democracy was largely inspired by Hegel. Its many critics damned its idea that history has direction, a notion that many events since (ethnic wars, 9/11, a deep recession) would seem to disprove. And yet, in the wake of more recent popular uprisings against totalitarian regimes, Hegel's suggestion that freedom inevitably seeks expression, and does so through the institutions of modernity (technology, art, liberal democracy), does make sense.

The Phenomenology of Spirit reminds us that consciousness (of ourselves, of political life, of history) is usually positive. Indeed, the book was written as Napoleon's forces were smashing up the old imperial system in Germany, which gave Hegel a rather scary and close-at-hand example of his own theories. He wrote:

> *"Spirit has broken with the world it has hitherto inhabited and imagined, and is of a mind to submerge it in the past, and in the labour of its own transformation. Spirit is indeed never at rest but always engaged in moving forward."*

As consciousness (manifested in people, institutions, customs, and laws) grows, it destroys or transforms what it has made, making way for replacements that display ever greater self-awareness. Of course there are apparent reversals in this flow of events, but the overall pattern is clear.

G.W.F. Hegel

Born Georg Wilhelm Friedrich Hegel in 1770, the son of a minor civil servant, Hegel's intellectual abilities led him to the University of Tübingen. There he met Friedrich von Schelling, later an idealist philosopher, and Friedrich Hölderlin, subsequently a celebrated poet. After university Hegel worked as a private tutor in Berne and Frankfurt, and then as a freelance lecturer at the University of Jena. As he completed Phenomenology of Spirit, *Napoleon's troops entered Jena and the university was shut down. Without a job, he became the editor of a newspaper in Bamburg, and then for many years (1808–15) was headmaster of a secondary school in Nürnberg. During this time he published the three volumes of* Science of Logic *and wrote his* Encyclopedia of the Philosophical Sciences.

In Nürnberg he married and started a family (a daughter died not long after birth, but the couple had two sons), and then in 1816 resumed his academic career with a professorship at Heidelberg University. He moved to the University of Berlin in 1818, where he died in 1831. After his death Hegel's followers separated into right and left factions, Karl Marx becoming a leading exponent of the latter.

Hegel's first book was The Difference between Fichte's and Schelling's System of Philosophy *(1801).* Science of Logic *(1812 and 1816) was the sequel to the* Phenomenology of Spirit. Philosophy of Right, *containing his political philosophy, was published in 1821, and* Philosophy of History *after his death in 1831.*

Being and Time

*"Why are there beings at all instead of nothing? That is the question
... Of course it is not the first question in the chronological sense
... And yet ... we are each touched once, maybe even every now
and then, by the concealed power of this question, without properly
grasping what is happening to us. In great despair, for example, when
all weight tends to dwindle away from things and the sense of things
grows dark, the question looms."*

*"We have defined the idea of existence as an ability-to-be,
as one which is in each case mine, is free either for
authenticity or for inauthenticity or for a mode in which
neither of these has been differentiated."*

In a nutshell

Human existence is a mystery, and the authentic person is one
who reflects on that mystery and yet lives in the real world,
making the most of their possibilities.

In a similar vein

Hannah Arendt *The Human Condition* (p 22)
René Descartes *Meditations on First Philosophy* (p 94)
Immanuel Kant *Critique of Pure Reason* (p 148)
Søren Kierkegaard *Fear and Trembling* (p 154)
Jean-Paul Sartre *Being and Nothingness* (p 272)

CHAPTER 20

Martin Heidegger

Martin Heidegger is often seen as the greatest philosopher of the twenti-eth century, and his forensic approach to apparently obvious questions or topics continues to have a big impact on contemporary philosophy. *Sein und Zeit* is his signature work, but it was famously preceded by a 12-year "period of silence" and seemed to come from nowhere. In fact, Heidegger had been lecturing to rapt audiences for years, building up an underground fame among German students as a truly original thinker. As Hannah Arendt (once his student) famously noted, "There was hardly more than a name, but the name travelled all over Germany like the rumour of a hidden king."

Being and Time was published to assist Heidegger's application for the chair of philosophy at Freiberg University, and was planned as the first part of a much larger work. With the book came international acclaim, and he rose to be Freiburg's Rector, replacing his mentor Edmund Husserl. Yet the position showed up Heidegger's naïve (or just plain dark, depending on your point of view) understanding of politics, for he became a public supporter of the Nazi party. After the humiliations of the First World War, he (along with many) wanted Germany to be great again, but whether he was truly anti-Semitic remains an open question. He had a campus affair with the Jewish Arendt, and she remained a loyal supporter throughout his life. However you see the controversy, that Heidegger's philosophy became caught up in his politics was, as it happens, a demonstration of his view that humans can never be divorced from their social environment, no matter how individuated they seem.

Notoriously difficult to understand, the best way to tackle *Being and Time* is to read around it with one of the many excellent commentaries. If you read it cold, you might find it a quicksand-like experience.

Being and personhood
At the start of *Being and Time*, Heidegger notes that the question of "being" had certainly been addressed by ancient and medieval philosophers, but that no one had explored it properly. It was almost taken for granted, because everyone "is" and therefore we know what it is to "be." Yet in terms of philo-sophical analysis, he writes, "the meaning of being is shrouded in darkness."

Commentators have struggled with Heidegger's answer to the question, as he wrapped it up in a variety of German terms that do not translate easily into English. The most important of these is *Dasein*, which in its literal translation is "being there," but which Heidegger took to mean a unit of self-reflective consciousness, of which a person is the most obvious example. His big question was: What is personhood? What is it like to be a human being in the world, bounded by space and time?

For him, philosophy's preoccupation with whether the external world exists and questions of what we can really know were a waste of time. What matters is "being-in-the-world," or the fact that we exist in a world rich in meaning and possibility. While previous philosophers had seen the self as an observing consciousness, Heidegger's placement of the self *in* the world led him on a completely different path, influenced by his study of medieval Christian theology. Whereas for Descartes the motto for the self was "I think," Heidegger's was "I care" – not the conventional meaning of emotional sympathy, but more like searching, exploring, making, dealing with, building something; that is, my place among others in a social or political sense (which includes concern for others) and my own development or unfolding.

For Heidegger there are three modes of seeing the world: *Umsicht*, "looking around"; *Rücksicht*, "considerateness" for other beings; and *Durchsichtigkeit*, "looking through" into our own selves. Each is fundamentally different and goes beyond the simple Cartesian duality of "mind" and "matter." Through such distinctions we begin to see why Heidegger felt there was much more to "being" than meets the eye.

Thrown into the world

Heidegger was a student of, and later assistant to, the founder of phenomenology (the philosophy of consciousness), Edmund Husserl. In his usual forensic way, Heidegger went back to the root of this word, the Greek *phainesthai*, meaning "to show itself," which in turn is derived from *phaino*, to bring something to light. Heidegger's phenomenology became an explication of how things show themselves, specifically how human beings "show" themselves in the world. In this he moved away from any kind of theological conception of a person being the manifestation of some eternal essence or soul, toward Being as it manifests itself now, in the theater of human life. The nature of *Dasein* is to be continually self-questioning and exploring its place, having to deal with uncertainties and yet affirming its identity. Part of this nature is showing or disclosing itself to the world, in the case of human beings through speech and action. Life is about exploring our possibilities within the environment in which we find ourselves.

"Thrownness" is a crucial idea in *Being and Time*. A human being is cast into a particular place, time, and family not of their choosing, and life is about making sense of this fall into the realm of space and time. How did I get here? Why am I here? What do I do now? Part of this perplexity is an inbuilt sense of "guilt" or "owing." We feel some responsibility to do something with our lives, and fortunately come equipped with the capacities for speech and action. In using them we find the meaning of our life; indeed, it would be impossible for life *not* to have meaning, given the raw materials of consciousness and environment before us. Death is also important to Heidegger, because it marks the end of one's self-showing. The nature of one's death can itself be a disclosure.

What are moods?

Heidegger presents a view of moods and emotions that is completely different to a conventional psychological interpretation. He sees the nature of Being for humans as a constant state of varying emotion. Our feelings and moods are not something to pass over or belittle in relation to our real life or work; rather, they are central to our being. At any one time we are experiencing an emotion, or at least are "feeling our way toward something."

Moods, either in a negative or a positive way, are enablers of our response to the world. With moods we cannot remain neutral; they make us ever mindful of what it is like to exist right now. Indeed, our understanding of the world does not happen through some neutral logical reasoning, but springs *from* our dispositions or moods. As Heidegger scholar Tom Greaves has noted, Heidegger would not support the idea of "emotional intelligence" as one of several kinds of intelligence. Rather, *all* intelligence emerges from the ground of feeling and disposition; or, as Heidegger puts it, "Understanding always has its mood."

In German the word for mood is *Stimmung*, which once meant the tuning of a musical instrument. A mood is an "attunement" of our being to the world around us. We may be out of tune with it (experiencing fear, anxiety, or dread), or in tune (things are going well), or we may come across an event or place or person that instills in us a new mood (a great speech or a beautiful forest). We are constantly attuning ourselves.

The authentic self

For Heidegger, authenticity means recognizing the unlikely fact of having consciousness, and yet still proceeding to "make sense" of our existence. Whereas the inauthentic person's life is shaped by a social "They," the authentic individual fully grasps their freedom to be master of their own Being, at least as far as the boundaries of time, space, and community allow. Authenticity is always a question of degree, for no one ever truly separates themselves from the communal or social voice, which Heidegger also calls the "One."

The essential nature of existence, Heidegger remarks, is that it is *mine*. There is an enormity to this realization; indeed, the weight of it is such that few people can grasp what an authentic life would mean for them. The more natural mode of being for a human is to exist as one among many, not to opt for a path of self-realization or tough self-examination. However, even for those who do, there is no such thing as a fully "self-made" person.

The appropriate response to life is to throw ourselves into it, along the way coming to conclusions about what is real or true, separate from public opinion. Paradoxically, it is only in admitting that we are very much part of the world that we can shrewdly see the points where we can make a difference. Only humans can help *form* a world, as well as simply existing in it.

Angst and resoluteness

The feeling of anxiety, Heidegger observes, is a natural result of the not-being-at-homeness that humans experience in the world. Yet angst is also part and parcel of an authentic life, because the nature of authenticity is not that we nullify or reduce this sense of isolation, but that we recognize it as a fact and carry on regardless. In fact, it is a sign of *in*authenticity when a person is fully at one with life and feels totally at home, because it suggests that they are not fully aware of their existence as being contingent and utterly mysterious. Greatness lies in questioning the mystery of our being, and yet taking that uncertainty (with all its fears) and choosing to do something with life in any case.

"Conscience" in Heidegger's terminology is not something moral, but is there to remind us continually to keep on the path of self-examination and original action. "Resoluteness" is the decision not to be subsumed by the "They" or the "One" of public mores and opinion, but to be clear about the unique role that we may play in relation to the world and to others.

Beings in time

For Heidegger, the crucial point about being is that it is played out within time. The nature of being human is our future orientation. Therefore, to be a being in time is the feeling of always moving toward something; the nature of being human is a future orientation. While we are creatures of the past and we dwell on the past, the true nature of man is to look ahead. We are our possibilities.

Heidegger rejected the idea that philosophy must be based on only what can be perceived by the senses, or on logic alone. He totally rejects the Schopenhauerian idea that the world is merely a projection of our minds. We clearly do exist in the world, and it is impossible for us to exist without our being having meaning in relation to the world: I love, I act, I have an impact – this is the nature of my being, and the sense of it becomes apparent across a lifetime.

Final comments

Heidegger was a big influence on Sartre and other existentialists, though he denied that he was himself one, saying that his focus was not humans and their existence, but rather Being itself, of which humans were the most advanced articulation. The general scholarly view is that Heidegger's exploration of Being was not designed to be useful for living. *Being and Time* is not a self-help book. However, it is difficult not to receive some inspiration from it.

Common sense would seem to bear out his distinction between authentic and inauthentic modes of being. At one level we demand that a person is social, accepts the mores of the time, and plays a part in political life. On the other, we accept that an authentic life is one where the person seizes what possibilities they have and makes something out of them. Indeed, despite its clinical style, running through *Being and Time* is a vein of passion about human possibility and the privilege of being. It is possible to forge a strong self in time, overcoming the perplexity at being thrown into existence.

Martin Heidegger

Heidegger was born in 1889 in the small southwestern German town of Messkirch, into a conservative Catholic household. At 14 he entered a seminary with a view to the priesthood, but left to pursue studies in literature, philosophy, and science. At 18 he had an epiphany reading a dissertation by the philosopher Brentano on "the manifold sense of being in Aristotle." This led him in turn to Husserl's writings. In his twenties he had articles published in Catholic journals and he received his philosophy PhD in 1913. His habilitation (postdoctoral thesis) on the medieval philosopher Duns Scotus was completed two years later.

In 1918, Heidegger became a Privatdozent *at Freiburg University and assistant to Husserl. In 1923 he was made an assistant professor at the University of Marburg, and in 1928 he gained a professorship at Freiburg University. A strong German nationalist, he was attracted to the strident "national socialism" of the Nazi party. As Rector at Freiburg he went along with Nazi guidelines to reorganize the university, which involved discrimination against Jewish students. Yet in "de-Nazification" hearings after the war, Hannah Arendt helped him form a defense that he had been a naïve believer in national socialism and had not foreseen what the Nazis would do in power. The two remained in contact until Heidegger died, in 1976.*

An Enquiry Concerning Human Understanding

"When we look about us towards external objects, and consider the operation of causes, we are never able, in a single instance, to discover any power or necessary connexion; any quality, which binds the effect to the cause, and renders one an infallible consequence of the other."

"The most perfect philosophy of the natural kind only staves off our ignorance a little longer: as perhaps the most perfect philosophy of the moral or metaphysical kind serves only to discover larger portions of it."

In a nutshell

We can never assume that an effect is the result of a certain cause, or that a certain cause will have a definite effect. Humans like to see patterns and interpret stories from events, but there is no causal necessity between objects (or at least not as far as the human senses are able to tell).

In a similar vein

CHAPTER 21

David Hume

D avid Hume is considered the greatest British philosopher and, through his influence on figures such as Kant (who famously said that Hume woke him from his "dogmatic slumber"), one of the major names in philosophy of the last 250 years.

Though his first book, *A Treatise of Human Nature*, "fell dead-born from the press," hardly noticed by anyone, it was a remarkable achievement, especially since it was written in his twenties. However, Hume's views on religion saw him passed over for academic philosophy posts, and it was only his *History of England and Political Discourses*, published in his forties, that led to him becoming well known and well off.

In terms of the history of philosophy, Hume's star really rose with the twentieth-century logical positivists like A.J. Ayer (who wrote a biography of him); today he is a patron saint of every kind of philosophical school that stands for empiricism and disavows metaphysical speculation. He can be interpreted in different ways, as we will see below.

An Enquiry Concerning Human Understanding is a mature version of the *Treatise*, and in its relatively easy, nonacademic style is an excellent starting point for exploring Hume.

We should be the real objects of study

While Hume is traditionally seen as a great philosophical skeptic who did not believe that his subject could achieve much, in the last few decades his work as a "scientist of human nature," attempting to do for philosophy what Newton did for natural science, is what has been emphasized.

Hume believed that our ability to reason was simply a result of language abilities, and that "human nature," or what we now call psychology, could be explained through knowing more about the brain and nervous system. He followed John Locke and George Berkeley in saying that experience, or the impressions that come to us through the five senses, and not reasoning should be the basis of philosophy.

Foreshadowing what the philosopher of science Thomas Kuhn would say in our time, Hume observed that "All sciences have a relation, greater or less, to human nature." We fool ourselves if we think that the natural sciences are an objective realm of knowledge outside humankind. In fact, by knowing human nature, Hume believed that you could create "a compleat system of the sciences." He felt that questions of logic, morals, and politics should be at least at the same level as natural science, and if he had been alive today he would no doubt have been a great supporter of psychology and the social sciences, because, as he put it in the *Treatise*, "The science of man is the only solid foundation for the other sciences."

The limits of knowledge

For Hume, ancient and modern philosophers had all thought too highly of the powers of human reason. Great systems had been built to understand humans, God, and the universe, while forgetting that, ultimately, all we can know is what we observe directly through our five senses. Going completely against Descartes, Hume argued that there are no timeless, abstract ideas. Rather, all concepts are a secondhand rendering of initial perceptions or impressions of things from our senses; we cannot have a notion of something until we have experienced it. We can only imagine a golden mountain (if we have never seen one), for instance, because we are able to take our previous experiences of gold and of mountains and combine them.

Hume's views on causation are central to his thinking. He noted that while things appear to cause one another, this is simply our mind drawing connections. We cannot ever really say with certainty that one thing caused another, only that two things often form a "customary conjunction." When fire meets skin, for instance, we can assume that there will be pain, or that snow normally means cold, but there is nothing actually linking them.

Neither can we say that because one thing appears to be true, it is always true. In fact, Hume claims, much of human "knowledge" is simply a reliance on custom, or accepting what everyone else says is true. Custom does not deliver truth, it merely makes life easier. It allows us to construct a meaningful world without having to recreate it through the senses anew every second.

Analyzing human perception, Hume observed that there is no real difference between imagination and reality save the level of belief we have in one or the other. "Reality" is simply what we believe in more strongly. He also rejected the idea that there is a solid, unitary self, an "I." We are, rather, merely a bundle of perceptions, our minds like a theater whose sets and scenes change every minute. (This is remarkably similar to the Buddhist view that there is no solid self, and that the "I" we experience is only a constant parade of ephemeral emotions and perceptions.) Hume doubted Descartes' idea that because we are thinking, we exist. All he felt could be said was that "thought exists," but it hardly proves the existence or permanence of the self, or of an individual soul.

The Hume debate

Hume has become a battleground for scholars.

The traditional positivist interpretation of Hume can be summed up in the "regularity theory" of causation: things don't cause each other to happen, and all we can say is that events can assume a certain regular pattern. To use Hume's example, we can see one billiard ball hitting another and assume that it is the cause of the second ball's movement, but we can never be certain about this. All we can say is that two objects are "contiguous, successive and constantly conjoined," and that there is no unseen "force" or "energy" moving things around. "An object may be contiguous and prior to another," he writes, "without being consider'd its cause."

The positivist camp supports Hume's view that anyone claiming to pinpoint a cause and its effect will have to talk in "unintelligible terms" (meaning metaphysical), which are an affront to philosophy. Indeed, Hume famously ends the *Enquiry* with a dramatic call for rigor in philosophy and for all metaphysical works to be taken with a grain of salt. Any book that does not contain "any abstract reasoning concerning quantity or number," or that does not rest in reasoning based "on matter of fact and existence," must be committed to the flames, "For it can contain nothing but sophistry and illusion."

The realist view of Hume (best represented by Galen Strawson) highlights the statements in the *Enquiry* that there probably *is* a connection between events, what Hume (perhaps contradictorily) called a "necessary connexion," but that our restricted ability to see the world through our senses means that we cannot see what these causes are. One of Hume's statements in support of this view is:

"Experience only teaches us, how one event constantly follows another; without instructing us in the secret connexion, which binds them together, and renders them inseparable."

For the realists, the claims of regularity theory that nothing ever causes anything are ridiculous. Hume was, after all, a strong believer in common sense, and the "natural beliefs" in things or ideas that people hold in common. If one of these natural beliefs is that in real life things cause other things to happen, why should that not be true in philosophy as well? As Hume put it:

"Nature has kept us a great difference from all her secrets, and has afforded us only the knowledge of a few superficial qualities of objects; which she conceals from us those powers and principles on which the influence of these objects entirely depends."

In pointing this out, Hume paved the way for philosophers such as Kant and Kierkegaard, who, while noting the impossibility of knowing for certain whether there was a first cause, supreme being, or unseen order behind things (limited as we are by our senses), claimed that this did not mean we could say that there is nothing beyond the physical world, or that there are no underlying causes.

Which interpretation is correct?

Hume's inquiry into what human beings can know about objects, causation, and the universe can be seen as a project in logic, in the manner of Descartes and his *Meditations*. His conclusions can be read simply as a logical "position" on the questions at which he chose to look, but do not necessarily define his personal beliefs. As he wrote in a letter to a friend, "I am not such a Sceptic as you may, perhaps, imagine."

Hume refuted the accusation that he was an atheist, though his extreme skepticism made him appear so to enraged theologians of his time. Perhaps the key to the debate is that he never said "There is no God," only that the various "proofs" for the existence of God were pure speculation of a very human kind and would take us nowhere.

Final comments

"Be a philosopher; but, amidst all your philosophy, be still a man."

As this quote suggests, Hume did not have any great faith in philosophy itself. After spending a merry few hours with his friends, he would sometimes go back to his rooms and read things he had written and note that they seemed ridiculous. Looking for certainties, he felt, was the work of a fool, and he continued with his philosophical work mainly because of the pleasure it gave him. He recognized that, compared with "superstition" and religion, the cold speculation of philosophy was uninteresting to most people.

If the refrain of the *Enquiry* is "What do we really know?" Hume does not return us reassuring answers. Nevertheless, he says that the lack of real knowledge should not make us give up on the world, and he admires philosophers like Cicero whose focus was not on meaning per se, but on living an honorable life and acting rationally according to thought-out beliefs.

For most people, this kind of philosophy is enough, and the other, more speculative type (in which Hume himself engages), while interesting, may not in the end lead us anywhere. In a droll defense of his pastime, however, Hume wrote in the *Treatise*: "Generally speaking, the errors in religion are dangerous; those in philosophy only ridiculous." Though he felt that our ability to have objective knowledge of the world was naturally limited by our senses, he nevertheless admitted that humans needed to make meaning from that experience, and that we have to live as if what we experience is real. We cannot go around thinking like a philosopher, doubting everything.

Hume was generally well liked (his nickname was "le bon David") and his writing style reflects his personality: undogmatic and compassionate. Like his friend and contemporary Adam Smith (economist and author of *The Wealth of Nations*), he wrote in such a way that as many people as possible could read him – which is one more reason to appreciate him.

David Hume

Hume was born in Edinburgh in 1711. He came from a good family on both sides, but he was not rich and his father died when he was a baby. While at Edinburgh University he began writing A Treatise of Human Nature, *and instead of graduating, went to Bristol to work as a clerk in a counting house. He then lived in France for three years, taking on a rigorous program of self-study.*

The Treatise *was published in 1739 with scarcely any recognition, but Hume's* Essays *(1741–42), including writings on political economy that foreshadowed Adam Smith's, were successful. Never a philosophy professor, his views on religion ruled him out of posts at Edinburgh and Glasgow Universities. His various positions included tutor for a year to a mad English nobleman, librarian, Undersecretary of State in London, and secretary to the British ambassador in Paris. This latter post enabled him to mix with other figures of the European Enlightenment outside Scotland, including Jean-Jacques Rousseau, whom he befriended but later fell out with. Hume was a supporter of the union between England and Scotland that had taken place in 1707.*

Books include An Enquiry Concerning the Principles of Morals *(1751),* Political Discourses *(1752), and* History of England *(6 volumes, 1754–62). His* Four Dissertations *of 1757 contained the controversial "Dialogues Concerning Natural Religion," which he arranged to be published posthumously (he died in 1776). James Boswell visited Hume on his deathbed and reported that the famous "atheist" remained in a jokey mood until his last breath.*

Pragmatism

"A pragmatist turns his back resolutely and once for all upon a lot of inveterate habits dear to professional philosophers. He turns away from abstraction and insufficiency, from verbal solutions, from bad a priori reasons, from fixed principles, closed systems, and pretended absolutes and origins. He turns towards concreteness and adequacy, towards facts, towards action, and towards power."

"[A]n idea is 'true' so long as to believe it is profitable to our lives … truth is ONE SPECIES OF GOOD, and not, as is usually supposed, a category distinct from good, and co-ordinate with it. THE TRUE IS THE NAME OF WHATEVER PROVES ITSELF TO BE GOOD."

"Rationalism sticks to logic and the empyrean. Empiricism sticks to the external senses. Pragmatism is willing to take anything, to follow either logic or the senses, and to count the humblest and most personal experiences. She will count mystical experiences if they have practical consequences."

In a nutshell

A belief or idea has value only if it "works" – that is, changes our world in some way. Other notions and ideas, however attractive or elegant, should be dismissed.

In a similar vein

A.J. Ayer *Language, Truth and Logic* (p 34)
Jeremy Bentham *Principles of Morals and Legislation* (p 50)
David Hume *An Enquiry Concerning Human Understanding* (p 136)
Iris Murdoch *The Sovereignty of Good* (p 212)

CHAPTER 22

William James

Pragmatism is a collection of unedited lectures that William James gave at New York's Columbia University in 1906–07, at the end of his career. One of America's great thinkers, he did not claim to have created the philosophy of pragmatism (this was Charles Sanders Peirce's achievement, and it was further developed by F.C.S. Schiller and John Dewey), but he did make it clearer and brought it to a general audience. James defines pragmatism as "the attitude of looking away from first things, principles, 'categories', supposed first necessities; and of looking towards last things, fruits, consequences, facts."

Pragmatism is a close intellectual cousin of utilitarianism. Both outlooks carry a deep suspicion of abstract academic philosophy, and an abiding interest only in the practical value of concepts. Indeed, James intended pragmatism as a way to see other philosophies. Today, academic iconoclasts such as Richard Rorty carry James's flame.

Philosophy is temperament

James starts by noting that every individual has a philosophy, which he describes as the

"more or less dumb sense of what life honestly and deeply means. It is only partly got from books; it is our individual way of just seeing and feeling the total push and pressure of the cosmos."

He notes G.K. Chesterton's remark that the landlady does not only want to know the lodger's income and job, they want a sense of the applicant's whole outlook on life. Personal philosophy is everything, a fact that academic philosophers, in their wish to be seen as objective discerners of truth, somehow gloss over.

James bluntly says, "The history of philosophy is to a great extent that of a certain clash of human temperaments." He means that the conclusions of philosophers come more from their personal biases than any objective findings. Their theories, perceived as "tough-minded" or "tender-minded," are a reflection of their emotional makeup and basic view of the world. A professional philosopher cannot make claims on the grounds of their temperament, so they try to hide their temperamental bias. At the heart of the philosopher is therefore a lie, because "the potentest of all our premises is never mentioned."

We as consumers of philosophy are not blameless either: we instinctively reject or warm to certain philosophies if they suit our own temperament.

The great divide

James divides philosophers into two basic categories: the empiricists, who wish to boil everything down to naked facts and observation; and the rationalists, who believe in abstract and eternal principles. The former tend to have an unsentimental, fatalistic, irreligious, and often dark view of the world, while the latter are optimists who tend to believe in free will, spiritual order, and the unity of all things. Naturally, each camp tends to have a low view of the other.

James notes that we live in an empirically minded age, yet this still does not cancel out the natural human impulse for religion. Many find themselves caught between philosophy that does not cover spiritual needs, that offers a completely materialistic universe, and religious philosophy that does not take account of facts. What most of us are after, he remarks, is "a philosophy that will not only exercise your powers of intellectual abstraction, but that will make some positive connexion with this actual world of finite human lives." It is no surprise that scientific types have turned their back on metaphysical philosophy as "something cloistered and spectral" that has no place in the modern world.

Yet unlike a pure empiricist, the pragmatist will be open to theological truths, or God-free metaphysical concepts such as Kant's transcendental idealism, if they are shown to have concrete benefit:

> "[J]ust as certain foods are not only agreeable to our taste, but good for our teeth, our stomach and our tissues; so certain ideas are not only agreeable to think about, or agreeable as supporting other ideas that we are fond of, but they are also helpful in life's practical struggles. If there be any life that it is really better we should lead, and if there be any idea which, if believed in, would help us to lead that life, then it would be really BETTER FOR US to believe in that idea, UNLESS, INDEED, BELIEF IN IT INCIDENTALLY CLASHED WITH OTHER GREATER VITAL BENEFITS."

James offers pragmatism as a way through, concerned with evidence and the facts, yet also open to religion if it provides concrete benefits for the believer. As a philosophy, pragmatism is rare in that it can be used both by "tough-minded" empiricists and "tender-minded" abstractionists.

What pragmatism can do for you

James refers to Peirce's idea that a belief or thought only has significance in terms of its effects. Any idea that is mere speculation, and would not if seen in practice change things in some way, has no value. We have to ask how the world would be different, assuming that idea were true. James tells his audience:

> "It is astonishing to see how many philosophical disputes collapse into insignificance the moment you subject them to this simple test of tracing a concrete consequence. There can BE no difference anywhere that doesn't MAKE a difference elsewhere – no difference in abstract truth that doesn't express itself in a difference in concrete fact ... The whole function of philosophy ought to be to find out what definite difference it will make to you and me, at definite instants of our life, if this world-formula or that world-formula be the true one."

Philosophers have always been looking for the one principle – call it God, Matter, Reason, the Absolute, or Energy – that would unlock all the universe's secrets, but with the pragmatic method, James notes, one can no longer rest in such things as self-evident, but must find out each concept's "cash-value," its practical worth. If we imagine philosophy as a hotel, with different philosophies inhabiting various rooms, pragmatism is not simply another room, but a corridor leading to the rooms, some of which might be religious, some scientific. Each philosophy can only be judged accurately if it is willing to leave its room and meet pragmatism in the corridor, and it will be able to expose their contentions to real worth and practicality.

Putting his finger on the dilemma for so many of us living in a scientific age, James says:

> "the greatest enemy of any one of our truths may be the rest of our truths. Truths have ... this desperate instinct of self-preservation and of desire to extinguish whatever contradicts them. My belief in the Absolute, based on the good it does me, must run the gauntlet of all my other beliefs."

In other words, a belief in God or an absolute of some kind provides us with a "moral holiday," but is it one we can afford, given the reality of everything else we have learned? If a person still finds that, despite all the evidence against it, their faith or belief in nonmaterial reality still brings strong benefits, then they are not being irrational at all; they are being pragmatic. Pragmatism differs totally from empiricism in that it has "no prejudices whatever, no rigid canons or what shall count as proof ... she will entertain any hypothesis" as long as its rational benefit can be shown.

Pragmatism, in short, "widens the field of search for God," following either logic or the senses, and will "count the humblest and most personal experiences. She will count mystical experiences if they have practical consequences." The latter point is a link to James's book *The Varieties of Religious Experience*, which fully admitted (even if James himself did not have the temperament for epiphanies) that conversion experiences could transform a person's life. Conversions showed beyond doubt that huge practical benefit could come from an abstract idea.

Final comments

James highlights the division between a monistic view of the universe, in which everything is seen as one, and a pluralistic one, which focuses on the astonishing diversity and plurality of life. The traditional view is that only the former is religious, the latter drawing a picture of chaos. But James maintains that we can still have a belief in the power of a pluralist cosmology even if we believe that there is no divine or other "logical necessity" in the unfolding of the world. Progress happens through "sheer desire," he says, occurring through individuals and "in spots." It is *we* who make the world what it is, and if we want a different life or a different world we must act.

In asking why anything should exist at all, James replies:

> "the only REAL reason I can think of why anything should ever come is that someone wishes it to be here. It is DEMANDED ... to give relief to no matter how small a fraction of the world's mass. This is living reason, and compared with it material causes and logical necessities are spectral things."

James's answer is not surprising when we consider his philosophy overall, which is that events themselves carry the truth (the proof is in the pudding, as it were). We can believe that God created the universe in seven days, or that it started on its own accord with the Big Bang, but either way our explanations do not really matter. The fact is that the universe is here, so in pragmatic terms it makes sense to study only what exists.

William James

Born in New York in 1842, James had a comfortable and cultured upbringing. In his teens the family, including Henry (later the famous writer), moved to Europe, where James learned several languages. Returning to the United States in 1860, he spent a year and a half trying to become a painter, then enrolled at Harvard, where he took courses in medicine. In 1865 he went on a scientific expedition with the well-known naturalist Louis Agassiz, but on the journey he suffered an array of health problems and was homesick.

In 1867 James went to Germany and studied physiology, and was exposed to thinkers and ideas in the new field of psychology. Two years later he returned to Harvard, where at 27 he finally received his medical degree. At 30 he obtained a post there teaching physiology, but only after having recovered from an emotional breakdown. In 1875 he began giving courses in psychology, and also established the first experimental psychology laboratory in America. In the year he began work on The Principles of Psychology, *1878, he married Alice Howe Gibbons, a Boston schoolteacher. They had five children.*

James met Sigmund Freud and Carl Jung on their visits to America, knew Bertrand Russell, Henri Bergson, Mark Twain, and Horatio Alger, and had among his students educationalist John Dewey and psychologist Edward Thorndike. Other key writings include The Will to Believe *(1897) and* The Varieties of Religious Experience *(1902). He died in 1910.*

Critique of Pure Reason

"Human reason has a peculiar fate ... it is troubled by questions that it cannot dismiss, because they are posed to it by the nature of reason itself, but that it also cannot answer, because they surpass human reason's every ability."

"No one, indeed, will be able to boast that he knows that there is a God and that there is a future life ... No, the conviction is not a logical but a moral certainty; and because it rests on subjective bases (of the moral attitude), I must not even say It is morally certain that there is a God, etc., but must say I am morally certain, etc."

In a nutshell

In a rational world based on science, is there a place for moral law?

In a similar vein

Aristotle *Nicomachean Ethics* (p 28)

Cicero *On Duties* (p 82)

Martin Heidegger *Being and Time* (p 130)

David Hume *An Enquiry Concerning Human Understanding* (p 136)

Arthur Schopenhauer *The World as Will and Representation* (p 280)

Ludwig Wittgenstein *Philosophical Investigations* (p 312)

CHAPTER 23

Immanuel Kant

Immanuel Kant was a product of the Enlightenment, in which everything – nature, law, politics – became subjected to the cold light of reason. The work of Newton, Hume, Rousseau, Leibniz, and Spinoza had signaled an end to the rabid superstition and irrationality of the Middle Ages. Kant not only accepted the scientific worldview, he began his career writing scientific books, including one on the origins of the solar system. Yet in this apparently clockwork universe, he wondered whether there was a place for morality. The attempt to reconcile the physical and the metaphysical might have seemed an impossible project, but this was the bold aim of *Critique of Pure Reason*.

The book grew out of Kant's dissatisfaction both with empiricists like Hume who argued that knowledge was only what we could confirm through our senses, and with the rational view that human reason was so powerful it could explain the universe. Kant's "third way" said that reason could indeed take us very far, but there were limits. We were wrong to think that, as beings existing in space and time, we could know anything definite about metaphysical matters. Yet our powers of reason had led us to metaphysics in the same way they had led us to natural science. Therefore, could our reasoning about morality, God, and the soul be so badly wrong, when our reasoning on physical, empirical matters was right?

The question was not whether metaphysics is legitimate, but how we could go about it in a rigorous, scientific way. His "critique of pure reason" would inquire into what we are capable of knowing about the nonmaterial world (God, for instance) *given the limits of our senses.*

The *Critique* is extremely difficult to read because Kant approached his subject like a forensic scientist, using precise, technical terms and proceeding by rigorous argument. Yet anyone who studies the book even a little will be rewarded by nuggets from one of the greatest minds in the history of philosophy.

Beings of space and time

Central to the book is the concept of "transcendental idealism," or the distinction Kant makes between the timeless essence, reality, or truth of a "thing in itself" and the world of appearances that we see around us.

As humans, we think of ourselves as observers of a real world of things (planets, furniture, etc.) and that time is something objective and outside of us. But Kant's radical idea is that space and time have no independent reality, but are simply the way humans perceive the world. Space and time allow us to filter and make sense of incoming data from our senses. We are hardwired to recognize patterns, for instance, and give a great deal of attention to any physical movement for survival's sake. We are built not to see things "as they are" – that is, their permanent, metaphysical reality – but what they might mean to *us*. Our knowledge of the world does not conform to how the world "really is"; rather, the world as we perceive it conforms to our knowledge of it.

Can spiritual belief ever be rational?

The younger Kant believed it was possible to gain metaphysical knowledge in a scientific way. However, after reading, and being unimpressed with, the work of the mystic Emmanuel Swedenborg, who described his visions of a spirit world, Kant changed course and concluded that we could not ever have real knowledge of metaphysical matters. The only firm ground we could find was to identify the limits of human reason.

Having reached this point, you might have expected Kant (as Hume did) to say that metaphysics was nonsensical, but he merely comments that it is a mistake, limited as we are by our five senses and living in the dimensions of space and time, to expect to talk about it intelligently. Because nothing of a spiritual nature could ever be proven in a rational or scientific way, theology could not be considered a proper, rational discipline. Yet he also concludes that while it was impossible to prove that God exists, it was also not possible to prove that God did not exist. It was in the nature of humankind to want some kind of firm footing on metaphysical matters, and the efforts to achieve certainty were therefore rational. Asking the big questions, even if the answers were beyond us, was essential to being human. What he was really against was dogmatism: blind belief minus rational thought.

Morality is real

The better use of reason, Kant believed, was to lead us toward a more objective morality. If something could not be shown to be good in a rational way, and could not be applied universally, then it probably was not good. This was his famous "categorical imperative":

"Act only according to that maxim by which you can at the same time will that it should become a universal law."

Your actions should be judged according to whether, if everyone did the same, it would be of benefit. People should never be seen as means to an end; they *are* the end. Of course, this is a basic principle of most religions, but Kant was determined to show that it made rational and philosophical sense.

For him, a person or society that acted according to the imperative could not go too badly wrong, because its morality would be based on reason. Kant believed it was right for us to try to discover all the laws and mysteries of the natural world, yet it was *also* humanity's destiny to identify and develop moral law. As the Kant scholar Sebastian Gardner expressed Kant's position, "As members of the sensible world we are subject to Newtonian laws, and as members of the spiritual world to moral laws."

Morality was not a lame-duck issue to be bulldozed by science, but rather could be seen as one of humankind's great achievements – as long as it was grounded in reason. This epitaph (taken from the *Critique of Practical Reason*) is chiseled onto Kant's gravestone:

> *"Two things fill the mind with ever new and increasing admiration and awe, the more often and steadily reflection is occupied with them: the starry heaven above me and the moral law within me."*

Morality is a sort of bridge between the experience of being human and the nonmaterial world. The feeling that something is right or wrong is not false or arbitrary, but suggests that we are bound to a set of metaphysical laws. Moral law is just as real as the planets and stars.

Kant on happiness

Unlike the Stoics, who believed that the pursuit of happiness was secondary to doing one's duty and accepting one's place in the universe, Kant believed that happiness was a legitimate goal for human beings, part of our physical nature as beings in space and time. Yet the happiness quest had to be seen within the larger quest for moral excellence. His solution was: "Do that which makes you *worthy* to be happy." Though this sounds like something he might have picked up from his Pietist upbringing, his point is that we should lead a moral life not because God is telling us to, but because, on a purely rational level, it is the life most likely to give us happiness. By going against moral law, we are destined to live unhappily; by doing what is right, we create for ourselves a world of order and peace. Kant himself lived by this and was said to have been a very happy man.

The glory of being human

In his last book, *The Conflict of the Faculties* (1798), Kant took pains to say that philosophy is not a science of ideas, or a "science of all sciences," but rather "it is a science of the human being, of its representing, thinking, and acting – it should present the human being in all of its components, as it is and ought to be, that is, in accordance with its natural determinations as well as its relationship of morality and freedom." While ancient philosophy had made human beings into machines that were a passive part of the universe, Kant's view was that humans had "a thoroughly *active* place in the world":

> "The human being itself is the original creator of all its representations and concepts and ought to be the sole author of all its actions."

We are not balls being shunted about in a Newtonian clockwork universe, but neither are our actions controlled by an external deity. Instead, we are autonomous beings who can improve ourselves by refining our own perceptions, and accordingly shape the world in a positive way.

Kant was a forerunner of Freud in recognizing that people's actions are often shaped by their unconscious inclinations, so that there seems little free will. And yet, through their reasoning power they could start to live according to higher ideas and ideals, fulfilling their potential and contributing to humankind.

The very essence of being human is freedom: we are free to see and organize the world as we see fit, based on our reason and experience. No other animal is even remotely capable of this, and indeed our greatest achievement is the realization that there exists a universal moral law that, in its timeless, spaceless nature, appears to us to come from somewhere else, and that we happily represent as "God." Whether God is an objective reality or not we will never know, but that is not the point. The point is the powerful freedom we have to organize our universe in a meaningful way, which includes the development of ethics based on universal moral law. This is humankind's destiny, and is Kant's central message.

Kant's assumption that human beings are essentially free and self-willing, and able to be seen separately from the cultural or political context, made him a philosophical inspiration for the French Revolution. From the perspective of contemporary research into free will, his position does not look too rigorous. Nevertheless, if you do believe in the individual's essential freedom, Kant is a great figure because he turned this simple idea into a fully worked-out philosophy.

Final comments

If such a supreme philosopher as Kant saw metaphysics as important, perhaps *the* important issue for philosophy, then it could never be dismissed easily, as an extreme empirical or rational view would want to do. Previous philosophers such as Berkeley and Leibniz had kept God at the center of philosophy by suggesting that the "real" world was metaphysical, while the natural world as we perceive it was a mere expression of this more important reality. No, said Kant, they are equally important.

For him, religion was not a pathway to connect with spiritual truth (which was impossible), but a validation of carefully reasoned moral positions. His thinking made it seem acceptable for a rational, modern person who accepts science and logic also to keep room in their life for spirituality. Yet in saying that nothing concrete could ever be said in theology (because it was a field of inquiry into a subject or reality that could not be known, or at least sensibly written or spoken of), Kant also laid the philosophical pavement for modern philosophy, including the logical positivists and Wittgenstein.

His work has remained compelling and influential because it manages to serve two camps: the empirically minded can say that Kant showed all talk of God and theology to be essentially guff; and believers can see in his work a rational foundation for moral law and metaphysics. Either way, because his system is so rigorous, comprehensive, and internally cohesive, no philosopher since has been able to ignore him.

Immanuel Kant

Kant was born in 1724 in Konigsberg, East Prussia (now Kaliningrad in Russia). His father was a craftsman and the family were poor, but Kant received a free education at a Pietist school. At Konigsberg University he took a variety of subjects, including science, philosophy, and mathematics. To earn money he worked as a private tutor for eight years, but in his spare time was busy writing scientific texts, including Universal Natural History and Theory of the Heavens, *about the origins of the solar system.*

The publication of his first philosophical work, A New Elucidation of the First Principles of Metaphysical Cognition, *allowed him to start giving lectures at the university, on everything from geography to law to physics. It was not until 1770, when he was 46, that he obtained a secure post as professor of philosophy in Konigsberg.*

Other texts include Dreams of a Spirit-Seer Elucidated by Dreams of Metaphysics *(1766),* Prolegomena to any Future Metaphysics *(1783),* Groundwork of the Metaphysics of Morals *(1785),* Critique of Practical Reason *(1788),* Critique of Judgement *(1790),* Religion within the Limits of Reason Alone *(1793), and* The Metaphysics of Morals *(1797).*

Kant never married and barely ever left Konigsberg. He was considered sociable and witty, and held lunchtime salons at his home. He died in 1804.

Fear and Trembling

"Faith is a marvel, and yet no human being is excluded from it; for that in which all human life is united is passion, and faith is a passion."

"The knight of faith knows it gives inspiration to surrender oneself to the universal, that it takes courage to do so, but also that there is a certain security in it, just because it is for the universal."

"No, no one shall be forgotten who was great in this world. But each hero was great in his own way, and each was eminent in proportion to the great things he loved. For he who loved himself became great through himself, and he who loved others became great through his devotion, but he who loved God became greater than all of these. Every one of them shall be remembered, but each one became great in proportion to his trust."

In a nutshell

Total trust in an absolute or spiritual reality is not a weakness, but is life's highest expression.

In a similar vein

Thomas Aquinas *Summa Theologica* (p 16)
Descartes *Meditations on First Philosophy* (p 94)
Immanuel Kant *Critique of Pure Reason* (p 148)
Blaise Pascal *Pensées* (p 224)
Plotinus *The Enneads* (p 236)

CHAPTER 24

Søren Kierkegaard

To Søren Kierkegaard, it seemed that in the modern age, everyone begins by doubting everything. This was exactly the approach taken by the arch doubter of modern philosophy, Descartes. Or was it? Descartes, Kierkegaard notes, was in fact "no doubter in matters of faith." In his *Principles of Philosophy*, for instance, Descartes supported the "natural light" of reason only if nothing contrary to it was revealed by God.

The opposite of doubt is faith, and Kierkegaard had long been fascinated by the story of the Old Testament's Abraham, the "father of faith." *Fear and Trembling* recounts the three-day journey of Abraham to Mount Moriah, where God has seemingly requested he go in order to sacrifice his son Isaac as an offering. Kierkegaard spends the book getting to grips with how Abraham could be willing to do such a thing. Isaac was not just any child, but the only son of Abraham and Sarah, who had miraculously been given him in their old age, after many years waiting. Thus he was especially loved and cherished.

Yet Abraham does not hesitate or question God's request, but saddles up his horses and sets off. When Isaac realizes what is happening he pleads with his father, but Abraham does not, as you might expect, blame his actions on God; instead, he assumes full responsibility. He reasons that it is better that his son believes him to be a monster "than that he lose faith in thee."

What happens? At the last minute, when Isaac is bound and a fire is being stoked, a ram comes into Abraham's vision, and it is clear that the animal, not Isaac, is to be offered up. Abraham has been tested and found to be a man of the greatest faith.

To Kierkegaard, Abraham's absolute willingness seems otherworldly, inhuman. At one level, Abraham is simply a murderer. However, because he is willing to follow through with what seems patently absurd just because God wills it, Kierkegaard argues that his actions represent the height of being human.

Levels of greatness

Everyone can be great in their own way, Kierkegaard says, according to what he loves and what he expects. People who love themselves can be "great in themselves"; those who love others can become great "through their devotion";

but those who love the Absolute or God stand above these. The first group become great through expecting the possible, the second through expecting the eternal, "but he who expected the impossible became greater than all." Beyond personal strength or self-sacrifice is the greatness of one who is willingly powerless, giving all power to the Absolute. As Kierkegaard puts it, "for he who always hopes for the best becomes old, deceived by life, and he who is always prepared for the worst becomes old prematurely; but he who has faith, retains eternal youth."

Such a person can, to the rest of humanity, seem to follow a path that is mad or absurd, but only because they are not depending on earthly wisdom or reason. If God moves in mysterious ways, then someone who is simply a vehicle for God will also, sometimes, seem to act beyond reason.

Believing the absurd

Resignation, Kierkegaard observes, is actually an act of the ego, making oneself seem heroic. Faith is in fact something much higher, since it means believing even *after* we have resigned ourselves. It means not giving up on our actions *in this world*.

On Mount Moriah, Abraham was willing to make the sacrifice "if that was indeed what was demanded." Because all human rationality had been suspended, Abraham had to believe in the absurd. He effectively had to say to himself, "I don't know the meaning of this, but I am leaving the meaning of it up to God."

Kierkegaard describes Abraham's leap of faith as a "movement," one that appears to demand the giving up of everything – and yet finally delivers everything to Abraham. Not only was Isaac given back to Abraham, he was a new Isaac, even more wonderful than before, who would fulfill the prophecy of prosperity and fertility over many generations. Because he had recognized God as the source of everything first, Abraham now had absolute security of knowledge.

Though a leap of faith is tremendously difficult, by uniting us with what is universal it is the only true security.

Knights of faith

A "knight of faith," Kierkegaard says, transforms the leap of faith into a gait – for this person it is simply a normal way of being. He will happily bet his whole life on a single love, or a great project. In contrast is a person whose life is simply "running errands."

Kierkegaard gives the example of a knight of faith in love with a woman. It seems that his quest is useless and he admits as much. But then he makes one more movement, saying, "I nevertheless believe that I shall get her, namely on the strength of the absurd, on the strength of the fact that for God all things are possible." On a purely human level he admits that his chances of getting the woman are zero, but this very impossibility forces him to make a leap of faith, knowing that only God can bring it about. He must believe the absurd in order for the Infinite to find expression.

The point about Abraham is that he suffers (obviously in great anguish, even going to the extent of tying Isaac up and starting a fire for the offering) while still believing. He is great not because he transcends fear, anguish, and agony, but because he lives through them. In doing so, he becomes a master of life. The mistake people make is to read the Abraham story and think his greatness is inevitable, only seeing the outcome while glossing over what he went through to arrive on the other side. If we want to be like Abraham, we should look to how he began, how he acted *before* he was the famous figure of the Bible.

Final comments

Philosophy, Kierkegaard notes, slights faith as something inconsequential. In fact, philosophy cannot really tell us anything about faith, because it is beyond words and concepts. Normal thought cannot comprehend Abraham's actions, because in such situations normal thought is redundant.

As Kierkegaard saw it, faith is in fact "the highest passion in a human being." The universal is expressed through a person, and that person expresses something timeless and limitless. We can all be knights of faith, he believed.

Søren Kierkegaard

Born in Copenhagen in 1813, Kierkegaard was from a well-off and deeply religious family. At 17 he enrolled in theology courses at the University of Copenhagen, but to his father's disappointment was drawn to philosophy and literature. His father died while he was still at university, and after being awarded his degree, he proposed to the daughter of a civil servant. The marriage never happened, however, and he remained a bachelor, living mainly off the proceeds of his father's estate.

He published Either/Or *in 1843, followed a few months later by* Fear and Trembling. *A year later came* Philosophical Fragments *and* The Concept of Anxiety, *and in 1846* Concluding Unscientific Postscript. *He also wrote books under pseudonyms,* The Sickness unto Death *and* Training in Christianity. *Edifying Discourses in Various Spirits (1847) presented what Kierkegaard believed was the true message of Christianity. He became a harsh critic of the Church of Denmark and its worldly outlook.*

Kierkegaard died in 1855. Wittgenstein described him to a friend as "by far the most profound thinker of the last century. Kierkegaard was a saint."

Naming and Necessity

"Could we discover that gold was not in fact yellow? Suppose an optical illusion were prevalent, due to peculiar properties of the atmosphere in South Africa and Russia and certain other areas where gold mines are common. Suppose there were an optical illusion which made the substance appear to be yellow; but, in fact, once the peculiar properties of the atmosphere were removed, we would see that it is actually blue ... Would there on this basis be an announcement in the newspapers: 'It has turned out that there is no gold. Gold does not exist. What we took to be gold is not in fact gold.'? ... It seems to me that there would be no such announcement. On the contrary, what would be announced would be that though it appeared that gold was yellow, in fact gold has turned out not to be yellow, but blue. The reason is, I think, that we use 'gold' as a term for a certain kind of thing. Others have discovered this kind of thing and we have heard of it. We thus as part of a community of speakers have a certain connection between ourselves and a certain kind of thing."

In a nutshell

The meaning of something is found not in the descriptions given of it, but in its essential properties.

In a similar vein

A.J. Ayer *Language, Truth and Logic* (p 34)
Ludwig Wittgenstein *Philosophical Investigations* (p 312)

CHAPTER 25

Saul Kripke

I n the twentieth century, Gottlob Frege, Bertrand Russell, Ludwig Wittgenstein, and others in the language-analyzing tradition saw themselves as saviors of philosophy, cutting it back to its basics. The misuse of language allowed "obviously" meaningless metaphysics to flourish, whereas if used well it could give us a more accurate picture of reality. The analytical philosophers *became* philosophy, and any alternative views were shouted down as being "not philosophy."

A challenge to the establishment can sometimes come from within its own ranks, and not many were as well equipped as Saul Kripke to point out that there were holes in the linguistic–materialist paradigm. In doing so, he allowed metaphysics to be taken seriously again.

Kripke was the son of a rabbi and a children's book writer from Omaha, Nebraska. His parents knew the legendary Omaha investor Warren Buffett, and became wealthy from an early investment in his company. A child prodigy, Kripke is said to have learned ancient Hebrew by 6, read the works of Shakespeare by 9, and read Descartes and mastered complex mathematical problems in his early teens. At 15 he developed a new theorem in modal logic, and at 18 had it published in the *Journal of Symbolic Logic*. He took an undergraduate degree in mathematics at Harvard, and while still a student was giving graduate-level courses in logic. At only 23 he became a Harvard Fellow, and went on to academic positions in logic and mathematics at Rockefeller and Princeton Universities.

Naming and Necessity is essentially a transcript of three lectures given by the 29-year-old Kripke at Princeton University in 1970, which he gave without notes. Though the book is short, it is not easy to understand.

Descriptions don't equal identity: The essentialist view
Kripke's modal logic was a reaction against the "descriptivist" view, expounded by Frege, Russell, Wittgenstein, and John Searle, which stated that all proper names of things had to correspond in some way to factual descriptions about them, whether confirmed by the senses, or shown to be true through unimpeachable logic (e.g., "all bachelors are unmarried"). This view also allowed for a *cluster* of statements such as "the first Postmaster General of the

United States," "the inventor of the bifocal lens," and "author of *Poor Richard's Almanacks*" to be brought together to arrive at an identity; in this example, Benjamin Franklin.

A proper name such as Benjamin Franklin is what Kripke calls a "rigid designator." Whereas information or descriptions about such a person may or may not be true, or may be proved to be untrue (we may discover that Franklin did not in fact invent the bifocal lens, or write the *Almanacks*, and by some mistake was never officially the Postmaster General), what does remain true is that the person we knew to be Benjamin Franklin *was* Franklin. In fact, Kripke argues, you can refer to someone without any of the descriptions of them being correct; there are "possible worlds" in which Franklin might have been none of the things mentioned above. And if this were so, taking descriptivist theory to its conclusion, Benjamin Franklin could not have existed. Yet he did exist, which suggests that there is some quality to Franklin that made him Franklin, irrespective of our descriptions, and irrespective of whether those descriptions turned out to be true.

Kripke's "essentialist" view says that Franklin's existence is determined by nothing other than that he existed. Though it sounds totally obvious to make this assertion, it nevertheless opened a divide between two views of "necessity." Whereas for the analytical-descriptivist philosophers, identity depended on accurate description, Kripke said that identity is only the relation "between something and itself." Another of his examples is someone having heard something about the physicist Richard Feynman and using his name to refer to him, even though the person knows nothing about Feynman. All the person's knowledge about him may in fact be *wrong*, but it is still Feynman, the real person, to whom they are referring.

A further example consists in the names "Cicero" and "Tully." Tully is the old-fashioned English name for Cicero (by virtue of his full name, Marcus Tullius Cicero), so they are simply different names for the same person. However, Kripke supposes that descriptions of "Tully" and of "Cicero" might have varied to such an extent that, in logical descriptivist terms, they might have been different people. The fact that they were not different identities shows up the weakness of wishing to link every name to descriptions of it. Here Kripke echoes John Stuart Mill's view on names: Mill argued that names *connote* an identity, rather than *denote* it.

When a child is born, Kripke notes, he or she is given a name, and through a "causal chain of usage" of that name it becomes our shorthand for that person. There may be hundreds of descriptions of them, but these are essentially irrelevant to their name, which tells us that the person exists, or once existed. We do not have to keep confirming their identity by coming up with accurate descriptions of them. In their zeal to make language more accurate, Kripke said, analytical-linguistic philosophers simply went too far.

To sum up his philosophy of identity, Kripke quotes Bishop Butler:

"Everything is what it is and not another thing."

A person is *who they are* – they have properties essential to them – and no amount of language accuracy is going to add, take away, or prove that identity.

Names and their meaning

Kripke notes that even if we have to change the name of something, we still know what the old name and the new name refer to. Names themselves do not describe, they are merely the means to convey the fact of something across time. Kripke's example is gold. If we discovered that gold only gets its yellow color due to the nature of the atmosphere in parts of the world where it is mined, and that taken out of this situation "gold" is in fact blue, does that mean that gold no longer exists? No, we would simply say that we made a mistake about gold's color; it is still gold.

Similarly, if we define a certain species, for example a tiger, as having certain features and properties, and it turns out that the animal to which we are referring does not in fact have these features or properties, does this mean that we no longer call it a tiger? No, we keep calling it what we have always called it, because actual descriptions and properties matter less than our wish to preserve a causal chain of meaning. What matters are the traits or properties that form a single, "natural kind" of animal. If we discover a new kind of animal that has the properties that we once associated with the old kind of animal, we do not transfer the old name to the new one, we invent a new name altogether. What matters is what *we* call something.

Returning to the example of gold, Kripke wonders what makes gold gold in a scientific sense. What essential quality does it have? We can describe gold in many ways: a metal, with a shiny yellow color, that does not rust, and so on. Yet such descriptions can easily lead to mistakes, such as people thinking that pyrite ("fool's gold") is the real thing. There needs to be something beyond such terms – beyond language itself – that tells us what gold is. This "essence of gold," Kripke says, is that it is the element with the atomic number 79. In this way, Kripke is able to show that his theory is not antiscientific; indeed, that looking for the essential qualities of things is what makes science. We can describe something to kingdom come, but only the presence of a specific microstructure tells us what that thing essentially, actually is.

Final comments

For most of the twentieth century, philosophy was dominated by the idea that only in analyzing language could one discover what was true, what was not true, and what one could not even talk about with any sense. Kripke's bombshell was to demonstrate that if descriptivism was flawed, and language could not even get to the heart of something's identity, why should it be considered the core of philosophy? Perhaps the materialist view of the world, which incorporated the idea that only what could be physically described was relevant or important, was only a bias.

These are the last lines of *Naming and Necessity*:

> *"Materialism, I think, must hold that a physical description of the world is a complete description of it, that any mental facts are 'ontologically dependent' on physical facts in the straightforward sense of following from them by necessity. No identity theorist seems to me to have made a convincing argument against the intuitive view that this is not the case."*

Such statements allow (at least in theory) for some order of reality to exist, mental or metaphysical, that cannot be defined by our descriptions of it. Kripke, who perhaps unusually for a mathematician and philosopher of logic is a religious Jew who upholds the Sabbath, told an interviewer:

> *"I don't have the prejudices many have today, I don't believe in a naturalist world view. I don't base my thinking on prejudices or a world view and do not believe in materialism."*

The naturalist–materialist paradigm (the basis of science and the modern world) as a mere prejudice or ideology? This is a startling statement from one so embedded in the rational establishment. Although Kripke has said that philosophy generally has little application to normal life, surely if he is correct it would mean the end of the "modern" materialist worldview. This would be the philosophical equivalent of a disruptive technology that changes everything.

Saul Kripke

Kripke was born in New York, but when he was still very young his family moved to Omaha, Nebraska. He received a bachelor's degree in Mathematics from Harvard in 1962, and in 1973 he was the youngest person ever to deliver the John Locke Lectures at Oxford University. He has held professorial positions at Harvard, Princeton, and Rockefeller Universities.

"Naming and Necessity" was first published in an edited collection, Semantics of Natural Language *(1972). Kripke does not write books as such, but edits talks that he gives so that they can be published. His controversial interpretation of Wittgenstein is expressed in* Wittgenstein on Rules and Private Language *(1982).*

Kripke is currently on the faculty of the Graduate Center of the City University of New York.

The Structure of Scientific Revolutions

"All historically significant theories have agreed with the facts, but only more or less."

"[The] new paradigm, or a sufficient hint to permit later articulation, emerges all at once, sometimes in the middle of the night, in the mind of a man deeply immersed in crisis."

"The transfer of allegiance from paradigm to paradigm is a conversion experience that cannot be forced."

"Assimilating a new sort of fact demands a more than additive adjustment of theory, and until that adjustment is completed – until the scientist has learned to see nature in a different way – the new fact is not quite scientific at all."

In a nutshell

Rather than a linear accumulation of facts, knowledge can be seen as the replacement of one worldview with another.

In a similar vein

Michel Foucault *The Order of Things* (p 112)
David Hume *An Enquiry Concerning Human Understanding* (p 136)
Karl Popper *The Logic of Scientific Discovery* (p 242)

CHAPTER 26

Thomas Kuhn

homas Kuhn was a graduate student in theoretical physics at Harvard, close to finishing his dissertation for his PhD, when he was asked to teach an experimental college course on science for nonscientists. It was his first real taste of the history of science.

To his surprise, the course altered some of his basic assumptions about science, and the result was a big shift in his career plans, from physics to history and then philosophy of science. In his mid-thirties he wrote a book on Copernicus, and five years later produced *The Structure of Scientific Revolutions*. A monograph of only 170 pages, the book sold over a million copies, was translated into 24 languages, and became one of the most cited works of all time in both the natural and social sciences. Its success was highly unusual for an academic work and was a shock to Kuhn himself.

The work is quite short because it was originally composed with the aim of being a long article in the *Encyclopedia of Unified Science*. Once published, this was expanded into a separate book. This limitation turned out to be a blessing, as Kuhn was prevented from going into lengthy and difficult scientific detail, making the book readable for the layperson.

Why has *The Structure of Scientific Revolutions* had such a huge impact? If its message had been restricted to science itself the work would still be very important, but it is the generic idea of paradigms, in which one worldview replaces another, that has been considered valuable across so many areas of knowledge. Indeed, at several points in the book Kuhn touches on the fact that paradigms do not only exist in science, but are the natural human way of comprehending the world. The roots of the book lay in an experience Kuhn had reading Aristotle, when he realized that Aristotle's laws of motion were not simply "bad Newton," but a completely *different* way of seeing the world.

Science is made by scientists

Kuhn starts by saying that the traditional textbook accounts of the development of science can tell us no more about reality than a tourist brochure can about a nation's culture. The textbooks present an incremental accumulation of facts, and describe theories borne out by successful experiments that lead to increasing amounts of knowledge. But does science really proceed in such a neat way?

Kuhn sought a less arrogant and more open view that understood scientific advance not as isolated individuals making great discoveries, but in terms of the scientific community and the intellectual environment of the day allowing (or disallowing) the reinterpretation of existing data. Central to his argument is the notion that scientists do not proceed by simply describing how nature works, but rather operate within paradigms of understanding that, once they turn out to be deficient in explaining phenomena, are replaced by new ones. He defines paradigms as "universally recognized scientific achievements that for a time provide model problems and solutions to a community of practitioners."

Why is this idea of scientific progress different? The conventional view of science is "here are the facts" about the world, and "here we are" (the scientists) uncovering them. However, facts do not exist without an observer, which means that the interests of the observer are all-important to what constitutes current science. Moreover, the progress of science is only partly about the discovery of the new; it also concerns changes to how we see what we already thought we knew. X-rays, Kuhn notes, "were greeted not only with surprise but with shock," because they did not fall into any existing theory. When a paradigm is replaced by another one, the world itself seems to change: "What were ducks in the scientist's world before the revolution are rabbits afterwards."

One of Kuhn's startling insights is that paradigms can have integrity, providing most of the answers to most of the questions asked of them in their day, and yet also be fundamentally wrong. For a long time the earth-centered view seemed to be a good explanation of cosmology, satisfying most people, until the various anomalies within the model became too obvious to ignore and a sun-centered paradigm became accepted. Nevertheless, the human affinity for certainty means that such revolutions are always resisted. Real discovery begins with the recognition of anomalies, or nature acting in a way that it is not meant to. Scientists do not know what to do with these facts, which are thus not "scientific" until they have found a home in an existing theory.

A paradigm starts to crumble when there is heightened insecurity about its capacity to solve the puzzles it has set for itself. Practitioners keep getting the "wrong" answers. The paradigm is in crisis mode, and it is at such points that breakthroughs to a new paradigm are possible, such as Copernican astronomy or Einstein's special theory of relativity.

Kuhn observes that in the early stages of a new discipline there is usually no established paradigm, only competing views trying to explain some aspect of nature. All of these views may be following established scientific method, but only one becomes the accepted way of seeing. This is not because everyone comes to agree on the facts, but because it is easier to work with a single paradigm; human psychology comes much more into play than we would like to admit. Science, Kuhn notes, does not progress coldly and clinically of its own volition, but is made by scien*tists*.

Normal and revolutionary science

Kuhn makes a distinction between "normal" science and the type of scientific thinking or research that can cause revolutions in how we see the world.

Normal science is based on the assumption "that the scientific community knows what the world is like" and, furthermore, "Much of the success of the enterprise derives from the community's willingness to defend that assumption, if necessary at considerable cost." Normal science tends to suppress anomalous facts because they are a roadblock in a precommitted theoretical path. Kuhn defines these novelties or anomalies within an existing paradigm as a "violation of expectation." The response to an anomaly is hardly ever to renounce the existing paradigm; it is to keep working within it to see what went wrong. Only a tiny minority of scientists can truly "think outside the box" and look at nature in a fresh way.

The basis of joining any scientific community is the study of its paradigm, and the vast majority of scientists will spend their lives working on things within that paradigm: smaller puzzles that need to be solved, or incremental research. Alternatively, they work to produce findings that can bring nature and the theory/paradigm closer together, as many scientists did in the wake of Newton's *Principia*. Normal science is

> *"an attempt to force nature into the preformed and relatively inflexible box that the paradigm supplies. No part of the aim of normal science is to call forth new sets of phenomena; indeed those that will not fit the box are often not seen at all."*

The problem is that when an unexpected novelty appears, scientists will either reject it out of hand as a "mistake" or put it down to a failure of method to prove what they were expecting. Thus the aim of normal science is not to find something new, but to make the existing paradigm more precise, to bring nature into perfect accord with theory.

Scientific revolutions, on the other hand, are the "tradition shattering complements to the tradition-bound activity of normal science." New theories are not simply new facts, but wholesale changes in how we see those facts.

This in turn leads to the reconstruction of theories, which is "an intrinsically revolutionary process that is seldom completed by a single man and never overnight."

Two different worlds: The incommensurability of paradigms

Since paradigm change is not a rational process, but rather a gulf between what different parties *see*, paradigms do not compete. They cannot agree on the methodology to tackle problems, or even on the language needed to describe them; the paradigms are "incommensurable," Kuhn says, because they have no common standard by which to judge each other.

Neither is it a case of each paradigm being closer or further away from an objective truth about the universe. The very essence of paradigms is that they are about the people who make and propose them, and each effectively inhabits a different world. Kuhn quotes Max Planck:

> *"[A] new scientific truth does not triumph by convincing its opponents and making them see the light, but rather because its opponents eventually die, and a new generation grows up that is familiar with it."*

Indeed, it took over a century following Copernicus' death for his views to really catch on, and Newton's ideas were not generally accepted for over 50 years after he published the *Principia*. Kuhn concludes, "The transfer of allegiance from paradigm to paradigm is a conversion experience that cannot be forced." Nevertheless, scientific communities do eventually catch on, and begin the process of "proving" what the new paradigm suggests must be right.

Final comments

The Structure of Scientific Revolutions was shocking in its suggestion that science does not take humanity on a neat, linear path toward some objective truth about the reality of the world via the accumulation of empirical observations (what can be called the Enlightenment view), but is in fact a human creation. If science is the attempt to make our theories fit nature, then it is human nature with which we have to contend first.

We like to weave advances or changes in scientific understanding into a grand story of progress, but Kuhn's implication is that science has no *aim*, simply adapting its explanations to reality as best it can. In the second edition of the book, Kuhn made it clear that he wasn't a relativist and that he believed in scientific progress. However, he also stated that science was like the theory of evolution: it evolves from something simpler, but one could not say that it has a final end or direction.

A common interpretation of Kuhn is that paradigms are "bad" and give people a blinkered view, when they should always be questioning the paradigm that underlies their discipline. In fact, Kuhn noted that the acquisition of a paradigm is a sign that a field has matured into something real, because at least it has a set of rules on which practitioners can agree. Paradigms are neither positive nor negative, they simply give us a lens to view the world. The real value lies in seeing paradigms objectively, and admitting the possibility that our truths may be mere assumptions.

Thomas S. Kuhn

Kuhn was born in 1922. His father was a hydraulic engineer turned investment consultant, and his mother was an editor. He grew up near New York City and attended various private schools before being accepted into Harvard University.

After graduating, Kuhn joined the war effort, working in radar in the United States and Europe, before returning to Harvard to do graduate work in physics. He also took philosophy courses and considered switching to philosophy, but felt it was too late to begin in this field. At 30 he began teaching the history of science, and his steep learning curve in a new field meant that he had little time for producing his own work. As a result, The Structure of Scientific Revolutions *was a decade in the making. Kuhn could not get tenure at Harvard, so took an assistant professorship at the University of California, Berkeley. In 1964, Princeton offered him a full professorial role in the history and philosophy of science, and he stayed there for 15 years before spending the final stage of his career at MIT (1979–91).*

Kuhn's first book was The Copernican Revolution: Planetary Astronomy in the Development of Western Thought *(1957). He also wrote* Sources for the History of Quantum Physics *(1967). In the years following publication of* The Structure of Scientific Revolutions *Kuhn revisited and clarified some of its concepts (see* The Road Since Structure: Philosophical Essays, 1970–1993, *which includes an autobiographical interview with Kuhn). He died in 1996.*

Theodicy

"[Since] God made the universe, it was not possible to do better."

"God, having chosen the most perfect of all possible worlds, had been prompted by his wisdom to permit the evil which was bound up with it, but which still did not prevent this world from being, all things considered, the best that could be chosen."

"It is true that one may imagine possible worlds without sin and without unhappiness, and one could make some like Utopian or Sevarambian romances: but these same worlds again would be very inferior to ours in goodness. I cannot show you this in detail. For can I know and can I present infinities to you and compare them together? But you must judge with me ab effectu [from the effect], since God has chosen this world as it is. We know, moreover, that often an evil brings forth a good whereto one would not have attained without that evil. Often indeed two evils have made one great good."

In a nutshell

The world that exists must be the best of all possible worlds.

In a similar vein

Thomas Aquinas *Summa Theologica* (p 16)

Blaise Pascal *Pensées* (p 224)

Plato *The Republic* (p 230)

Baruch Spinoza *Ethics* (p 298)

CHAPTER 27

Gottfried Leibniz

Gottfried Leibniz was a well-connected man of the world, usually to be found crisscrossing Europe on political missions for his employers. Among the friends he made was a young queen, Sophia Charlotte of the house of Hanover. On visits to the royal court in Berlin, he would spend hours in conversation with Sophia, making observations on the religious, philosophical, and political controversies of the day.

For the queen's benefit, Leibniz responded at length to the ideas of French Calvinist pastor Pierre Bayle, author of the famous *Historical and Critical Dictionary*. Bayle argued that Christianity was a matter of faith and not something that could be penetrated by reason, and that the question of human suffering could only remain a mystery.

When Sophia died at only 36, as a legacy to her Leibniz pulled together the notes she had encouraged him to make and published the *Theodicy*. Divided into three essays on the "goodness of God," the "freedom of man," and the "origin of evil," the work sought to make an elegant defense of a just and benevolent Supreme Being, while reconciling this with the fact of evil in the world. At a time when science was on the rise and the old religious assumptions were being challenged, the book was a rejoinder to Bayle's belief in the incompatibility of faith and reason.

In addition to his role as a senior bureaucrat and political adviser, Leibniz was one of the great polymaths, making major contributions to mathematics (he discovered infinitesimal calculus separately to Isaac Newton, and built one of the first mechanical calculators), jurisprudence, physics, optics, and philosophy. Despite being at the cutting edge of secular thought in his day, however, Leibniz was not ready to throw centuries of reasoning about the nature of God onto the heap, and considered it his mission to refute the ideas of Descartes, Locke, and particularly Spinoza, who pictured a universe run by impersonal natural laws, with no room for the judgment or intentions of God, and little attention to human choice and freedom. The seventeenth-century world was still very much based around God, even if science and modernity were coming to the fore. Yet Leibniz did not want to see science and metaphysics as separate, and his proofs for the role of a Supreme Being are still quite convincing.

"Theodicy" was a word that Leibniz coined, combining the Greek *theos* (god) and *dike* (justice). Literally "justifying god," the title expresses the intent of the book: to explain how God can allow evil if he is all-powerful. As this is a question that people today continually ask, Leibniz's book remains relevant, and seems designed for anyone who unthinkingly accepts the view that "because there is so much evil or suffering in the world, there can be no God."

Leibniz's idea of the "best of all possible worlds" was famously satirized by Voltaire in his play *Candide* (1759), in which the character of the perpetually optimistic Dr. Pangloss was partly a parody of Leibniz. Voltaire's understanding of Leibniz's philosophy is somewhat superficial and yet Leibniz himself was keen to note that his notion of divine benevolence and the best of all possible worlds *did* make him a genuinely happy man. This is unsurprising, as the idea provides a sense of security and order in an apparently random and meaningless universe.

How we live in the best of all possible worlds

Leibniz's concept that we live in the best of all possible worlds carries with it the acceptance of God's perfection. Put simply, if God is perfect, then any world that he makes must be perfect, even if at the human level it may seem the very picture of imperfection. Yet God could not make *us* perfect, since he would then be making other gods. Rather, there are different degrees in the perfection of things; human beings are not an example of corrupted divinity, but of perfection slightly limited. Leibniz extols the near-perfection of the human body, writing: "I am not astonished men are sometimes sick, but that … they are sick so little and not always."

The universe is organized according to "sufficient reason," which includes divine intentions. The world that exists must exist for very particular reasons, even if we – with our limited knowledge – cannot understand them. Indeed, Leibniz says (and this contradicts the caricature of him as a foolish optimist), the best possible world is often *not* the one that delivers immediate human happiness. Human beings are driven by self-interest and are not aware of the good result of everything that happens. We see things in terms of cause and effect, but our appreciation of the relationship between things is naturally limited.

Leibniz suggests that the universe is composed of trillions of "monads," self-sufficient entities or forms of existence (including human souls). They do not influence each other as such, but God orders everything in the universe to work harmoniously together. This is the principle of "pre-established harmony." Only God has an overview of how everything is knitted together and of the wisdom behind events. Our role is to trust in this infinite wisdom and benevolence of intention.

The world that God has created is not some mindless Utopia where nothing negative ever happens, but a real world, rich and varied, and full of meaning. It is a place in which bad things may be needed for the good to finally manifest, or in which "an imperfection in the part may be required for a greater perfection in the whole." Leibniz cites St. Augustine and Thomas Aquinas, who both noted that God permits evils in order that a good may come of them; indeed, that sometimes an evil is necessary for the world to head in the direction it must. A world with evil may in fact be the best possible world, even if it is not always good for every person all the time. "It is not that we ought to take pleasure in sin, God forbid!" Leibniz is careful to say, but that sin allows for "grace to abound" and lift people up, where they might have stayed undeveloped. Despite apparent negatives in the short term, everything does truly work out for the best.

How free will can exist

Leibniz goes to some lengths to show how free will is possible within a divinely ordered universe. There is no "absolute necessity" in human actions, he says: "I am of the opinion that the will is always more inclined towards the course it adopts, but that it is never bound by necessity to adopt it." God gave humans freedom to act, so for God to come down and right wrongs before they happen, or just after, would cancel out that freedom. This would lead to less of a world. This freedom means that although God creates everything we see, at the same time he is not the "author of sin." Indeed, God allows for many possible worlds to come into being, based on humankind's freedom to think and act:

> "[A]lthough his will is always indefectible and always tends towards the best, the evil or the lesser good which he rejects will still be possible in itself. Otherwise ... the contingency of things would be destroyed, and there would be no choice."

Leibniz qualifies his discussion of free will by noting that although human beings have a choice to create one of several possible worlds for themselves, their past actions will cause only one to come into being. However, knowing humanity's will and past actions as he does, the Supreme Being knows which world is likely to manifest.

The line that Leibniz walks between free will and necessity is a fine one, illustrated by his example of the "Fatum Mahometanum." Islamic peoples in his time would not try to avoid places ravaged by the plague, on the grounds that fate had decreed whether they would catch it or not, so their actions would not make a difference. However, such "lazy reason," as it was called by the ancient philosophers, took no account of the role that causes play in life, or of the notion that by changing the present new possible worlds open up. Even if the future is determined in some way by a Supreme Being, Leibniz says, this should not stop us living according to good intentions and behavior, and creating new, good causes now. We can then leave the rest up to God. We should presume, too, that God wants for us what we want for ourselves, unless he has some even greater good in mind for us. Either way, a beneficial outcome is never in doubt.

Final comments

Ironically for someone now associated with providing a rationale for belief in God, in his lifetime Leibniz was accused of being an atheist. He was not a great churchgoer and opposed some beliefs of his time, such as that unbaptized children would be sent to hell. An important part of his work, both in his political roles and as a philosopher, was reconciling the Catholic and Protestant churches, and the *Theodicy* was a pan-Christian work written to that end (though Leibniz was Protestant, the book makes copious reference to "Papist" philosophers Aquinas and Augustine).

One of the great stories of modern philosophy is Leibniz's trip to the Netherlands to visit Baruch Spinoza, well told in Matthew Stewart's *The Heretic and the Courtier*. The pair could not have been more different: Leibniz was a young, suave "spin doctor" and up-and-coming science guru, and Spinoza was a brilliant philosopher-recluse, despised by many as the "atheist Jew." Stewart depicts the meeting as the defining moment in Leibniz's life and philosophy, because he felt compelled to accommodate what were apparently opposite views to his own. Stewart suggests, "Even today, the two men who met in the Hague stand for a choice that we all must make and have implicitly already made."

What is that choice? Belief in a universe run according to strict natural laws that do not require a Supreme Being; or one in which God is the driver of everything (including humanity's progress toward scientific knowledge). Anyone who opts for the former on the basis that "if God existed, evil would not exist" should at least suspend judgment until they have read Leibniz's arguments.

Gottfried Wilhelm Leibniz

Leibniz was born in 1646 in Leipzig. His father was a philosophy professor, but died when Leibniz was 6. A brilliant school student with a remarkable fluency in Latin, at Leipzig University Leibniz studied Latin, Greek, philosophy, and mathematics before specializing in law. He was subsequently awarded a doctorate by the University of Altdorf.

His first job was as an adviser and librarian to a politician, Baron von Boineburg. At only 21 he wrote a celebrated book on the reform of German law, and at 24 was appointed privy counsellor of justice to the Elector of Mainz, a senior bureaucratic post. In his mid-thirties Leibniz went to Paris as an envoy, and there studied mathematics, made friends with two of France's great philosophers, Nicolas Malebranche and Antoine Arnauld, and became acquainted with the thinking of Descartes.

It was in November 1676 that he journeyed to the Hague to meet Spinoza, staying for three days of discussion. Though he left no details of the meetings, a single page with a "proof of God" survives, probably written in Spinoza's presence. In the same year Leibniz took on a job as librarian, adviser, and historian in the administration of the Duke of Hanover. The position, which he held until his death, gave him the opportunity to travel on the pretext of researching a never-finished history of Hanover's ruling Brunswick family, and make scientific contacts in Paris, London, Italy, Russia, and within Germany.

Other writings include The Philosopher's Confession *(1672–73) and* Discourse on Metaphysics *(1686). His* New Essays on Human Understanding *was written in 1704 but not published until 1765. The* Monadology *was published in 1714, the year of his death. Leibniz never married.*

1689

Essay Concerning Human Understanding

"From what has been said, I think it past doubt, that there are no practical principles wherein all men agree; and therefore none innate."

"If it shall be demanded then, WHEN a man BEGINS to have any ideas, I think the true answer is, – WHEN HE FIRST HAS ANY SENSATION. For, since there appear not to be any ideas in the mind before the senses have conveyed any in, I conceive that ideas in the understanding are coeval with SENSATION."

"If by this inquiry into the nature of the understanding, I can discover the powers thereof; how far they reach; to what things they are in any degree proportionate; and where they fail us, I suppose it may be of use to prevail with the busy mind of man to be more cautious in meddling with things exceeding its comprehension."

In a nutshell

All our ideas, simple or complex, originate in sensory experience. We are blank slates; morality and character are not innate.

In a similar vein

A.J. Ayer *Language, Truth and Logic* (p 34)
David Hume *An Enquiry Concerning Human Understanding* (p 136)
William James *Pragmatism* (p 142)
Jean-Jacques Rousseau *The Social Contract* (p 252)
Nassim Nicholas Taleb *The Black Swan* (p 306)

CHAPTER 28

John Locke

John Locke studied medicine at Oxford and began his adult life as the personal physician to a Whig politician, the 1st Earl of Shaftesbury. He was credited with saving his boss's life via a liver operation, but his interest in medicine could not compete with his passion for politics and philosophy.

For most of his life, Locke was best known as a political adviser and intellectual force in the Whig party. His liberal views were expressed in *Two Treatises on Government* (published anonymously a year after the *Essay Concerning Human Understanding*), which made a brilliant case for individual freedoms and the natural rights of the people as opposed to the "divine right of kings" and Thomas Hobbes' absolutism. The *Treatises* became a major influence on French revolutionaries and the founding of the American republic, and the Lockean concept of the pursuit of happiness found its way into the American constitution.

During his political career Locke had been working on his *Essay Concerning Human Understanding*, a purely philosophical work. Francis Bacon was the developer of the scientific method, and famously died of pneumonia in 1626 while experimenting with freezing meat. Locke, born six years later, would become his intellectual heir, expanding the British empirical view into a fullblown philosophy. The *Essay Concerning Human Understanding* created the ground on which Hume could walk, and the latter in turn paved the way for twentieth-century analytical philosophers such as Russell and Wittgenstein. In its first pages Locke modestly notes,

> *"in an age that produces such masters as the great Huygenius [Dutch mathematician and astronomer] and the incomparable Mr. Newton [as in Isaac, whom he knew] … it is ambition enough to be employed as an under-labourer in clearing the ground a little, and removing some of the rubbish that lies in the way to knowledge."*

This "under-labourer" was a very modern kind of philosopher. He averred the building of a big system in favor of finding out what a single individual could actually know, and, like today's philosophers, was very concerned with precision in language itself:

"Vague and insignificant forms of speech, and abuse of language, have so long passed for mysteries of science; and hard and misapplied words, with little or no meaning, have, by prescription, such a right to be mistaken for deep learning and height of speculation, that it will not be easy to persuade either those who speak or those who hear them, that they are but the covers of ignorance, and hindrance of true knowledge."

Yet the contemporary philosophers who claim Locke as one of their own often ignore that he still carried many of the views of his time. The *Essay*, for instance, has a fair amount of what today we would call theology, and the line he walks between skepticism and seeing the world as the product of a creator makes for some interesting explanations, as we will see. Recent scholarship has focused on his ideas about the self, which we also consider.

If we all perceive differently, where is hard truth?

The common view since Aristotle had been that there are certain principles or universal truths that are agreed to be true by "common assent," and therefore they must be innate. But Locke argues that humans possess no innate knowledge: we are blank slates. All our knowledge comes to us through our sight, hearing, smell, touch, and taste, and the ideas or concepts (for example "whiteness, hardness, sweetness, thinking, motion, man, elephant, army, drunkenness") that we form from them simply result from this sensory input. As he puts it:

"To ask, at what TIME a man has first any ideas, is to ask, when he begins to perceive; – HAVING IDEAS, and PERCEPTION, being the same thing."

We cannot experience anything without having first had a sensory experience of it. Even a complex idea finds its roots in the senses.

In Locke's terminology, "simple" ideas are the basic experiences given to us by our senses, for example the coldness and hardness felt at once on touching a block of ice, or the whiteness and smell experienced when holding a lily. These simple ideas form the basis of any number of complex, more abstract ideas about how the world works. The sight of a horse galloping, for instance, eventually leads us to reflections on the nature of motion. Yet we must always first have the experience of simple ideas before we can create complex ones. Even an abstract concept such as power originally derives from our awareness that we can move our limbs to do something. From this simple knowledge of what power is, we can understand why a government or an army can have power. Locke further separates things according to their primary and secondary qualities. The primary qualities of a rock, for instance, are its bulk and motion, which are true even if they are not perceived. Its secondary qualities are the way we perceive it, for instance its blackness, its hardness.

Locke's belief that all ideas must come originally from sensation led him to an interesting insight: if the senses can give one person a widely different view of the world than the person sitting next to them (for instance, the same bathtub of water can be cold to one person, yet warm to another), how can there be any certainty or truth in the ideas spoken by individual philosophers, which are much more complex? Every view of the world, he suggests, must be a personal one, and abstractions and ideas, however attractive, must remain suspect, particularly if they make spurious claims to universality.

Is morality innate?

In Locke's time it was assumed that morality was innate (people are born good or evil) and that there exists a set of universal moral principles. He attempts to show that morality cannot be universal by pointing out the wide variation among individuals and peoples in terms of beliefs. For example, practices such as leaving children out in the wild or bad weather, or burying them along with their mother if she dies, have been normal practice in various cultures, but in the England of his day they were considered abhorrent.

"Where then," he asks, "are those innate principles of justice, piety, gratitude, equity, chastity?" If such principles, including the "innate" acceptance of God, are lacking in children, "idiots," and various foreign peoples, it suggests that they are created by humans. Locke then addresses the argument that our reason, given to us by God, enables us to discover the timeless moral truths. Reason is a creation of human minds, he concludes, and therefore cannot be relied on to reveal eternal truth.

Principles seem innate, he says, only because "we do not remember when we first accepted them." Children soak up what they are told, only questioning it in adulthood. Perhaps the only thing innate in us is our wish to live according to principles, *any* principles, so long as they give life some order or meaning. Yet "[i]deas and notions are no more born with us than arts and sciences," and they are often used by one person against another. Therefore, the route to freedom must be each person testing truths for themselves, so that they may be under no one's false dominion.

In Locke's empirical view, where stands spiritual belief? He sees it simply as a complex idea, drawn from other complex ideas such as existence, duration, knowledge, power, and goodness. We take these and multiply them by infinity to arrive at the comprehension of a Supreme Being. Though Locke cannot "prove" God's existence, he somehow manages to show that belief in God is perfectly natural and logical, something worked out from our direct experience of the world around us.

Personhood

In the second edition of the book (1694), Locke included a new chapter, "Of Ideas of Identity and Diversity." For many scholars this has become the most fascinating part of the work, as it is an early attempt to explain questions of consciousness and identity.

Identity, Locke says, is always based on our perceptions of something over time. The identity of living creatures does not simply depend on their being the same mass of particles they were two years ago. An oak tree is the same plant that was once a sapling, and a horse is the same horse it was as a colt. This tells Locke that identity is not based in matter alone, which constantly changes, but in something's organization.

But how does this work in relation to human beings? Locke raises the fascinating question of souls, which may inhabit successive bodies and take on new identities across many lifetimes. Even assuming, for instance, that each of these incarnations is male, one could not say that such a succession of identities is the same "man." Central to his argument is the separation of the concepts of "man" and "person." While a man or woman is an expression of the human species – a body, an animal, who is also combined with a consciousness – personhood implies a duration of consciousness that expresses an identity, transcending the physical. Thus we could almost say that a very intelligent cat or parrot seems like a person and we ascribe it a personality, whereas we might consider someone who has lost their memory more as a body who has lost their personhood. Locke mentions everyday sayings such as he is "not himself" or is "beside himself," which imply that "the selfsame person was no longer in that man." These sayings confirm that consciousness, not physicality, is identity.

Final comments

Though Locke's refutation of innateness seemed to be a step toward truth, science has been less kind to it. The idea of the mind as a *tabula rasa* has had a huge effect on culture and public policy (giving us the notion, for instance, that boys and girls act differently only because of societal conditioning), but research into the brain shows that a significant number of behavioral tendencies are, in fact, innate. Moral action itself is considered by many to be an evolutionary trait that helps human beings live better in communities.

Locke's *Essay Concerning Human Understanding* is still, however, a great expression of the empirical view, and was very bold for its times. It is also quite readable (more so than a lot of contemporary philosophy) and covers many ideas that we do not have space for here, such as his position on free will and ethics.

Locke also wrote in defense of religious toleration (*Letters Concerning Toleration*, 1689–92), primarily to bridge the Catholic–Protestant divide, and his vision of an open, tolerant, and democratic society has been influential. Specifically, his modest view of humans as beings shaped by their senses who naturally pursue their own happiness and avoid pain has been a long-lasting influence on modern political institutions, particularly those of the United States. His conception of human beings as moral animals was very modern and realistic, and has been successful because it gives full credit to our ability to create positive change, yet does not try to make us into something we are not.

John Locke

Locke was born in 1632 in Somerset, England. His father was a lawyer and minor official and Locke attended the prestigious Westminster School in London. He won a studentship to Oxford, and after earning two degrees stayed on to research and teach on theological and political issues, living in the city for a total of 15 years. In 1665 he transferred his interests to medicine, and the following year met Anthony Ashley Cooper, Lord Ashley (later the Earl of Shaftesbury), whose household in London he joined. It was in 1668 that he supervised the liver operation on Cooper.

When Cooper became Lord Chancellor in the English government, Locke worked with him as an adviser, and after this period helped to organize the new American colony of Carolina. Given that its constitution (which he helped draft) set up a feudal aristocracy based on the slave trade, many have pointed out the apparent hypocrisy of Locke's work there in contrast to his broad political views.

From 1683 to 1689 he exiled himself to Holland for political reasons, but returned after the Glorious Revolution, which saw William of Orange installed as Britain's monarch. Never marrying, Locke spent his last years in Essex living with his friend Lady Damaris Masham and her husband. He worked on a committee advising the government on monetary matters, and anonymously published The Reasonableness of Christianity *(1695). The following year he was appointed to a salaried position with the Board of Trade, and engaged in a prolonged public debate with cleric Edward Stillingfleet on the theological implications of the* Essay. *Locke died in 1704.*

The Prince

"And you are to understand that a Prince, and most of all a new Prince, cannot observe all those rules of conduct considered good, being often forced, in order to preserve his Princedom, to act in opposition to good faith, charity, humanity, and religion. He must therefore keep his mind ready to shift as the winds and tides of Fortune turn, and, as I have already said, he ought not to quit being good if he can help it, but should know how to follow evil courses if he must."

In a nutshell

The good ruler will build a strong and successful state that provides prosperity and peace for its citizens; maintaining it sometimes requires action at odds with the morals of the day.

In a similar vein

CHAPTER 29

Niccolò Machiavelli

The *Prince* is said to have been bedtime reading for Napoleon, Hitler, and Stalin, and Shakespeare used the term "Machiavel" to mean a schemer who was happy to sacrifice people for evil aims. The book was put on the Catholic Church's index of prohibited works and was equally reviled by Protestant reformers. It is shocking because it attempts to tell things as they are, instead of trying to align political life with some spiritual or ethical ideal. Only by doing this, Niccolò Machiavelli felt, would his book be truly *useful*.

Machiavelli was a government adviser at the highest levels of Renaissance Florence, and it was only after the political winds turned against him that he sat down to write. *The Prince* was dedicated to a member of Florence's ruling aristocracy, the Medici, in an effort to gain employment, and though it was perhaps written with an eye to a larger audience, its author could not have guessed its impact on later generations.

Is this really a handbook of evil? As Yale's Erica Benner has suggested in *Machiavelli's Ethics*, *The Prince* is best considered not as a guide on how to be ruthless or self-serving, but rather as a lens through which to see objectively the prevailing views of the day, as a device to open the reader's eyes to others' motives. It can therefore be used as a handbook of effectiveness for any contemporary leader who wants to keep their essentially noble goals on track – or, at a general level, as one of the great philosophies of power. Having said that, it is still a very disturbing work when set next to utopian political philosophies.

Let's be honest

In the fourteenth to sixteenth centuries there was a genre of guidebooks, "mirrors for princes," written for young men who were about to inherit a kingdom. Erasmus's *The Education of a Christian Prince*, published only a couple of years after Machiavelli had finished *The Prince*, exhorted rulers to act as if they were saints, arguing that successful rule naturally corresponds with the goodness of the ruler. Centuries before, Augustine's *The City of God* had provided a stark contrast to the flawed political structures of humans, proposing that true fulfillment lay in turning inward to God.

Yet not only did Machiavelli believe that, given human nature, a truly good ruler or perfect state could not exist, he viewed the incursion of religious ideals into politics as damaging to a state's effectiveness. Though he appreciated the value of religion in creating a cohesive society, he felt that the direct involvement of the church in state affairs ultimately corrupted both state *and* church. There was no better example of this than the papal or ecclesiastical states, which in his time became very powerful, able to make even large states like France tremble. Some popes had several mistresses, sired illegitimate children, and grew rich through their conquests. Machiavelli devotes a chapter to these states, but he weighs his words carefully, noting with some sarcasm that since they are "set up and supported by God himself ... he would be a rash and presumptuous man who should venture to discuss them."

His view is that politics and religion are two different realms; "the good," while a noble aim, was best left to the private and religious spheres, while the effectiveness of a ruler should be measured by *virtù*, the decisive strength or prowess needed to build and preserve a state.

Machiavelli wished to counter the idealized state that Plato had set forth in *The Republic*, and also disagreed with the code for principled political action established by the Roman statesman Cicero. His conclusion is that a leader cannot be effective operating in a Ciceronian way if all about him are unscrupulous or rapacious. To preserve his good aims, Machiavelli famously says, the Prince must learn "how to be other than good." A ruler has to make choices that the normal citizen never does, such as whether to go to war or what to do about people trying to kill or overthrow you. To maintain order and peace, and preserve the honor of your state, it may be necessary to act in a way that, as a private citizen, you never would.

Why force is justified

While Machiavelli was working for the Florentine city-state, the town of Pistoia was being ravaged by infighting. He proposed that Florence take it over to subdue it and bring order, but the public did not have a taste for such an enterprise and nothing was done. Left to its own devices, however, there was a bloodbath on the streets. Thus, Machiavelli argues:

> *"he who quells disorder by a very few signal examples will in the end be more merciful than he who from too great leniency permits things to take their course and so to result in rapine and bloodshed; for these hurt the whole State, whereas the severities of the Prince injure individuals only."*

The fact is that any ruler, no matter how benign, must face up to the state's use of violence to maintain its existence. Machiavelli notes that "all armed Prophets have been victorious, and all unarmed Prophets have been destroyed." He refers to Savonarola, the clerical Florentine leader whose fatal mistake was to possess no forceful means to see his vision of the city become real. Though a good man by any measure, who tried to bring back morality and republican ideals in contrast to the ruthless Medicis, in the end Savonarola was powerless to stop his own demise.

A prince must be able to act both as man and beast, Machiavelli states; an effective ruler must be "a fox to discern snares, and a lion to drive off wolves." He imagines the wise leader as spending many of his hours during peacetime considering various scenarios of war, and working out how the kingdom will respond if the event actually happens. A prince could fool himself into believing that his energies should be spent on other things, but ultimately his role is to protect and preserve the state.

This necessarily involves taking action that would normally be considered bad, but "if it be permitted to speak well of things evil," as Machiavelli delicately puts it, there is a distinction between violence that is committed for the reason of creating or preserving a good state, and wanton cruelty that is performed merely to preserve an individual ruler's power. He gives low marks to the Roman emperors Commodus, Caracalla, and Maximus, who made cruelty a way of life. They became so hated that their premature deaths were inevitable. Not only is excess cruelty bad, therefore, it is politically unwise.

When it comes to seizing a principality or state, Machiavelli's general rule is that "the usurper should be quick to inflict what injuries he must, at a stroke, that he may not have to renew them daily." If you are going to take or attack something, do it as quickly as possible and with maximum force, so that your foes give up early and, paradoxically, violence can be minimized. In doing so you will be feared, and can later be seen to be magnanimous by your favors. In contrast, a half-hearted coup will allow your enemies to live on, and you will forever be fearful of being overthrown.

To understand Machiavelli one must appreciate the geopolitics of his time. Italy, he laments, "has been overrun by Charles, plundered by Louis, wasted by Ferdinand, and insulted by the Swiss," a state of affairs that would have been prevented had its rulers had strong national armies. Yet rather than power for power's sake, Machiavelli's purpose is the establishment of strong government that allows the private economy to flourish, works according to laws and institutions, and preserves culture. He believes that God would want a strong and united Italy that is able to bring security and prosperity to its people, with a flourishing national culture and identity. The Prince is, from its author's standpoint, a work with a clear moral foundation.

Of the people, by the people

This was Machiavelli's vision, but what did it mean in terms of the flavor of an actual government? He heaped praise on Cesare Borgia, the Italian ruler, cardinal, and son of Pope Alexander VI, whose famously ruthless actions provide a sense of what Machiavelli was willing to accept for the sake of power.

Still, Machiavelli believed that a successful state could bring out the best in people, providing a stage on which individuals could find glory through great acts. As Hannah Arendt noted, *The Prince* is an "extraordinary effort to restore the old dignity to politics," bringing back the classical Roman and Greek idea of glory to sixteenth-century Italy. Machiavelli admires the self-made men who rise from humble private stations by their deeds, risking all for public esteem and the chance of power.

Yet how does this adulation of strong individual action fit with the Republican ethos that runs through Machiavelli's other writings (*Florentine Histories, Discourses*), and in fact his lengthy experience working for a republic? *The Prince* can be seen as largely a manual for *founding* a state, a great enterprise that is inevitably the inspiration and work of a single person. Once established, the ruler's power would then be properly checked and balanced by an array of democratic institutions.

Machiavelli was acutely sensitive of the delicate dance of power between the ruler, the noble class, and the people. He states his wariness of a prince ever depending for his power on the nobility, since they will desire many favors for installing you, or want to replace you altogether. The support of the people, on the other hand, may be more fickle and less able to be controlled, yet in difficult times it is worth a great deal, providing a source of legitimacy: "For however strong you may be in respect of your army, it is essential that in entering a new Province you should have the good will of its inhabitants." Later he tackles the issue of how a prince can control a state that has previously lived under its own laws. He notes that the people, no matter how long they are subverted, will not forget the freedoms they once enjoyed or the laws and institutions that made them a proud state. Here Machiavelli veils his republican sympathies thinly, noting that despite the apparent power of usurpers and conquering rulers, the rule of law and democratic freedoms are so conducive to the natural state of humankind that they have an abiding power that is not easily forgotten or extinguished.

In summary, the ideal state is one that is open enough for remarkable individuals of any station to fulfill their ambitions, and these largely selfish motives can lead to good outcomes for all, since these special individuals, to succeed over the longer term, must shape their designs in a way that also satisfies the natural wants of the people.

Final comments

The Prince continues to fascinate, shock, and inspire people today as much as it did readers in the sixteenth century. Though written as a kind of showcase of its author's knowledge of statecraft, and very much concerned with the events of his time, the book's timeless insights into the nature of power and human motivation have transcended its original setting.

The usual accusation against the book is that it is evil or immoral. Yet it is best seen as a founding text of political science, clinically analyzing political situations as they are and providing prescriptions for action. In seeking to minimize upheaval and misery by promoting a strong state that can secure prosperity and security for all within it, Machiavelli's aim was an ethical one, even if it allowed for institutionalized force or violence.

Machiavelli remains essential reading for anyone in a leadership position. Each of us must make decisions that may not be welcomed, or may even hurt, those in our charge. Yet we must act for the benefit and long-term wellbeing of the body that we administer, whether it be a business, some other organization, or even a family. In this respect the leader's role can be lonely and often brings with it dark responsibilities. Such is the nature of power.

Niccolò Machiavelli

Machiavelli was born in Florence in 1469. His father was a lawyer, and he received a good education in Latin, rhetoric, and grammar. He lived through the reign of Savonarola and his Christian republic, and in the years following the friar's execution rose through the ranks of Florentine government. In 1498 he was made Secretary of the Second Chancery of the Republic, and Secretary of the Ten of Liberty and Peace. Two years later he went on his first diplomatic mission, meeting King Louis XII of France. In 1501, he married Marietta Corsini, with whom he would have six children.

In 1502–03 he spent a four-month period at the court of Cesare Borgia, Duke Valentino, a fearful ruler who is considered by many to be the model for Machiavelli's prince. He was also part of missions to Pope Julius II and Emperor Maximilian. With the fall of the Florentine republic in 1512, Machiavelli was dismissed from his positions, accused of conspiracy, imprisoned, tortured, and then released, allowing him time to compose The Prince.

Other writings include the Discourses, *a commentary on the work of Roman historian Livy that reveals Machiavelli's republican sympathies;* The Mandrake, *a satirical play concerning Florentine society;* The Art of War, *a treatise in the form of a Socratic dialogue that was the only historical or political work to be published in his lifetime (in 1521); and his* History of Florence, *commissioned by Cardinal Giulio de' Medici in 1520 but not published until 1532. Machiavelli died in 1527.*

The Medium Is the Massage

"The family circle has widened. The worldpool of information fathered by electric media … far surpasses any possible influence mom and dad can now bring to bear. Character is no longer shaped by only two earnest, fumbling experts. Now all the world's a sage."

"Societies have always been shaped more by the nature of the media by which men communicated than by the content of the communication."

"The wheel is an extension of the foot, the book is an extension of the eye, clothing an extension of the skin … electric circuitry, an extension of the central nervous system … Media, by altering the environment, evoke in us unique ratios of sense perceptions. The extension of any one sense alters the way we think and act – the way we perceive the world. When these ratios change, men change."

In a nutshell

The mass media and communications technology are not neutral inventions but change the way we are.

In a similar vein

Jean Baudrillard *Simulacra and Simulation* (p 38)
Noam Chomsky *Understanding Power* (p 76)

CHAPTER 30

Marshall McLuhan

Marshall McLuhan was the original media guru. He achieved international fame in the 1960s and 1970s, coining the phrase "global village" in his 1962 book *The Gutenberg Galaxy: The Making of Typographic Man*. His star dipped slightly in the 1980s before rising again with the advent of the internet, which he predicted.

The Medium Is the Massage is not a typical philosophy book. First, it was not actually written by McLuhan. A talented book designer, Quentin Fiore, took some of McLuhan's key quotes and placed them in a very striking visual order, with lots of images, changes of font, and devices such as upside-down print, consistent with McLuhan's own ideas about print being too restrictive a medium. The book seems very "hip 'n' happening" in a sixties way, but this disguises McLuhan's deep literary and metaphysical learning. He was, after all, a college professor.

Why was the book called *The Medium Is the Massage*, when McLuhan is more commonly known for his catchphrase "the medium is the *message*"? The change was actually a typo that crept into the editing process, but McLuhan thought it was very apt (and insisted that it stayed) because, he felt, "All media work us over completely" – media technology so changes our personal, political, aesthetic, ethical, and social lives that "no part of us is untouched, unaffected, unaltered."

The global village

Today, every child learns the alphabet, and we teach it without really thinking about it. And yet, says McLuhan, words and their meaning make a child act and think in particular ways. He explains this in greater length in *The Gutenberg Galaxy*, but his point is that the alphabet and the advent of printing created a much more mentally fragmented, detached, and specialized kind of human being. However, the electronic age and its technologies have reinvigorated social involvement, bringing us together again. Telephones and the internet allow us to have hundreds of friends and connections around the world. While we are still using the alphabet, the different media for its expression allow for exponentially greater influence on others, and for us to be influenced by others endlessly as well. A learned person in the late Middle Ages might have had access to a library of a few hundred volumes; today, the average person has millions of books at their disposal at the push of a button. How would such changes *not* alter who and what we are? As McLuhan famously says:

> *"Ours is a brand new world of allatonceness. 'Time' has ceased, 'space' has vanished. We now live in a global village ... a simultaneous happening."*

Before the advent of the alphabet, he argues, humankind's main sensory organ was the ear. After it, the eye became dominant. The alphabet made us think in the way that a sentence is constructed: linear, with each letter connected in an order. "The continuum became the organizing principle of life." Rationality came to mean the sequential connection of facts or concepts.

Yet the new media environment is multidimensional – no longer detached, and involving more of our senses again. Media information now comes to us so thick and fast that we no longer have the ability to categorize it properly and deal with it in our minds. It is more a case of recognizing patterns as quickly as we can. Influenced by his reading of Lao Tzu, McLuhan says:

> *"Electric circuitry is Orientalizing the West. The contained, the distinct, the separate – our Western legacy – are being replaced by the flowing, the unified, the fused."*

Self and social changes

Early in *The Medium Is the Massage*, McLuhan notes that media students are often attacked for "idly concentrating on means or processes" rather than on substance. In fact, in the era in which we live it is these very means and processes that are rapidly and deeply changing what is "known." "Electric technology," as he describes it, is reshaping every aspect of social and personal life, "forcing us to reconsider and reevaluate practically every thought, every action, and every institution formerly taken for granted." He warns: "Everything is changing – you, your family, your neighbourhood, your education, your job, your government, your relation to 'the others'. And they're changing dramatically."

A child growing up in the modern media environment does not only have their parents and teachers to influence them, they are exposed to the whole world: "Character is no longer shaped by only two earnest, fumbling experts. Now all the world's a sage." Every child is exposed to a barrage of adult information through the media that makes the very idea of "childhood" seem quaint. On the plus side, technology is making learning more fun and gives some control back to the student. Education no longer has to mean rote learning, blackboards, and regimented schooldays.

The relationship between "public" and "private" has also changed:

"Electrical information devices for universal, tyrannical womb-to-tomb surveillance are causing a very serious dilemma between our claim to privacy and the community's need to know. The older, traditional ideas of private, isolated thoughts and actions ... are very seriously threatened by new methods of instantaneous electric information retrieval."

Social media sites have indeed blurred the distinction between what is private and public. Facebook's founder Mark Zuckerberg naturally sees this in a positive light – he thinks that people's public and private faces should be one and the same. That is a fair point, but the larger question in the hyperlinked, connected world is to what degree a person can be said to exist if their actions and thoughts are not frequently updated online. If the self is not always on show, *is* there a self? Such thoughts validate McLuhan's claim that the new media environment changes everything: self, family, society.

One of his points is that the technology of each age induces ways of thinking and conditioned responses in people, responses that become incompatible in a subsequent age. New technologies do not merely wreck the old commercial order, they render *mindsets* useless too. In the face of the new, we hark back to the old. It is only "the artist, the poet and the sleuth" who are willing to tell things as they really are.

The world of work

McLuhan also calls time on the conventional idea of "jobs," which were an outgrowth of the industrial era's mechanization and specialization and in which people were reduced to cogs in a machine. In the new world, he says:

"fragmented job patterns tend to blend once more into involving and demanding roles or forms of work that more and more resemble teaching, learning, and 'human' service, in the older sense of dedicated loyalty."

This sounds very much like today's increasingly freelance, "consultant," "expert" economy, in which people create dedicated followings for their ideas or products, and in which their highest offering is guidance or training for others who would like to do the same (e.g., write, cook, be an online marketer). All of this happens outside corporations and the usual organizational structures – another case of the medium (the internet) dictating the changes.

Politics

The media environment also changes politics in a fundamental way. Where once there was a "public" consisting of many separate and distinct viewpoints, this has been replaced by an "audience" that gives instant feedback to any political decision. Through television and other media, we can see what is going on in real time anywhere in the world and react to it. Emotions are sprayed across our screens and one person's plight might be felt by millions.

Almost universal access to these media forms has another effect:

"In an electric information environment, minority groups can no longer be contained – ignored. Too many people know too much about each other. Our new environment compels commitment and participation. We have become irrevocably involved with, and responsible for, each other."

This point about minority groups becoming the mainstream was picked up by Noam Chomsky. If they have access to information and can express their points of view using the media, they can exert the same power as a mainstream political party or a large corporation.

Final comments

McLuhan was wrong on some things. He believed that in the information age cities – monuments to the railway – would become less important, museum-like places, not where people lived and worked. For a time he seemed to be right, as people fled from cities into the suburbs, but the new fashionableness of city living has emerged out of a desire for real experience (the possibility of chance meetings, access to live music, and so on), not only the virtual. Generally, though, it is astonishing how someone who died in 1980 could have so well foreshadowed how we live now.

McLuhan notes that before the invention of printing, authorship of a book was secondary to the information it contained. It was only after Gutenberg that "literary fame and the habit of considering intellectual effort as private property" came to the fore. Yet he also says, "As new technologies come into play, people are less and less convinced of the importance of self-expression. Teamwork succeeds private effort." Does Wikipedia come to mind? Though the fame of individual authors has not altered, McLuhan was essentially right in his feeling that collaboration and the text itself would rise back to prominence.

According to his reasoning, online social media applications like Twitter and Facebook do not simply assist revolutions, they are at the heart of them. More than merely connecting people who would otherwise have remained unconnected, they actually change the weight of power toward the people. Whereas some commentators have tried to downplay the role of social media, McLuhan would likely have argued that this is a reaction of the old guard. The new applications *are* the message, and they will continue to transform the world.

Near the end of the book is a spread of the front page of the *New York Times* from September 1965, the day after the great electrical failure that plunged the city into darkness. McLuhan notes that "were [the blackout] to have continued for half a year, there would be no doubt how electric technology shapes, works over, alters – massages – every instant of our lives." And this was in 1965, when plenty of people did not even have televisions. Zoom forward to the present and imagine if the internet ceased to work for six months – would we live in the same world? Would we be the same people?

Marshall McLuhan

McLuhan was born in 1911. His mother was a Baptist schoolteacher who later became an actress, and his father had a real estate business in Edmonton, Canada.

McLuhan attended the University of Manitoba, earning his MA in English in 1934, and in the same year was accepted as an undergraduate at the University of Cambridge. In 1936 he returned to Canada for a job as a teaching assistant at the University of Wisconsin. In the early 1950s, he began the Communication and Culture seminars, funded by the Ford Foundation, at the University of Toronto. During this period his reputation grew, and in 1963 the university created the Centre for Culture and Technology, which he would head until 1979.

His first major work, The Mechanical Bride *(1951), was an examination of the effect of advertising on society and culture. McLuhan pointed out that the means of communication itself creates an impact, regardless of what is being said, instead of the commonly accepted attitude that the content of a message is more important than its form. His other key books are* Understanding Media *(1964) and* War and Peace in the Global Village *(1968). He died in 1980.*

The Myths We Live By

"Myths are not lies. Nor are they detached stories. They are imaginative patterns, networks of powerful symbols that suggest particular ways of interpreting the world. They shape its meaning. For instance, machine imagery, which began to pervade our thought in the seventeenth century, is still potent today. We still often tend to see ourselves, and the living things around us, as pieces of clockwork: items of a kind that we ourselves could make, and might decide to remake if it suits us better. Hence the confident language of 'genetic engineering' and 'the building-blocks of life'."

In a nutshell

Science is not the end of knowledge, but simply one way of approaching it.

In a similar vein

Isaiah Berlin *The Hedgehog and the Fox* (p 56)
Michel Foucault *The Order of Things* (p 112)
Iris Murdoch *The Sovereignty of Good* (p 212)

CHAPTER 31

Mary Midgley

I n the last few decades, evolutionary biologists such as Richard Dawkins and Daniel Dennett have captured the public's imagination with their ideas about "selfish genes" as the source of human action, and "memes" (a sort of social gene) as the maker of culture. Because the ideas are "scientific," and we live in a scientific age, this way of seeing humanity has gone surprisingly unchallenged.

One of the voices of dissent has been Mary Midgley, a non-academic philosopher. At a time when Dawkins, Dennett and their ilk were achieving fame, her *Evolution as a Religion* (1985) compared them to prophets selling a new religion. Though never anti-science per se, her gripe is with science held up as salvation for all human ills, and the reduction of everything to scientific terminology. These are the themes of *The Myths We Live By*, a collection of short essays and an excellent introduction to her thinking.

Not slaves to science

In a scientific and technological culture, how we see our lives becomes expressed in scientific and technological terms. While on one hand we see science as "value free: objective, unbiased, neutral, a pure source of facts," we also make it the source of our values, because we see it as the only thing that can truly explain everything – in the same way that religion once appeared to explain everything. A scientific culture assumes that the best way to understand anything is to break things down to their smallest parts; truth lies at the other end of a microscope, and any idea of a larger whole is suspect. Midgley writes:

> *"Our dominant technology shapes our symbolism and thereby our metaphysics, our view about what is real ... Just as in times past people bowed down to wood and stone, today it is silicon, plastic, steel and glass that shape our truths."*

One of our overriding modern myths is evolution, but not as Darwin intended it. His theory of adaptation has become metaphysics, and it is promulgated with missionary zeal in order to replace all other metaphysical concepts. (Think, for example, of those "Darwin" bumper stickers on cars which mimic the fish symbol used by Christians). As modern people we think we are just sorting facts, but any kind of fact is seen through the prism of beliefs – and the scientific way of seeing the universe is just as much a mythology as other ones. Science is not just a huge storehouse of facts, but must be viewed from certain angles, organized and adapted for our understanding.

It is possible to be very thankful for science and what it has given us, yet refrain from a total and slavish adaption of its imagery and symbols. We don't need science to take over areas that involve human judgements and values, such as the ethical, historical or linguistic. Marxism and behaviourism are examples of human theories that borrowed scientific ideology, yet we now see both with more realistic eyes. Midgley suggests an alternative way of seeing science:

> *"Lovers of physical science can be happy to see it as it is, as one great department of human thought among others which all cooperate in our efforts at understanding the world. This is a far more honourable status than that of a nineteenth-century political power trying to enlarge its empire by universal conquest."*

Midgley herself is not religious, but rejects the idea that things such as art, poetry, God, history and nature can simply be declared "dead," or cultural concepts be reduced to "memes" that fight for supremacy. All these things are important; they are fundamental structures we use for perceiving and shaping our lives.

Rejecting science as an absolute

Midgely quotes Rudolf Carnap, the Positivist philosopher: "When we say that scientific knowledge is unlimited, we mean that there is no question whose answer is in principle unattainable by science." Today, scientists have an equal hubris. Stephen Hawking claimed, for instance, that "philosophy is dead" because it does not rest on science.

But as Midgley points out, "science" in this context is not just the store-house of facts about the universe; it is an ideology which says that the scientific way is the *only* approach to dealing with the world's problems. Science is not seen simply as correct information, but "a moral signpost that could take the place of religion." Some scientific thinkers, such as Dawkins, do not see themselves as the furnishers of neutral facts, but as promoters of a particular world view.

But science doesn't give us everything. It doesn't provide "good laws, effective administrators, honest and intelligent politicians, good new customs to replace old ones." And might not history and anthropology provide us with some understanding? Science can certainly make our world much better, but it doesn't replace values and judgements. We expect technology to bring us a clean, new world, and when it doesn't happen we can see that these things cannot be a moral or spiritual project; we still have to rely on ourselves – to *use* science to bring such a world into being – not take it uncritically as an absolute.

From the eighteenth century on, Midgley argues, many scientific "prophets" turned against religion, particularly Christianity, pointing out that it had not transformed the world as was claimed, and so should be replaced by science. But then we saw in the Russian Revolution how this worked in practice: "State atheism turned out to be every bit as convenient an excuse for crime and folly as state religion had been."

Science and religion can only be seen as adversaries when they are caricatured, or if either are held up as the answer to everything. They are not; both have their place, and only a place.

Let's be scientific

Midgley discusses the work of the behaviourists B.F. Skinner and J.B. Watson, who believed that psychology could only be scientific if it took motivation, thoughts and feelings out of the equation, and looked only at visible behaviour. Yet by dismissing subjectivity, they ended up with pat theories (like parents shouldn't hug or kiss their children) that helped no one, and could even cause damage. Their focus on "objectivity" ended up turning people into things.

You are seen as "scientific," Midgely notes, if you talk in terms of quantities and not qualities. As long as you count or measure something you are considered objective, even if the *interpretation* of the data is oh-so human. The other way to be appear scientific is to use metaphors of the human as machine. Most commonly, the brain is a "computer." We have become so used to this mechanistic terminology that many people accept is as fact, not metaphor. Yet mechanistic models of the universe can prove to be ill-founded. We once thought of the universe running like clockwork, only to replace this view with a much more complex understanding involving space–time relativity. Now, the talk is of even more complex extra dimensions, nonlocality and multiple universes. However, the hope for a "theory of everything," even if it exists, may never be explicable by theoretical physics itself. Indeed, as the physicist Paul Davies points out, if physics wants to be seen as a universal discipline, it must account for *consciousness*, or the connection between the mental and the physical world. And most likely, this means going beyond physics itself.

Midgley argues that objectivity is just one direction in which thought can move, and subjectivity is the other. Neither cancel each other out, as Descartes thought, but can have equal validity in our world:

"... increased objectivity is not always a virtue, nor is it always useful for explanation. A dentist or psychiatrist who decides to become more objective by ignoring the pain of his patients will not thereby become more skilled or more successful in his profession."

The fashionable reductive view puts folk wisdom and stories at the bottom of a linear sequence of truth, and physics at the top. The former are "soft," the latter "hard," and the general metaphor is *building* towards truth. But what if the construction metaphor is wrong, another example of our hubris? What if it is more accurate to say that truth is about interaction with our world and growth in appreciation and awareness, instead of a movement "up"?

Midgley also highlights the dangers of reductionism. Can boiling everything down to a single cause (for Nietzsche, it was the "will to power," for Dawkins, it is "selfish genes") ever give us a realistic understanding of reality? The universe is surely a lot more complex than we know.

The abuse of Darwin

In a chapter titled 'The sleep of reason produces monsters', Midgley notes how seventeenth-century philosophy involved an attempt to collapse all of reality into one "system" that would seek to explain everything, as in the ideas of Descartes and Spinoza. More open-minded thinkers like Hume, Locke and Kant knew that the "subject matter" – us – was "far more radically complex ... than supposed."

Yet contemporary philosophers like Daniel Dennett hark back to the seventh century in their belief in uniformity; for Dennett, for instance, everything must be seen in terms of the theory of natural selection, which is a "universal acid ... it eats through just about every traditional concept and leaves in its wake a revolutionised world view, with most of the old landmarks still recognisable, but transformed in fundamental ways." He is not satisfied to have Darwin explain the natural world; language, art, religion and ethics also fall under its spell. In this, Midgley argues, Dennett is more akin to the grandiose claims made by Herbert Spencer than Darwin himself. Darwin "understood that large ideas do indeed become dangerous if they are inflated beyond their proper use." He emphasized in his autobiography that his theory was only intended for biology, and even then not as a cover-all explanation; natural selection was only one means of modification. Darwin rued the fact that his ideas had been misrepresented and inflated beyond their original intention.

Final comments

Midgley makes clear that she isn't attacking science, rather defending it against "dangerous misconstructions," a kind of scientific imperialism that will not rest until it has conquered everything. The scientific fundamentalists of today may well become tomorrow's "communists" – that is, people who once fervently believed in a single approach to all the world's problems, yet who found the world to actually be more complex than they imagined.

The wish to put science at the centre of our politics and ethics is a wish for purity, but human nature is messy and eludes simple solutions. We should use science all we can to make life better, but to accept it as our *only* philosophy brings the danger of seeing the world as one of competing objects. We should remember that we are people.

Mary Midgley

Born in 1919 to an Anglican minister father and Jewish mother, Midgley displayed a keen interest in philosophy in her school years, reading Plato. At Somerville College at Oxford University she took the advanced humanities course and became friends with Iris Murdoch.

After graduating with honours, Midgley worked in the civil service for the Ministry of Production, a common choice for women college graduates during the Second World War. She taught at Downe School and Bedford School before working for the philosopher Gilbert Murray at Oxford. She began her career as a lecturer at Reading University and moved to Newcastle University, where she taught philosophy.

Midgley was married to the late Geoffrey Midgley, and they had three children. She did not publish her first books until her fifties. The first was Beast and Man: The Roots of Human Nature *(1978), followed by* Heart and Mind: The Varieties of Moral Experience *(1981),* Animals And Why They Matter *(1983),* Wickedness *(1984),* Evolution as a Religion *(1985) and* Science and Poetry *(1994). There is a memoir,* The Owl of Minerva: A Memoir *(2001).*

Midgley enjoyed friendships with some of Britain's famous women philosophers including Elizabeth Anscombe, Philippa Foot and Mary Warnock, who were at Oxford around the same time. She died in 2018.

On Liberty

"The only freedom which deserves the name, is that of pursuing our own good in our own way, so long as we do not attempt to deprive others of theirs, or impede their efforts to obtain it."

"[T]he individual is not accountable to society for his actions, in so far as these concern the interests of no person but himself. Advice, instruction, persuasion, and avoidance by other people, if thought necessary by them for their own good, are the only measures by which society can justifiably express its dislike or disapprobation of his conduct."

"In proportion to the development of his individuality, each person becomes more valuable to himself, and is therefore capable of being more valuable to others."

In a nutshell

Unless a person's actions cause direct harm to others, they must be allowed. The priority in any open society must be freedom, not policies that purport to be for people's own good.

In a similar vein

Jeremy Bentham *Principles of Morals and Legislation* (p 50)
John Rawls *A Theory of Justice* (p 246)

CHAPTER 32

John Stuart Mill

hat is the correct balance between personal freedom and state control? Writing in 1859, John Stuart Mill described this as "the question of the future," and his thoughts remain vital reading on the matter. At the start of *On Liberty*, his most famous work, Mill complains that "owing to the absence of any recognized general principles, liberty is often granted where it should be withheld, as well as withheld where it should be granted." He sought to redress such confusion, and the book became a political counterpart to Adam Smith's *Wealth of Nations* in outlining the rightful extent of individual freedom and the bounds of government.

Mill's father James was a disciple of Jeremy Bentham and John was groomed to lead the Utilitarians. However, by the time Mill was 30 both his father and Bentham were dead, and he was free to find his own philosophical way. At 35 he became friends with Harriet Taylor, and he considered *On Liberty* to be a "joint production" with her. Her influence on his other famous essay, *The Subjection of Women* (1869), is also clear. Their intense yet chaste romance ultimately resulted in marriage, though only after Taylor's merchant husband had died.

What is the connection between the Mills' ideas on personal freedom and political liberty? The book reasons that liberty allows for the flowering of the individual, but results in a whole society fulfilling its potential, since all questions are open for debate and therefore advances – both social and scientific – can more easily happen. Ultimately, every aspect of life benefits from greater liberty.

Genuine freedom

At the time Mill was writing, he admitted that quite a few countries could be described as democratic, yet this structure of government was no guarantee of real liberty, because those in power became a class removed from the people. Moreover, a popularly elected government could still oppress some group within the society – known as the "tyranny of the majority." This, he felt, could be an even worse kind of rule than regular political oppression, because it becomes a social tyranny, forcing a "right" way of acting onto everyone. In saying this, Mill perfectly presages twentieth-century communist states, in which those who did not conform to the new social norms had to be "reeducated." Such regimes, he notes, focus on enslavement not of the body, but of the mind and soul.

In a democratic society, the vital question is where the limit should be placed between a need for social control, and the freedom of the individual to think and believe as they wish. The rule of the majority does not establish any kind of universal morality; it is, rather, the expression of the likes and dislikes of the ascendant class. Mill notes that religious freedom only became enacted when multiple minority groups, knowing that they could never be dominant, fought for the principle of religious freedom in law. Humans are by nature intolerant, therefore a policy or law of tolerance comes into being only when there are so many competing beliefs that no group is willing for another to become dominant.

All of this leads Mill to his famous criterion or principle for ensuring freedom, the avoidance of harm:

> *"The only purpose for which power can be rightfully exercised over any member of a civilized community, against his will, is to prevent harm to others. His own good, either physical or moral, is not a sufficient warrant. He cannot rightfully be compelled to do or forbear because it will be better for him to do so, because it will make him happier, because, in the opinions of others, to do so would be wise, or even right."*

A government or dominant body in society cannot impose a law on people merely because it is considered "for their own good." Rather, freedom is to be seen in a negative sense: unless a citizen's action is shown to be demonstrably bad for others, he or she should be allowed to do it. "In the part which merely concerns himself, his independence is, of right, absolute," Mill says. "Over himself, over his own body and mind, the individual is sovereign."

Specific freedoms

Mill outlines the areas of individual liberty that should be assumed to be a basic right as long as they involve no harm to others:

* Freedom of conscience.
* Freedom of thought and feeling, including "opinion and sentiment on all subjects, practical or speculative, scientific, moral, or theological."
* Freedom to publish those opinions.
* Freedom of tastes and pursuits, or "framing the plan of our life to suit our own character," even if others should think our conduct "foolish, perverse, or wrong."
* Freedom to associate with whom we want, and to unite people behind a particular purpose.

Mill notes that even in the Britain of the 1850s, people were being sent to jail for professing no belief in God, and furthermore those same people had no right of redress in relation to crimes committed against them. Believing differently to what was socially accepted put a person outside the law.

The stupidity of regulating thought and belief is witnessed in the persecution of Socrates and Jesus, Mill says, who now are held up as two of history's greatest figures. If every age sees that people who were considered "bad" are now "good," they must perceive that current opinion is usually flawed. Whenever there has existed in history a society or nation that has held some principles beyond dispute, or prevented discussion of some big question, Mill observes, "we cannot hope to find that generally high scale of mental activity which has made some periods of history so remarkable." A nation becomes great not by a mere imposition of order and power, but by letting go, knowing that there is much to gain by open discussion. Indeed, this is what frees the best minds to come up with the greatest advances.

Individuality as the basis of a good society

Mill argues that "pagan self-assertion" is as valid as "Christian self-denial" in terms of personal development. A person becomes more valuable to society in direct proportion to the flowering of their individuality: "The initiation of all wise or noble things, comes and must come from individuals; generally at first from some one individual."

Mill writes that the amount of eccentricity in a nation will mirror the "genius, mental vigour and moral courage" contained within it. Victorian Britain became famous for a set of values, but it was also known as a land of eccentrics. He notes that people are just like plants: they differ greatly in the conditions needed for their flourishing. Europe's success, he ventures, is the result of its fostering or acceptance of individuality, in contrast to the Chinese or Japanese outlook, which is that everyone should conform.

Mill was writing at a time when Mormonism was new (rather like the Scientology of its day) and people wanted to ban it because of its allowance of polygamy, which one writer called "a retrograde step in civilization." Notwithstanding Mill's own dislike of the religion, he writes, "I am not aware that any community has a right to force another to be civilized." If the rest of society is not directly hurt by it, there is no grounds for a law against it. He frames the issue this way:

"No person ought to be punished simply for being drunk; but a soldier or a policeman should be punished for being drunk on duty.

Whenever, in short, there is a definite damage, or a definite risk of damage, either to an individual or to the public, the case is taken out of the province of liberty, and placed in that of morality or law."

However, such damage has to be overt and clear. If it is not, people should be left to follow their beliefs, life projects, causes, and interests without hindrance.

Applying the principles

Mill includes a long section on questions of government policy arising from his principles. For instance, while noting that in a free society one cannot really defend a ban on prostitution or gambling – people should be free to fornicate or gamble as far as their conscience allows – "should a person be free to be a pimp, or to keep a gambling-house?" Mill does not give a clear answer on this, but generally he repeats that government's role is not to enact laws for people's "own good," only to prevent direct harm; if people want to drink or gamble (with all the downsides), that is their choice. Government can play a role in preventing harm, however, through taxation and licensing, and Mill approves of taxing alcohol to make people likely to drink less. He also supports the state requiring people who wish to marry to prove that they have sufficient resources to have children, to prevent babies coming into the world who face a wretched life because of poverty.

Today, behavioral economics and psychology offer ways of achieving socially useful outcomes without reducing personal freedoms. In their book *Nudge* (2008), Cass Sunstein and Richard Thaler outline "liberal paternalism," a way for governments to influence people's decisions without actually forcing them to do anything. For instance, organ donation forms can assume that a person holding a driver's license will donate in the event that they are killed, unless they specifically opt out. This simple change can dramatically affect the number of organs that become available in a country, saving hundreds of lives a year. Yet there is no regulation involved, simply a tinkering of the "choice architecture," as the authors describe it.

Final comments

Mill noted the natural human disposition (whether in rulers or fellow citizens) to want to impose our will on others. This results in the tendency for government power to increase and individual freedoms to be eroded, unless it is monitored and held in check. Yet this fact, and its warning of government creep, did not mean that governments had no legitimacy, as some of today's extreme libertarians believe. The Harvard philosopher Robert Nozick outlined in his classic *Anarchy, State and Utopia* (1974) a vision of government's core role: protection of life and property, and the enforcement of contracts. Anything beyond this would involve the diminution of rights and freedoms.

While it might be thought that Mill's heirs are today's libertarians, Mill was never an extremist, and was much more in the commonsense mold of Adam Smith; though both warned against the creep of government into every area of society and economy, neither denied or questioned that government did play an important role. The accurate way to see Mill is as a great beacon of progressive politics. The progressive principle, he writes, "whether as the love of liberty or of improvement, is antagonistic to the sway of Custom, involving at least emancipation from that yoke; and the contest between the two constitutes the chief interest of the history of mankind."

Though both left and right have claimed Mill as their own, his expression of what freedom means is beyond the various shades of politics. *On Liberty* is best seen as a manifesto for an open society.

John Stuart Mill

Born in 1806 in London, Mill had a famously intensive education thanks to his Benthamite father James. Largely excluded from play with other children, he learned Greek at 3 and Latin at 8; by 12 he was well versed in logic, and at 16 he was writing on economic matters.

After further studies in France in history, law, and philosophy, while still in his teens Mill began a career at the East India Company, where his father had a senior position. He served in the Company until the Mutiny of 1857, when he retired as a Chief Examiner. Concurrently with his bureaucratic career he started the Utilitarian Society, which met in Bentham's house, and with Bentham also established (in 1825) University College, London. Mill was an editor and contributor of the Westminster Review *and other magazines. His activism in social reform led to an arrest for handing out birth-control information to London's poor.*

Mill was elected to parliament in 1865, and campaigned for women's right to vote and other liberal issues. His large body of writings covers logic, economics, religion, metaphysics, epistemology, current affairs, and social and political philosophy. Titles include A System of Logic *(1843),* Principles of Political Economy *(1848),* Three Essays on Religion *(1874), and his* Autobiography *(1873). Mill's* Utilitarianism *(1863) refined the Benthamite philosophy and kept it influential for a new generation.*

In 1872 Mill became godfather to his friend Lord Amberley's second son, Bertrand Russell. He died the following year in Avignon, France.

Essays

"So, reader, I am myself the substance of my book, and there is no reason why you should waste your leisure on so frivolous and unrewarding a subject. Farewell then, from Montaigne, this first day of March, 1580."

"Let the man who is in search of knowledge fish for it where it lies; there is nothing that I lay less claim to. These are my fancies, in which I make no attempt to convey information about things, only about myself."

"We are all convention; convention carries us away, and we neglect the substance of things ... We have taught ladies to blush at the mere mention of things they are not in the least afraid to do. We dare not call our parts by their right names, but are not afraid to use them for every sort of debauchery ... Convention forbids us to express in words things that are lawful and natural; and we obey it. Reason forbids us to do what is unlawful or wicked, and no one obeys it."

In a nutshell

Most forms of knowledge are a conceit; it is a big enough task trying to know something of ourselves.

In a similar vein

René Descartes *Meditations on First Philosophy* (p 94)
Iris Murdoch *The Sovereignty of Good* (p 212)
Blaise Pascal *Pensées* (p 224)
Nassim Nicholas Taleb *The Black Swan* (p 306)

CHAPTER 33

Michel de Montaigne

W hen Michel de Montaigne was 42, which he considered to be the start of old age, he had a medal made with *Que sçais-je?* (What do I know?) inscribed on one side.

Though he lived in an age of emerging science, he was no scientist himself, but a man of letters and a country gentleman, and he fell back on himself in his quest for knowledge. If I do have any knowledge or opinions, he wondered, what are they based on? What is this thing I call my "self"? Am I merely a flurry of passing emotions and thoughts, or something more substantial?

Montaigne used the word *essai*, meaning "trial," to test out what seemed to be true, about both the world and himself. His collection of essays is a sort of autobiography, but he is at pains that it not be a self-glorifying one; the tone of the *Essays* is more curiosity than anything else. In a prefacing letter, he notes:

> *"Had it been my purpose to seek the world's favour, I should have put on finer clothes, and presented myself in a studied attitude. But I want to appear in my simple, natural, and everyday dress, without strain or artifice."*

Indeed, the *Essays* often read like a catalogue of his deficiencies. For the first few years of his life Montaigne was steeped in Latin, and the book is littered with quotes from his heroes Virgil, Ovid, Seneca, Plutarch, Cicero, Cato, and Catullus. He does not reference them to show his learning, but rather, he says, uses their virtues "as a cloak for my weakness."

His quirky subjects include "On smells," "On the affection of fathers for their children," "On the custom of wearing clothes," "On the power of the imagination," "On three kinds of relationships," and "On cannibals." Here we look at a handful of essays that seem to encapsulate Montaigne's worldview, which influenced William Shakespeare, Blaise Pascal, Ralph Waldo Emerson, and Friedrich Nietzsche, among others.

Human weakness and vanity
The longest of the essays, "On presumption," is arguably the best and can be summed up in this sentence:

"It is my opinion that the nurse and mother of the falsest opinions, both public and private, is the excessive opinion that man has of himself."

Montaigne is no great fan of scientists, or at least not their air of certainty: "Those people who bestraddle the epicycle of Mercury and see so far into the heavens make me grind my teeth." With his own study of humankind telling him that we are often wrong on even the most basic of matters, Montaigne wonders why we should give so much credence to those who "set out the causes of the rise and fall of the Nile." If we so repeatedly lack self-knowledge, he argues, why should our "facts" about the universe be considered reliable?

Montaigne confesses that nothing he has written has satisfied him, and that other people's good opinions are no compensation. He is hopeless at telling entertaining stories, or small talk, and bad at giving speeches or making arguments. His prose is simple and dry, with none of the arts of Plato or Xenophon. He is short in stature, which he considers a drawback for those who try to hold high positions, because "a fine presence and dignity is lacking." Other skill gaps include tennis, wrestling, and control of animals. Of his work ethic he says: "I am extremely idle and extremely independent both by nature and by intention. I would as willingly lend my blood as my pains." He discusses his poor memory ("It takes me three hours to learn three lines"), which means that he can never remember his servants' names. Among further defects are "a slow and lazy mind," which allows him to understand only the most simple of plays and games, and blurred eyesight when he reads too much. Despite having been left a country estate to manage, he admits that he is hopeless with finance, cannot tell one grain from another, and only a month before he had been caught out not knowing that yeast is needed to make bread.

Overall, Montaigne writes,

"I think it would be difficult for any man to have a poorer opinion of himself, or indeed to have a poorer opinion of me, than I have of myself ... I plead guilty to the meanest and most ordinary of failings; I neither disown nor excuse them."

Yet in fully admitting the range and extent of his ignorance and defects, he hopes to be able to reveal some things about himself that are true, noting that "whatever I make myself out to be, provided that I show myself as I am, I am fulfilling my purpose."

All that he is finally left with is his own judgment, or reason. Perhaps surprisingly, Montaigne seems to have had a high regard for this faculty in himself, but also admits it as a source of vanity: "We readily recognize in others a superiority in courage, physical strength, experience, agility or beauty. But a superior judgment we concede to nobody." Our "vainglory" has two sides, he observes, "the over-estimation of ourselves, and the under-estimation of others."

Enough with the masks

Boldness of action is considered to be "manly," so we know that Montaigne is laying himself bare when he admits his indecisiveness. He recalls Petrarch's honest remark: "Neither yes nor no rings clearly in my heart." He is good at defending points of view, but has trouble developing opinions of his own, with the result that decisions might just as well be made by the throw of a dice: "So I am only fitted for following, and easily allow myself to be carried along by the crowd. I have not sufficient confidence in my own abilities to set up as a commander or guide; I am very pleased to find my path marked out by others."

The result of this furtiveness is that Montaigne is skeptical when others make claims for certainty and absolute truth. This relates not only to scientists, but to philosophers, and here he sums up his motivation for the *Essays*:

"It is a cowardly and servile characteristic, to go about in disguise, concealed behind a mask, without the courage to show oneself as one is ... A generous heart should never disguise its thoughts, but willingly reveal its inmost depths. It is either all good, or all human."

As William James notes in *Pragmatism*, the claim of philosophers to be offering objective theories is weak, because a philosophy is usually merely someone's character writ large. Montaigne also understood that so-called objective science and philosophy were often just a projection of human minds, and trying to keep one's personal view hidden meant that one had something to hide.

In political life, Montaigne is critical of Machiavelli's idea that one needs to become a master of trickery and falsehood to succeed; what tends to happen is that an initial gain made for the wrong reasons will be followed by a stream of losses. Instead, he quotes Cicero: "Nothing is as popular as goodness." Montaigne would rather be seen as a tactless bore who says what is on his mind than someone who schemes, lies, and flatters.

The mystery of the self

In the use of our minds, Montaigne says, we "have usually more need of lead than wings." Our normal state is constant desire and agitation, so we must bring ourselves down to earth and see the way that things actually are. Meditation or contemplation is perhaps best in this regard, which he describes as "a rich and powerful method of study for anyone who knows how to examine his mind, and to employ it vigorously."

The "chief talent" of humans is their adaptability and flexibility. Just as life itself is unequal and irregular, so it is madness to stick to our rigid habits of mind, which lead us to become a slave to ourselves. "The best minds," Montaigne says, "are those that are the most various and supple."

The *Essays* continually evoke the transitory and unreliable nature of this thing we call the "self." In "On books," Montaigne dismisses the idea that a person grows in knowledge and wisdom as they get older and becomes "all of a piece":

> *"I may have some objective knowledge one day, or may perhaps have had it in the past when I happened to light on passages that explained things. But I have forgotten it all; for though I am a man of reading, I am one who retains nothing."*

All he can do, Montaigne says, is say what he appears to know at any given moment. In any case, he does not even want to know everything. It is more important to him to live pleasantly and without great labor. When he reads, it is only for entertainment; or if the tome is more serious, it must show him a clearer way to self-knowledge, or how to live and die well.

Montaigne contradicts himself in various places, though this is not necessarily a sign of weakness. As Walt Whitman would say several centuries later, "I am large, I contain multitudes," and those selves will see things differently at different times.

Final comments

In the absence of a carefully worked-out worldview, some have suggested that Montaigne was not a philosopher at all. However, his aversion to big philosophical or theological systems actually made him a philosopher of a very modern type, questioning the scientific and religious certainties of his day. On the issue of free will, for instance, he casts aside church dogma to take the position of the Stoics that we are part of a completed universe. In his essay "On repentance," he wonders why repenting of anything makes sense: "Your mind cannot, by wish or thought, alter the smallest part without upsetting the whole order of things, both past and future."

With this outlook, it made sense that Montaigne could not take himself too seriously, and in doing so he avoided the lies that most people tell themselves. He contrasts two philosophers, Democritus and Heraclitus. The former was known for his mocking and wry view of human life, while the latter was known as the weeping philosopher, so deep were his pity and compassion for the human condition. Montaigne sides with Democritus, because man is so worthy of derision, as a vessel not of sin or misery, but simply of folly. "We are not so full of evil," he remarks, "as of inanity."

Yet skepticism and fatalism are no excuse for a dissolute life, and through avoiding passions and extremes ("Restraint" was inscribed on the other side of his medal), Montaigne freed himself up for contemplation and meditation, practices that he felt revealed something about himself, others, and the world. One of the many amusing lines in the book is: "It is good to be born in very depraved times; for, compared with others, you gain a reputation for virtue at a small cost."

While Montaigne noted the Roman satirist Persius' remark "No man attempts to descend into himself," by doing exactly this he created a template for a more personal kind of philosophy. Anyone writing an autobiography would do well to read him; they will learn that it is less interesting to record "how I did it" than "what it has been like to be me" – that is, a person living in this time and this place with these limitations and this potential.

Montaigne

Michel de Montaigne was born in 1533, the son of a Dordogne landowner and his Sephardic Jewish wife. He received an excellent education, knowing Latin by 7, and in his teens studied at the Universities of Bordeaux and Toulouse. He practiced law and was a counselor at the Bordeaux parliament, where he met his mentor Etienne de la Boetie, and for a time worked at the court of Charles IX.

In 1570 Montaigne moved back to the family estate in Perigord, which he had inherited, and minimized his obligations so that he could focus on study; for the next nine years he spent his time reading, writing, and thinking. His library was in a circular tower above his estate buildings, so that he could see what was going on without getting too involved. He wrote: "Miserable, to my mind, is the man who has no place in his house where he can be alone, where he can privately attend to his needs, where he can conceal himself!"

After journeying around Europe from one spa to another seeking a cure for his often painful gallstones, Montaigne was recalled home when elected (against his will) as Mayor of Bordeaux, a position once held by his father. He served for two terms.

His marriage was arranged, and his wife is barely mentioned in the Essays. *Late in life he adopted as his daughter Marie de Gournay, a young woman who had come to know him through his writings. He died of a tonsil abscess in 1592.*

The Sovereignty of Good

"We need a moral philosophy in which the concept of love, so rarely mentioned now by philosophers, can once again be made central."

"[W]hat is at stake here is the liberation of morality, and of philosophy as a study of human nature, from the domination of science: or rather from the domination of inexact ideas of science which haunt philosophers and other thinkers."

"'Self-knowledge', in the sense of a minute understanding of one's own machinery, seems to me, except at a fairly simple level, usually a delusion ... Self is as hard to see justly as other things, and when clear vision has been achieved, self is a correspondingly smaller and less interesting object."

In a nutshell

The efforts we make to improve ourselves morally
are real and important.

In a similar vein

Immanuel Kant *Critique of Pure Reason* (p 148)
Plato *The Republic* (p 230)
Ludwig Wittgenstein *Philosophical Investigations* (p 312)

CHAPTER 34

Iris Murdoch

Better known as a novelist (*Time* magazine included *Under the Net* as one of the top 100 books of the twentieth century), Iris Murdoch also wrote two important works of philosophy, *Metaphysics as Morals* and *The Sovereignty of Good*. The latter was written when existentialism was very much in vogue and seemed to be the intellectual heir of Western philosophy.

Yet Murdoch describes existentialism as "an unrealistic and over-optimistic doctrine and the purveyor of certain false values." She also rejects fashionable behaviorism and utilitarianism because of their focus on external results, instead suggesting that the development of inner qualities, if a less obvious project, is just as valuable.

The book's title relates to Plato's notion of Good, a formless reality or order that underlies the universe, of which humans can only have glimpses, yet which they nevertheless spend their lives pursuing in usually unconscious ways. Though modern philosophers have debunked it with relish, Murdoch believed Good to be the central concept in moral philosophy (and indeed in life itself, even in a universe that does not appear to have any meaning).

The points below loosely follow the organization of *The Sovereignty of Good*, which consists of three chapters originally composed as articles or lectures.

The idea of perfection

"For all our frailty the command 'be perfect' has sense for us. The concept of Good resists collapse into the selfish empirical consciousness."

Murdoch begins with a discussion of the philosopher G.E. Moore, who believed that Good had a reality beyond personal experience, and that goodness was a real component of the world. Later philosophers convincingly refuted this idea, suggesting that goodness had no objective reality but simply depended on the individual's perception. According to this view, "Good must be thought of, not as part of the world, but as a moveable label affixed to the world."

Murdoch draws a picture of the "typical man" represented by modern moral philosophy: this person has clarity of intention; is self-willing, knowing what they are doing and what they want; they are focused on results and public acts; and their mental life is essentially without value. Finally, because their will is sovereign, they have responsibility for their actions. Murdoch calls this image "existentialist-behaviourist-utilitarian": existential because it emphasizes the primacy of the will as the sole means of causality in an otherwise meaningless universe, and behaviorist and utilitarian in its focus on outcomes and action, as opposed to the inner person.

Murdoch notes Wittgenstein's observation that because inner thoughts have no internal checking procedure, whatever "seems" to us to be is irrelevant. His analogy of the mind in relation to action is that "a wheel that can be turned though nothing else moves is not part of the mechanism." As beliefs, feelings, and thoughts have no test of accuracy, all that matters is our actions, and all kinds of abstract visions of goodness are thus suspicious, or valueless.

Murdoch also notes the view of moral philosopher Stuart Hampshire that "anything which is to count as a definite reality must be open to several observers." All such ideas are wrong, she counters. Consider the example of a mother-in-law who works to change the opinion she has of her son's new wife, challenging her own prejudices in order to see her daughter-in-law in a more correct or loving light. It is this kind of struggle, so clearly portrayed in literature, that surely *is* real, whether it can be objectively observed or not. It is an inner moral act of freedom, whose aim is clear perception. This attempt to take the "highest view" of another person involves a progress toward perfection, and this very idea of perfecting oneself in a moral sense is surely basic to being human, and central to moral philosophy.

Morality is not science

Murdoch points out that the whole vocabulary of empiricism "is blunt and crude when applied to the human individual." While psychoanalysis was meant to be the objective "science" that laid bare the history of an individual, Murdoch is skeptical of the idea that a psychoanalyst can be a scientific observer and judge. (Time has of course proved her correct: psychoanalysis is now considered so subjective that it lies outside the bounds of mainstream therapeutic treatment.) Her alternative view of the individual rests on this observation:

> *"Moral concepts do not move about within a hard world set up by science and logic. They set up, for different purposes, a different world."*

She argues that moral terms can be treated as concrete and universal, even though moral language involves a reality that is "infinitely more complex and various than that of science." While the language used to describe moral reality is "often unavoidably idiosyncratic and inaccessible," it is "infinitely more complex and various than that of science" and can still be treated as concrete and universal.

Moreover, it is a mistake to put "science" in one basket and "culture" in another, for science is a part of our culture. "We are men and we are moral agents before we are scientists," Murdoch says, "and the place of science in human life must be discussed in *words*." This is why it will always be more important to know about Shakespeare before we know about a particular scientist. Literature is the lens through which we can see and understand all human efforts, moral or scientific.

In place of willing, seeing

Both existentialism and humanism Murdoch views as hollow creeds: the former believes too much in the self and nothing else, and the latter asks people to live according to an "everyday reasonableness" from which any kind of moral gravitas is absent. The individual becomes either "an isolated principle of will" or "a lump of being which has been handed over to other disciplines, such as psychology or sociology." Such philosophies of self-assertion are wrapped up in a kind of "pseudo-scientific determinism" and, although they promote some good values – freedom, rationality, responsibility, self-awareness, sincerity, common sense – "There is of course no mention of sin, and no mention of love."

In the world of Wittgenstein's *Tractatus*, Murdoch notes, moral judgments had no place because nothing of factual value could be said about them. With other philosophers, moral judgments were simply seen as "emotion." In the existentialist view, a person is a lonely "will" in a sea of physical facts. Though there is no moral vision of life, the upside is a freedom to act. Yet Murdoch considers this view unrealistic and simplistic. The reality is that a person's morality is a very real and consequential project that spans a lifetime:

"Moral change and moral achievement are slow; we are not free in the sense of being able suddenly to alter ourselves since we cannot suddenly alter what we can see and ergo what we desire and are compelled by."

The opposite view to this is to see ourselves as beings presented with an infinity of choices, willing a life course into being. Murdoch clearly sees this as an inferior way to live. Her alternative is a kind of "necessity" that saints and artists know well; that is, "a patient, loving regard, directed upon a person, a thing, a situation," which is not so much a case of conscious will but of *obedience*. This attention takes place over many years, in fact is lifelong, and lessens the importance of single acts of decision. If our attention is on a person, for instance, over a long time, "at crucial moments of choice most of the business of choosing is already over." Willing is not conscious resolve, but rather being true to what one *loves* or *sees*.

This view allows for the greatness of art, which the existentialist-behaviorist model sees as a mere indulgent by-product of human irrationality. In Plato's opinion, beauty and art are part of the same thing; the act of being open to see beauty is selfless, and so is in itself moral. What is Good, what is Real, and Love are closely connected for Murdoch. Where one gives one's attention is found one's morality. In looking with love, we find what is real or true or good.

What art makes us see

"Art pierces the veil and gives sense to the notion of a reality which lies beyond appearance; it exhibits virtue in its true guise in the context of death and chance."

Murdoch openly assumes that human beings are selfish, and that there is no external end or point in any divine sense of our existence. Rather, we are "transient mortal creatures subject to necessity and chance." She does not believe in a God, but neither does she deify reason, science, or history. In the post-Kantian age, the freedom, will, and power of the individual are everything, a position taken to its extreme in the moral philosophy of Nietzsche. Yet what do we do with this responsibility?

Murdoch's answer is that life must be about how we can make ourselves better, and part of this project is reducing the size of our ego so that we can see others and the world clearly. The most obvious way to "unselfing" is appreciation of beauty and truth: in nature, art, and literature. We may be brooding over some affront, gazing absentmindedly out the window, when we see a kestrel in flight and suddenly we forget ourselves. Good art, not the type that simply aims to console by providing fantasy, "affords us a pure delight in the independent existence of what is excellent." In a world that seems "chancy and incomplete," beauty, goodness and love are the only things that have meaning. Furthermore, contrary to common belief, art and literature are not about the artist or writer; rather, for them to be good, the creator's self must be taken *out* of the equation.

Final comments

"Freedom," Murdoch writes, "is not an inconsequential chucking of one's weight about, it is the disciplined overcoming of self. Humility is not a peculiar habit of self-effacement ... it is selfless respect for reality." Her prescription is to look away from the self toward Good, as the man in Plato's allegory of the cave looked toward the sun. This movement is also away from the particularity, variety, and randomness of the world.

One of the implications is that the quest for self-knowledge is somewhat of a delusion. Even if we are to find this elusive self and see it correctly, we may find it to be a "smaller and less interesting object" than we had imagined. It is much more valuable to go beyond the personal, using our attention and love to try to see the world and people in their true light.

The elevation of the will, or the power of decision, by the behaviourist-existentialist school is a mistake, because only "Good, not will, is transcendent," Murdoch says. While will is the "natural energy of the psyche" that can be put toward good ends, Good reveals things as they really are. There is no comparison in terms of power: will is part of the person, Good is a universal. Therefore, she says, "what should be aimed at is goodness, and not freedom or right action." Having said this, "right action, and freedom in the sense of humility, are the natural products of attention to the Good." In other words, seek the good first, and everything else worthwhile will come to you naturally. Seek only to have muscular will, and that is all you will have.

Iris Murdoch

Born in 1919, as a child Murdoch was passionate about animals, singing, and reading. She excelled at the coeducational Froebel Demonstration School in London and Bristol's Badminton Girls' School. She read Plato and Sophocles in preparation for Oxford University, and was accepted to Somerville College, where she befriended Mary Midgley (see The Myths We Live By, *Chapter 31). At Oxford she was influenced by Marxism and subsequently joined the Communist party.*

Murdoch had a variety of relationships and lovers, including the poet Frank Thompson, military historian and soldier Michael Foot, and Nobel laureate Elias Canetti. She married John Bayley, an Oxford English scholar, in 1956. The couple lived in London and Oxford and remained childless so that Iris could focus on her writing. Other key works include A Severed Head *(1961),* The Unicorn *(1963), and* The Sea, the Sea *(1978), which won her the Booker Prize. Philosophical works include* Sartre: Romantic Rationalist *(1953),* The Fire and the Sun *(1977), and* Metaphysics as a Guide to Morals *(1992).*

Murdoch was diagnosed with Alzheimer's disease in 1996, and died in Oxford at 79. A biography, Iris Murdoch: A Life *by Peter Conradi, inspired the 2001 film* Iris, *starring Judi Dench as Murdoch.*

Beyond Good and Evil

"Psychologists should bethink themselves before putting down the instinct of self-preservation as the cardinal instinct of an organic being. A living thing seeks above all to discharge its strength – life itself is Will to Power; self-preservation is only one of the indirect and most frequent results thereof."

"The falseness of an opinion is not for us any objection to it: it is here, perhaps, that our new language sounds most strangely. The question is, how far an opinion is life-furthering, life-preserving, species-preserving."

In a nutshell

Human beings have a natural and healthy urge to be creative and powerful, and morality only suppresses and distorts this.

In a similar vein

Martin Heidegger *Being and Time* (p 130)
Niccolò Machiavelli *The Prince* (p 182)
Arthur Schopenhauer *The World as Will and Representation* (p 280)

CHAPTER 35

Friedrich Nietzsche

Friedrich Nietzsche saw the history of philosophy as an expression of the "will to Truth," yet this obsession with truth was simply an arbitrary prejudice. Why are philosophers not as interested in *un*truth or *un*certainty, he wondered?

As he writes in *Beyond Good and Evil*, "In spite of all the value which may belong to the true, the positive and the unselfish, it might be possible that a higher and more fundamental value for life should generally be assigned to pretence, to the will to delusion, to selfishness and cupidity." Perhaps good and evil are more knitted together than we think, though (in the interests of purity) we like to see them as separate.

Good and evil are a creation of humankind: "There is no such thing as moral phenomena, but only a moral interpretation of phenomena." And if this is so, it frees us to live according to our natural wish to be more, have more, do more, not worrying too much about others. Selfishness, including evasion, distrust, and a love of dissembling and irony, Nietzsche says, is a sign of health – it is the people who are always after some pure and objective absolute (whether in religion or philosophy) who are the sick ones.

While the common reaction to reading Nietzsche is shock, there are few philosophers who can be more entertaining, or who carry the potential to really change your view of things. The list of people he influenced is long, and includes Sigmund Freud, Rainer Maria Rilke, Thomas Mann, Heidegger, W.B. Yeats, Sartre, and Foucault. Among contemporary philosophers, Nassim Nicholas Taleb and Slavoj Žižek, though very different in their content, borrow some of their free-flowing, idiosyncratic, subjective style from Nietzsche. His startling originality and emotion-charged, nontechnical prose could not be more different to today's dry, overspecialized academic writings.

After a promising early start (he became a philosophy professor at only 24), illness and a truly independent spirit saw Nietzsche fall outside the mainstream, and his dismissal of philosophy as an objective science allowed him to write in a brilliantly personal and often mad style. Though in *Beyond Good and Evil* some of the people or events he mentions are of his time and not so relevant to today, generally his insights – including how to view science and religion – seem very fresh.

Why "truth" in the first place?

Philosophers make an assumption that "the certain is worth more than the uncertain, that illusion is less valuable than 'truth,'" but such valuations, Nietzsche says, may only be superficial, necessary to a sense of self and part of our need to create a feeling of certainty for our very survival. We want to generate logical fictions in order to understand reality. He further argues that what most people see as conscious thinking is in fact mere instinct. We think much less than we would like to believe.

Philosophers too, though they see themselves as independent minds creating new systems of cold, objective logic, are most of the time merely spouting who and what they are; they are not machines generating truth, but rather defenders of a prejudice. Kant, for instance, fashioned the guise of a scientific philosopher to convey his moralistic "categorical imperative," but Nietzsche sees him as just another in a long line of "old moralists and ethical preachers." And Spinoza's wish to make his philosophy seem more scientific led him to clad it in a "hocus-pocus" mathematical format. In sum, philosophers are not lovers of wisdom, but lovers of *their* wisdom. At the heart of each of their worldviews is a moral position, and "knowledge" is the costume in which it is dressed. Yet Nietzsche admits that he is not the first to suggest such a thing; Epicurus, a down-to-earth ex-slave, also pointed out the grandiosity and vanity of philosophers such as Plato who presented apparently "self-evident" truths.

The will to power, and free will

Nietzsche thought that psychologists were wrong in saying that the strongest instinct in living things was for self-preservation or survival. Rather, their chief aim is to *discharge their strength*. This is his famous Will to Power (a concept in part derived from Schopenhauer's "Will"). In short, we want to keep living not for its own sake, but so that we can express our powers.

Given this, what Nietzsche has to say about free will is perhaps surprising, summed up in the statement:

"I shall never tire of emphasising a small, terse fact, namely, that a thought comes when 'it' wishes, and not when 'I' wish."

The idea of a self-willing ego is an assumption; it is more accurate to speak of things that "one" does rather than "I," because we are a complex of sensation, emotion, and thinking. The "strangest thing about the will," Nietzsche says, is that it is a mechanism that both gives orders and accepts them. We identify ourselves with the order-giver (what we call "I"), but in reality our body is "a social structure composed of many souls." We believe that our decisions are the basis of our success, but this is like assuming that the ruler of a land is alone responsible for outcomes, forgetting all the other factors involved. We are neither totally in control of what happens nor totally irresponsible. The truth lies in between, and the belief in pure free will, or what Nietzsche calls "intention-morality," should be put in the same category as astrology or alchemy.

But how do Nietzsche's thoughts on free will square with the Will to Power, and indeed his concept of the *Übermensch* ("superman"), the sovereign actor who is free of all the usual moral conventions and ways of seeing? The answer is that Nietzsche believes that people think too much, when they should give free rein to their instinctive Will to create and dominate. The idea of free will is a Christian nicety based on a belief in the sanctity of every soul, when in fact a human is better seen as a higher animal that grasps what it wants from life. The nature of the *Übermensch* is not contemplating or rationalizing, but energetic doing and creating.

Science, philosophy, and the true philosopher

Nietzsche enjoys pointing out the hubris and insolence of science as claiming to be the only discipline that matters in the modern age, replacing both philosophy and religion. Philosophy is the "master-task," he asserts, supreme among all areas of learning. He despairs over modern philosophy's relinquishing of its noble role, specializing as a mere "theory of knowledge," for instance; and he is not surprised that the average person sees philosophy as having a rather downbeat face, while the countenance of science is happy and confident, claiming to be the measure of all things. In fact, he says, science explains little; it is merely a way of arranging the world according to human perception.

Nietzsche notes that it would be dangerous, revolutionary, for a modern philosopher to say that he is not a skeptic. The philosopher prefers instead to say that he knows nothing, or that nothing can be known. Yet skepticism is a "pleasing, lulling poppy" that comforts the user and makes him feel part of his world. This outlook comes about, Nietzsche says, through the person being an amalgam of different races and classes, in which nothing is stable and everything is relative. Everything is thought through, and nothing is done through pure Will. "Objectivity" and the "scientific spirit" are simply expressions of paralysis of the Will, a disease that spreads wherever civilization lasts longest. Nietzsche distinguishes between "philosophical workers" and "scientific men," on the one hand, and real philosophers on the other. Among philosophical workers he includes Kant and Hegel, who have sought to identify values and truths and put them in some order. But Nietzsche's real philosopher is a "commander and law-giver," a creator whose motto is "Thus *shall* it be!"

The conventional view of the philosopher is that he or she is wise, prudent, and lives apart from normal life. But Nietzsche draws an alternative picture: "the *genuine* philosopher ... lives 'unphilosophically' and 'unwisely', above all 'imprudently', and feels the obligation and burden of a hundred attempts and temptations of life – he risks *himself* constantly, he plays *this* bad game." Real philosophers should be "the bad conscience" of their time and culture, their job to apply a "vivisector's knife to the breast of the very virtues of their age."

In asking the question "Is greatness *possible*, nowadays?" Nietzsche must contend with the nature of modern society, which he says is "a general war against everything rare, strange, and privileged, against the higher man, the higher soul, the higher duty, the higher responsibility, the creative plenipotence and lordliness." Above all, the modern person seeks a life free from fear or pain. This is a sad dereliction of our potential. Instead, we should be throwing ourselves into life at whatever risk, without getting permission for anything.

Slave morality and master morality

There is a natural hierarchy to humankind, a kind of natural justice. The "noble soul," Nietzsche says, does not like to look above for anything; it looks forward, or down, because "he knows that he is on a height." Nietzsche admits that this is the opposite of what many moralities and religions suggest – that we are fulfilled when we make ourselves *smaller* than others. This to him seems like fakery. Modern education and culture are about deception, trying to exalt the plebeian and mediocre at the cost of a true aristocracy of spirit.

Nietzsche despised democracy and notions of "equality of rights" and "sympathy with all sufferers," because he believed that this attempt to level the playing field robbed people of the conditions that could make them great. Oppression, poverty, violence, and severity of every kind carried the opportunity of making the mediocre into something substantial, as it called on their inventive powers, daring, and spirit.

He called Christianity a "slave morality" because it emphasized "the sacrifice of all freedom, all pride, all self-confidence of spirit" and made the believer into a self-deriding shadow of what they could be. However, he admires the Old Testament as a great work of divine justice.

Morality was designed to make human beings seem simple and intelligible; if there are common rules, then we can all be judged the same way. But if we look beyond the usual categories of "good" and "evil," we can see people in their true light: having a natural belief in and reverence for themselves. And when people have to answer to us, this is as it should be. Rather than being some flight of vanity, power over others is simply a sign of the "noble soul."

Final comments

Nietzsche's disavowal of the traditional philosophical project – the search for fundamental truths – had a big influence on existentialism and also the deconstructionist philosophies. Unfortunately, his aversion to the "blending of races," as well as his disavowal of traditional morality and democratic ideals, made him ripe to be taken up by Nazi ideology (though he was not an anti-Semite). Given the many horrible events of the twentieth century, Nietzsche's attitude to many matters now seems naïve, but perhaps because he was so little read in his lifetime, he clearly felt he had nothing to lose by putting his philosophical explosives under the bed of Europe.

The book has two sections of aphorisms, where can be found gems such as "Insanity in individuals is something rare – but in groups, parties, nations and epochs it is the rule" and "The thought of suicide gets one through many a bad night." Nietzsche had little luck with women and therefore disdained them, but his aphorisms contain some interesting observations on relationships, including "In revenge and in love woman is more barbarous than man." But just when one has come to the view that he is a little too hard-edged or even nasty, there is this: "What is done out of love always takes place beyond good and evil." Love transcends any classifications of morality. It is neither good nor bad but just is – that is its power. Nietzsche's wish to go beyond opposites is little different to the concept of "duality" in Eastern religions, in which light and dark, good and bad are mental constructions. Ultimately, everything just "is" and requires no labels.

Friedrich Nietzsche

Nietzsche was born in Röcken, Prussia in 1844. His father (who died when Nietzsche was 5) and grandfather had been Lutheran ministers. He attended a boarding school in Pforta, then studied classical philology at the University of Bonn. The young Nietzsche was considered so brilliant that at only 24 he was made a professor at the University of Basle. After a stint as a medical orderly in the Franco-Prussian War, he wrote The Birth of Tragedy.

Dogged by ill health, he had to resign from his professorship and thereafter lived on a modest pension in a series of rented rooms around Europe. In 1889 he suffered a mental breakdown (perhaps brought on by syphilis or depression) and was thereafter nursed by his mother, then his sister, until his death in 1900.

Major works include Human All-too-Human *(1878),* The Gay Science *(1882),* Thus Spake Zarathustra *(1883–85),* On the Genealogy of Morality *(1887),* Twilight of the Idols *(1888),* The Antichrist *(1888), and the auto-biographical* Ecce Homo *(1888).*

Pensées

"Let us weigh the gain and the loss in wagering that God is. Let us estimate these two chances. If you gain, you gain all; if you lose, you lose nothing. Wager, then, without hesitation that He is."

"The only thing that consoles us for our miseries is diversion, and yet this is the greatest of our miseries. For it is mainly what prevents us from thinking about ourselves ... diversion amuses us and guides us imperceptibly towards death."

"For after all what is man in nature? A nothing in relation to infinity, all in relation to nothing, a central point between nothing and all and infinitely far from understanding either ... He is equally incapable of seeing the nothingness out of which he was drawn and the infinite in which he is engulfed."

In a nutshell

As we have little to lose by a belief in a higher power, and plenty to gain if it is true, it is rational that we believe.

In a similar vein

Thomas Aquinas *Summa Theologica* (p 16)
René Descartes *Meditations on First Philosophy* (p 94)
Søren Kierkegaard *Fear and Trembling* (p 154)
Gottfried Leibniz *Theodicy* (p 170)
Michel de Montaigne *Essays* (p 206)

CHAPTER 36

Blaise Pascal

B laise Pascal possessed a great scientific mind. After building 50 proto-
types he invented the mechanical calculator, the Pascaline, which inspired Leibniz to build his own. Through correspondence with Fermat
Pascal developed probability, and he had brilliant insights in the philosophy
of mathematics. He invented the hydraulic press and the syringe, and showed
clearly how mercury barometers work. Pascal's law relates to a unit of pressure, and his famous wager is appreciated as a seminal contribution to game
theory, probability, and decision theory. The Pascal computer programming
language is named after him.

How did this staunch defender of the scientific method come to be so
intense a defender of spiritual faith?

When Pascal died, a note was found sewn into his coat. It recorded
a mystical experience on November 23, 1654, after which he gave up his
work in mathematics and science and devoted himself to matters of spirit
and philosophy. In a short but busy life, Pascal had already in his twenties
converted to a more intense form of Christianity (Jansenism, under the
influence of his sister Jacqueline), but ill health in his thirties prompted him
further to questions of human beings' place in the universe.

In private, he wrote reams of notes that he aimed to work into an apology
for Christianity, and after his death these *Pensées* (thoughts) were put into
some order by his family. In a time of growing skepticism toward established religion, Pascal felt it his mission to address the nonchalant, irreverent
worldview of Montaigne, on the one hand, and the overly rational stance of
figures like Descartes, who had died only ten years before the *Pensées* was
compiled. He wished to show the reader that both skepticism and the resignation to fate that Stoic philosophy offered lead to directionless misery. His
answer to both was simple faith. However, because people in his time increasingly sought a rational basis for their beliefs, he hatched the idea of a wager
that would put the benefits of religion beyond doubt.

Pascal's wager

*"If you gain, you gain all; if you lose, you lose nothing. Wager, then,
without hesitation that He is."*

Pascal drew on his mastery of probability and mathematics to create his wager. He starts with the question of whether God exists. This is something for which reason can never provide an answer; indeed, something it cannot confirm either way. Yet he asks us to wager that it is true. Surely, he reasons, we would be mad not to take a chance in a game in which there was potentially so much to gain ("an eternity of life and happiness") and so little to lose (a belief proved wrong).

Noting that wagering for the existence of God is likely to make you act in accordance with your belief – that is, to be a better person who is convinced of God's love – Pascal goes on to ask:

"Now, what harm will befall you in taking this side? You will be faithful, honest, humble, grateful, generous, a sincere friend, truthful. Certainly you will not have those poisonous pleasures, glory and luxury; but will you not have others? I will tell you that you will thereby gain in this life, and that, at each step you take on this road, you will see so great certainty of gain, so much nothingness in what you risk, that you will at last recognise that you have wagered for something certain and infinite, for which you have given nothing."

This may sound attractive, the nonbeliever may say, but still there is nothing *certain* in it. That is right, Pascal says, we cannot be absolutely certain, but then the outcomes of battles and sea voyages are never certain either, and we cannot know whether we will still be alive tomorrow. However, is it not wise to make a small bet on something with shortish odds, which if it is true will deliver huge benefits? For himself, he says,

"I would have far more fear of being mistaken, and of finding that the Christian religion was true, than of not being mistaken in believing it true."

We can apply Pascal's wager without believing that there is a God as such. Rather, we can bet that there exists some form of absolute or universal truth, and that this truth is positive. If we see its effects in our life and community, it is quite rational to make it central to our existence.

The downside of doubt

Pascal foresaw that in a secular age, the default position for most people would not be "I have no reason to believe, so I don't." He understood doubt, because he had seen enough things to suggest that there was no God. But he also came to the view that life could not be explained satisfactorily on a purely physical plane. In a section titled "The misery of man without God," Pascal asserts that only by giving ourselves up totally to a higher power can we find peace, truth, and happiness. Not doing so brings despair, darkness, confusion, and error. Answering those who ask why, if God is real, he is not more evident, Pascal retorts, "Instead of complaining that God has hidden himself, you will thank him for revealing so much of himself."

He notes that there are only three kinds of people:

"Those who serve God, having found Him; others who are occupied in seeking Him, not having found Him; while the remainder live without seeking Him, and without having found Him. The first are reasonable and happy, the last are foolish and unhappy; those between are unhappy and reasonable."

For Pascal, lack of faith was a kind of laziness, a view summed up by T.S. Eliot in his introduction to the *Pensées*:

"The majority of mankind is lazy-minded, incurious, absorbed in vanities, and tepid in emotion, and is therefore incapable of either much doubt or much faith; and when the ordinary man calls himself a sceptic or an unbeliever, that is ordinarily a simple pose, cloaking a disinclination to think anything out to a conclusion."

To go beyond doubt was in Pascal's mind a great human achievement. Humble people believe cheerfully, in contrast to others "who have sufficient understanding to see the truth, whatever they may have against it." This is his pointed challenge to the "smart" people of his time to think through their beliefs instead of falling into a lazy, ironic doubting of everything.

Overcoming our vanity

Despite his opposition to Montaigne, Pascal was nevertheless highly influenced by his fellow Frenchman's ironic, "I give up" view of human nature. We assume an air of certainty, reasonableness, and knowledge, but humanity's general condition, Pascal writes, is "Inconstancy, boredom, anxiety," and, above all, vanity. If you cannot see just how vain the world is, he said, then you must be very vain yourself.

He observes, "We have such a lofty view of man's soul that we cannot bear being despised and not esteemed by some soul. And all the happiness of men consists in this esteem." People do crazy things for love, or rather to be loved, and this action frequently "disturbs the whole earth, princes, armies, the entire world." Pascal makes a famous remark about the face of an Egyptian ruler: "Cleopatra's nose: had it been shorter, the whole face of the earth would have been changed." Minor things (the beauty of one woman, for instance) can be the point on which history turns.

The scholarly Pascal observes the folly of people spending their precious days "chasing a ball or a hare." It is not the object that matters, but the chase itself, because people go to extraordinary lengths to avoid thinking properly about themselves. He offers an alternative recipe for happiness:

> *"To bid a man live quietly is to bid him live happily ... in which he can think at leisure without finding therein a cause of distress."*

This thought is sometimes rendered as, "All man's miseries come from not being able to sit alone in a room." We are miserable unless we are diverted, but diversion, while it amuses us, is all the time guiding us "imperceptibly towards death." In truth, our best moments are those spent examining our motives and our purpose, since they correct wrong action and open us up to divine order, truth, and intention.

Yet Pascal notes that humans are potentially great because we can recognize our own wretchedness, something a dog or a tree cannot do. From our concupiscence (our natural lust for people and things) we have somehow, nevertheless, managed to draw a moral order:

> *"Man must not think he is on a level with either beasts or angels, and he must not be ignorant of those levels, but should know both."*

Believing that we are simply smart animals debases us, but neither can we say that we are purely spiritual beings. The goal of life is to accept the fact of the body and our natural inclinations, and still recognize our divine origins.

Final comments

The *Pensées* includes Pascal's well-known distinction between the mathematical and the intuitive mind, the *esprit de géométrie* and the *esprit de finesse*. The problem with someone of the mathematical mind is that, because they are used to knowing clear and unchallenged principles, they do not trust intuitive knowledge. They can only talk in terms of definitions and axioms, but as a result of this narrow and over-exacting mindset they miss out on other kinds of knowing. (For Pascal, Descartes was a good example of such a mind.) Intuitive principles – the laws of life, if you like – are "felt rather than seen," and "there is the greatest difficulty in making them felt by those who do not of themselves perceive them." Yet they are real nonetheless.

This, then, is how Pascal bridges the scientific and spiritual worldviews at the level of the person: we should nurture our intuition or metaphysical sense, which saves much time in making our way in the world, taking us to the heart of things, yet also be open to accepting abstract principles appreciated through reason.

Perhaps the most famous line in the *Pensées* is "*Le cœur a ses raisons que la raison ne connaît point,*" usually translated as "The heart has its reasons, which reason knows nothing of." Though the phrase is often appropriated to explain the actions of those in love, Pascal's meaning was more general. We should not doubt when we can use our reasoning powers, and when we can use rational human judgment then we should do so. However, the highest kind of reasoning admits that there are matters where reason stops, submitting to a different order of reality.

Pascal, scientist and mathematician, wanted passionately to know all there was to know of the world, but was wise enough to admit that not everything could be known. God seems to want both from us: the highest use of our reason to act and create in the world, and acceptance that we are "spiritual beings having a human experience." On the biggest questions we need ultimately to submit to a greater intelligence, to which our "heart" provides a link.

Blaise Pascal

Pascal was born in 1623 in Clermont, France. His mother died when he was 3 and his father Etienne moved the family, including two sisters, to Paris. Pascal was precociously bright and attended meetings on mathematics and philosophical matters with his father. When he was 17 the family moved again to Rouen, where Etienne was made tax commissioner. To assist him in tax calculations, Pascal invented his mechanical calculators.

In his twenties Pascal and his saintly sister Jacqueline converted to Jansenism, a stricter form of Christianity, and became affiliated with the monastery of Port-Royal. Two years after his mystical experience he published his religious and political polemics the "Provincial Letters" to defend Jansenism against attack by the Jesuits. In the same year he saw his niece Marguerite miraculously healed of a lachrymal fistula at Port-Royal.

Pascal died in 1662, at only 39. The cause of his death is uncertain, but was probably tuberculosis or stomach cancer.

The Republic

"[The form of the Good is] the universal author of all things beautiful and right, parent of light and of the lord of light in this visible world, and the immediate source of reason and truth in the intellectual … this is the power upon which he who would act rationally either in public or private life must have his eye fixed."

"Until kings are philosophers, or philosophers are kings, cities will never cease from ill: no, nor the human race; nor will our ideal polity ever come into being."

"The State in which the rulers are most reluctant to govern is always the best and most quietly governed, and the State in which they are most eager, the worst."

In a nutshell

What you believe to be true may be only a poor and distorted reflection of reality. Philosophy opens the door to higher knowledge, which can be used to serve your state and community.

In a similar vein

CHAPTER 37

Plato

Plato came from an aristocratic family that had long played its part in the Athenian state. Though we don't know much about his early life, it is said that he had an initial love for poetry before his teacher Socrates guided him toward philosophy. The major event of his early life was the death of Socrates (in 399 BC), whose awkward questions had become a threat to the Athenian establishment. Plato was present immediately before his teacher's demise, and would later write accounts of his trial, final days in a prison cell, and death, in the *Apology, Crito*, and *Phaedo*.

After Socrates' death, Plato traveled widely across Greece, Italy, and Egypt, spending time with the philosopher Eucleides and Pythagorean thinkers. In his forties, he returned to Athens and founded his famous academy, which became the center of intellectual life in the city, pushing the boundaries of philosophy, mathematics, and science.

Before Socrates died Plato had made a couple of attempts to enter politics, first after Athens' defeat in the Peloponnesian War, and a year later when democracy was restored. But the experience disillusioned him regarding political life, and he concluded that change could only come through a totally new approach to government. *The Republic* is his outline of an ideal state, but also carries his theory of justice, his explanation of the "three parts of the soul," and his famous allegory of the cave.

Despite being one of the great works of Western philosophy it is a relatively easy read, requiring no special knowledge, and is one of the best expressions of the Socratic method; that is, questions and answers designed to lead the reader to inescapable conclusions. Across 10 books, Plato describes how Socrates responded with powerful logic to the questions and counter-arguments of a cast of characters including Glaucon and Adeimantus, older brothers of Plato, Polemarchus, whose home in Piraeus (the port of Athens) is where the dialogue takes place, his father Cephalus, a city elder, and Thrasymachus, an orator.

Allegory of the cave
While much of *The Republic* is an expression of what Plato had learned from Socrates, his theory of forms, or essential ideas, is his own. It is best expressed in his allegory of the cave. Though ostensibly unconnected to Plato's theory

of justice and government, the allegory provides its metaphysical heart and carries a timeless message.

Socrates has his friends imagine a group of people living in a cave that has only a small opening to the light of the outside world. They have spent their whole lives in the cave, chained in such a way that they can only see the walls, and cannot turn around to see the light. Behind them is a perpetual fire, and between the fire and the walls walks a parade of people carrying various things, including models of animals, whose shadow is cast onto the wall in front of the prisoners. The chained people can only ever see the shadows of this procession and their own shadows, ensuring that "reality" is for them a two-dimensional film of shadows, never the original forms that cast them.

Then, someone comes to release one of the prisoners from their bondage. Rather than the prisoner being delighted to see that what they had perceived was just a projection, the sudden shift in perception is too much. The prisoner is dazzled by the light of the fire before being brought out of the cave and shown the sun, which appears horribly bright and pains his eyes. Yet in time the prisoner comes to appreciate that the sun is the real light of the world and the source of all perception. He pities his fellow prisoners back in the cave, who still believe that what they dimly see is "reality."

When the prisoner returns to the cave and cannot see so well in the dark any more, his fellow captives contend that his journey into the light was a waste of time that only damaged his eyes. They cannot comprehend that his world has changed for ever, and he himself cannot imagine going back to his former life in which mere appearances count for truth.

Here Plato is using the sun as a metaphor for the Form of the Good, and stressing the fact that appreciation of the Good is not arrived at easily. Elsewhere, he describes the journey out of the cave as a movement from "becoming" to "being," from conditional to absolute reality – from the worldly experience of being human to the pure light of reality.

The rewards of being just

The book actually begins with Plato's discussion of the meaning of justice. Cephalus argues that justice is simply telling the truth and making sure that one's debts are paid. He will die a comparatively rich man, and says that one of the benefits of wealth is that one can die in peace, knowing that all accounts are settled. But, Socrates asks, is there not something more to truth and a good life than that?

Glaucon and Adeimantus make a case for *in*justice, saying that we can live to suit ourselves and escape criticism, even prosper. Glaucon grants that justice is good in itself, but challenges Socrates to show how justice can be good at an individual level. He mentions the story of Gyges and his magical ring, which gave him the power to make himself invisible at will; Gyges, naturally enough, employed the ring to do things that he could not get away with if he were visible. People only act justly when they fear they will be caught, Glaucon suggests, and have no interest in being good for its own sake.

Socrates replies that acting justly is not an optional extra, but the axis around which human existence must turn; life is meaningless if it lacks wellintentioned action. And while justice is an absolute necessity for the individual, it is also the central plank of a good state.

The three parts of the soul

Plato divides the human soul into three parts: reason, spirit, and desire. Reason is the overseer of the soul and seeks the best overall outcomes; it gives us the ability to make decisions and provides our conscience. Spirit generates ambition and enterprise, but also gives rise to feelings like anger, pride, and shame. Desire is simply the basic urges for food, sleep, and sex. The individual becomes just when spirit and desire are not given free rein, but shaped and guided by reason, which in turn is influenced by knowledge of the Good, a basic universal form. Thus we achieve balance, and our actions are naturally in harmony with the world around us.

Plato has Socrates retell the myth of Er, a man whom the gods allowed to see what happens to souls between lives. Er discovered that souls were often swayed by the chance of being rich or famous in their next life, while failing to choose on the basis of whether a life was *just* or not. Those who made the most progress over many lifetimes naturally chose the just way. The message? Always seeking to do the right thing is the eternal route to a happy and fulfilled life. Plato thus presents his final nail in the coffin of the idea that justice is a noble but impractical notion. In fact, it is the *only* route to the good life.

Only a "philosopher" can develop the right balance between the parts of the soul, says Socrates. The philosopher's chief desire is for the world to be as good as it possibly can, and to help achieve this he is willing to forgo what he might naturally desire. Those who have knowledge of absolute truths, and who are psychologically and spiritually in balance, have a duty to serve the rest of society who lack these things. This is the link between Plato's theory of justice and the bulk of *The Republic*, which outlines his vision for an ideal state.

The ideal state

Plato goes through the failings of types of government in his time – timarchy, oligarchy, and tyranny – but his real focus is Athenian democracy. This was a popular assembly of free male citizens who met regularly to vote on specific issues, and who devolved administration to a Council of Five Hundred. Plato's problem with this kind of direct democracy is that complex issues relating to foreign policy or economics, for instance, become subject to the irrational whim of the voting bloc on any given day. Moreover, since membership of the Council was limited to a year, and no citizen could be a member more than twice, there was little strategic or long-term thinking. Athenian leaders gained power by telling voters what they wanted to hear, when they should have been charting a plan for the health of the state. The result was "a pleasing, lawless, various sort of government, distributing equality to equals and unequals alike."

Plato's alternative is an elite governing body of philosophers whose sole purpose is to work for the good of the state. Brilliant, highly educated, spiritually advanced, and incorruptible, these individuals would probably rather spend their time in contemplation, considering the eternal forms (of the Good, Beauty, or Truth) that underlie the world of appearances. Instead, they are asked to relinquish their all-knowing state of bliss and choose to return to the prosaic world to govern for the benefit of all.

Plato suggests that we should not expect a nation or state to be run properly by merchants, tradesman, or soldiers, but only by those who have the best general overview of what constitutes the good in society. A society run by soldiers would be always at war and limit freedom to its citizens; a state run by businessmen would course with envy and materialism; and a state run by workers would lack the intellectual breadth and depth to know what good governance is, or properly to manage relations with other states. Only a highly educated generalist, trained over many years in abstract subjects (Socrates suggests 10 years' study of mathematics before moving on to philosophy), can govern well. Practical knowledge of administration is the least of their requirements, the basic condition of superiority and fitness to govern being knowledge of the essential spiritual forms of Justice, the Good, Beauty, and Temperance, which manifest themselves in actual circumstances.

The link that Plato makes between the quality of the state and the quality of the individual, also known as his analogy between the city and the soul, can seem somewhat strange to the modern reader. Today, it is probably more usual to think that the nature or quality of a nation arises from the combined attributes of its citizens, but Plato took the opposite view. He saw the ethics of the state as the driver and shaper of individual action.

Social engineering

A controversial part of *The Republic* is Plato's discussion of the control of culture. He believed that the great poets and stories of his time did not inculcate the right moral values. Rather, education must focus on instilling the idea of the Good. Stories told to children should be censored so that their brains are not filled with negative images. The citizenry should be exposed only to literature that does not glorify lying, lack of self-control, or violence, for these will naturally weaken and corrupt minds, leading to the wrecking of the ship of state. Even worse are stories in which unjust characters are said to be happy, or to win at the cost of the just, or those suggesting that being good is a disadvantage.

Though he may seem overbearing on the cultural front, Plato was remarkably far-sighted when it came to sexual equality. He demonstrates that the estimation of women as weak is usually wrong, and provides a case that women who seem cut out for ruling should receive the same education and have similar opportunities as men. Yet he was hard-hearted when it came to family life, which he did not see as a private domain but rather existing for the benefit of the state. He has Socrates voice a proposal for the regulation of marriage and sex so that the "right" people are brought together. The children of this elite are then looked after in state nurseries, leaving their parents free to devote themselves to government. Plato himself never married, which perhaps says something about his views in this area.

Final comments

Does Plato's template for the just and balanced individual still work for us? In a culture that seems to offer easy routes to every kind of pleasure, and encourages us to express emotions with abandon, his emphasis on allowing reason to be our ruler can seem austere. Yet the fruits of self-discipline and reason are the same for a person today as they were for the individual of ancient Greece. The Republic's power lies not in its provision of a template for government (it is unlikely that we will ever see states run by "philosopher kings"), but in showing how the qualities of wisdom, courage, self-discipline, and justice make for well-balanced individuals. If the three parts of the soul are in harmony, it is good for us personally, for our community, and for the state to which we belong.

Plato's allegory of the cave is a precious reminder that most of us go through life chasing shadows and believing in appearances, when behind the superficial world of the senses awaits a more permanent realm of truth. Plato has Socrates make the case for philosophers being the only ones who can ascertain this truth through their study of the Forms, but in truth every person can get a sense of what is changeless and perfect. Each of us lives in a cave of wrongful perception and illusion, which, if we make the effort, we can leave behind.

The Enneads

"Of men, some enter into life as fragments of the All ...
they are victims of a sort of fascination, and are hardly,
or not at all, themselves: but others ... head towards the Higher ...
preserve still the nobility and the ancient privilege
of the Soul's essential being."

"All our ideas will be determined by a chain of previous causes;
our doings will be determined by those ideas; personal action
becomes a mere word. That we are the agents does not save our
freedom when our action is prescribed by those causes; we have
precisely what belongs to everything that lives, to infants guided by
blind impulses, to lunatics; all these act; why, even fire acts; there is
act in everything that follows the plan of its being, servilely."

"But humanity, in reality, is poised midway between gods and
beasts, and inclines now to the one order, now to the other;
some men grow like to the divine, others to the brute, the greater
number stand neutral."

In a nutshell

The goal of human life is to remind ourselves that
we are part of a perfect and changeless One, and to act in a
way that confirms this truth.

In a similar vein

Thomas Aquinas *Summa Theologica* (p 16)
Isaiah Berlin *The Hedgehog and the Fox* (p 56)
David Bohm *Wholeness and the Implicate Order* (p 62)
Plato *The Republic* (p 230)

CHAPTER 38

Plotinus

Plotinus was the greatest exponent of what modern philosophy calls "Neo-Platonism," the most influential philosophical outlook in late antiquity (roughly the third century AD to the fourth). The Neo-Platonists mainly differ from Plato in their focus on metaphysics. They see humans as a spiritual and earthly entity, and go beyond Plato's strong interest in politics and how to live in society.

Compiled by his student Porphyry, the six "enneads," or books, present Plotinus' idea of human beings as part of the indescribable and divine One, which can be partially glimpsed and understood through contemplation, intuition and reasoning.

The Enneads is a major work of Western metaphysics, and Plotinus is sometimes called the last great pagan philosopher. His thinking was a huge influence on early Christian thinkers including St Augustine and Boethius, and later figures such as Marsilio Ficino.

The constituents of reality

Plato had divided all reality into two realms: the Intelligible (the realm of ideas, a non-physical changeless and timeless reality) and the Sensible (the realm of bodies and matter, experienced by us through the senses). Plotinus took this basic division and expanded on it, laying out the constituents of reality as a hierarchy.

Plotinus saw something called the "One," or Good, sitting at the top of the hierarchy, and underneath it the "Intellect," or Soul. The One is the source of everything, and from it comes the universal mind/Soul/Intellect. At the bottom of the scale is the world of matter and bodies. While the One is a perfect Unity and sufficient unto itself, the world of matter is only a reflection of a higher unity or level of reality, and therefore has no unity or reality of its own. The body and the soul are a microcosm of this: our bodies are simply an expression of the greater unity of our souls.

The modern, scientific view of the universe (expressed through the writings of Hume, for instance) is that only what can be experienced through the senses is real, and there are no metaphysical or spiritual realities. Plotinus, like most thinkers of his era, had completely the opposite view, believing that only the Intelligible world really exists, because it exists independently of anything, and is caused by nothing. The Sensible realm, because it exists only as an expression or mirror of the Intelligible world, is formless, compared to the perfect, timeless and unchanging form of the One. Human beings have a foot in both camps: we are souls belonging to the Intelligible world, but obviously are also part of the Sensible world. The world around us that we call "reality" is in fact just an expression of the real, Intelligible world; it is one big illusion, or at least a poor, chaotic reflection of the Intelligible. Only when a human being is attuned to eternal forms, principles or ideas (represented by the Good or the One) can they be in touch with (capital "R") Reality.

Plotinus' view of time is that it does not really exist, at least not in the Intelligible realm. It only exists in the Sensible, where souls generate a physical world that seems to evolve or develop in stages. But the knowledge or truth found in these stages is, in the Intelligible realm, known all at once. From the perspective of the Intelligible, past, present and future are all one.

'On Beauty', the first treatise of *The Enneads*, was a big influence on art in the Middle Ages and Renaissance, specifically the idea that the multifarious beautiful things in this world are simply the expression of a single, changeless "principle" of Beauty. This idea, which comes from Plato's theory of forms, suggests that things in themselves have no reality, but are only representations or expressions of a higher principle. The principle behind the universe itself is the One; at a lower level the principle behind human lives is the Soul. While Plotinus granted that each person has an individualized soul, we are deluded if we believe too much in our separateness. The wise person realizes that a good life is one in which we shed this illusion and focus instead on our connection to the greater Soul from which all individual souls emanate.

The purpose of life

Plotinus identified three types of soul: the major ("capital S") Soul in the Intelligible realm; individuals souls (animals as well as humans, some which incarnate, some which don't); and a "world-soul." There are also lower souls that inhabit nature and the cosmos itself. But ultimately all souls are derived from the same unity or principle of Soul.

Human souls inhabiting a body remain connected to their source in the Intelligible world, and yet "I" as a person am not aware of everything that is going on with my soul and what it is trying to achieve through me. And though we can't really know anything about the One, by self-surrender and cultivation of ethical virtues we put ourselves on a path that can lead us to experience an "ecstasy" in which our soul unifies with the One. In doing so we are returning ourselves to source.

Plotinus asks, "How we can know our true self?" We cannot know anything of ourselves in isolation (or to put it in contemporary terms, the ego can only give us wrong answers). We receive the right answer only when we willingly return ourselves to the Intelligence from which we sprang. Our natural state as a soul is to be joyful, because we are always part of Intelligence. It is just that as a body we do not always realize it. Plotinus's analogy is that the soul when incarnated is covered in mud, but it is mud which does not penetrate the soul. Through the "purifications" (wisdom, self-control, justice, courage, and contemplation), we rediscover the truth about us that was there from the beginning.

The human soul has a higher part which is unchangeable and divine, and a lower part where the "personality" resides. The lower part is the source of problems, while the higher part redeems us. We tend to believe only in the information that comes through our senses. They seem to provide us with truth about the world, but in fact they simply provide us with images of things, instead of revealing the truth behind appearances. In contrast, identification with our soul or the Intellect is identification with our higher selves. Through philosophy we can learn to be clear about this choice (body/senses vs. soul/Intellect), and it helps us towards a way of life that brings us closer to the One.

Plotinus wonders: how can evil exist in the world, if the One or source which gives rise to it is perfect? His answer is that while the One is perfect "form," the physical world is (paradoxically) "formless." Being by its nature an imperfect and formless expression of truth, the real world is naturally "evil," because the beings in it are ignorant of the One's perfect nature. Matter is far away from the good and perfect unity of the One, and with this distance it is obvious that evil will exist. Yet evil is not concrete or real, it is just a deficiency of good. A person avoids being evil by reminding themselves constantly, through philosophy and contemplation, of the perfection of the One, and resolving to live by principles that make them more attuned to the Intelligible realm.

The goal of human life is simple: to remind ourselves that we part of the perfect and changeless One and its goodness, and to act in a way that confirms this truth. This means identifying fully with that part of ourselves connected to our eternal source, and disidentifying with that part of us which belongs in the world of mere matter, i.e., our bodies.

Happiness and freedom

In the first Ennead, Plotinus discusses *eudaimonia*, or happiness.

He disagrees with the view that happiness is to be found in pleasure, but also rejects the Stoic idea that we find happiness in living a rational life. Instead, Plotinus argues that the only true happiness is found in the Intelligible realm, and our therefore earthly life will be happy or otherwise according to our attunement with the Intelligible. A focus on external forms of happiness is a dead end; it takes us further away from what is eternal and changeless, and by its nature free of any unhappiness.

Plotinus agrees with the Stoics in saying that you don't need happy events or great things to be happy, and neither should adverse events take away your happiness. Because genuine happiness is connected to our attunement with the timeless One, how long we live doesn't affect the level of happiness we reach in life. The real question is whether or not, during a lifetime, we can see what is real or true (the spiritual realm) and distinguish it from what is corruptible and ephemeral (the physical world and the body).

Plotinus also addresses the question of how free human beings can be. Given that we exist in bodies and experience most things through our senses, we do not have access to all levels of truth or fact; therefore, our judgement and decisions will reflect this limited appreciation of reality. However, those who work to identify themselves with what is eternal (or more accurately, to forget the self and melt into the One) naturally make themselves open to perceiving truth. They will therefore will act in the best and most appropriate way, most of the time. Such people are naturally free, and their actions autonomous and spontaneous.

Final comments

The Enneads is a difficult and not especially enjoyable read, but the message itself – that the purpose of life is to attune ourselves to what is changeless and eternal, and in doing so transcend our body and senses – is powerful and uplifting.

Plotinus' impact on early Christian theology we have mentioned. His concept of the One was for the Christians just another way of saying "God," and his emphasis on contemplation and virtues, plus clear separation between the perfection of the One compared with the corruptibility of the body, also gelled with Christian morality. Yet his focus on the eternal and unchangeable, and the idea that the "real" world as we believe it to be is simply a poor reflection of non-physical truth, Intelligence or Mind, is also a mainstay of Buddhist thought.

It is easy to see Plotinus' ideas as fuzzy mysticism, yet his attempt to pare metaphysics back to its essentials was a great enterprise, and he went about it in a rational, secular, and systematic way (as you would expect from a classically trained scholar). Modern science, with its focus on universal, unchanging laws contrasted with the difficulty of isolating the "reality" of particles of matter, may yet bear out Plotinus' implication that the physical world is at base an elaborate set-up that lacks fundamental reality.

What *is* real has no physical form, but can only be intuited in moments of reflection or in the perfection of our virtues. We are not just our bodies, and the purpose of life is to remember that we are part of something much larger that is free of the restrictions of time and space.

Plotinus

Plotinus was born in Egypt, and his approximate dates of birth and death are 205 to 270 AD.

He was 28 by the time he began his formal study of philosophy, under Ammonius, and was under his tutelage for 11 years. To learn more about the philosophy of Persia and India he joined Roman emperor Gordian's campaign in Persia, and was lucky to return in one piece after Gordian's death.

At 40, Plotinus settled in Rome, starting his own philosophy school, and only after a decade there began to write. He is rare among ancient philosophers in that he left a large body of intact work. Plotinus' student and friend Porphyry edited The Enneads, *and wrote a biography,* On the Life of Plotinus and the Order of His Books.

The Logic of Scientific Discovery

"According to my proposal, what characterizes the empirical method is its manner of exposing to falsification, in every conceivable way, the system to be tested. Its aim is not to save the lives of untenable systems but, on the contrary, to select the one which is by comparison the fittest, by exposing them all to the fiercest struggle for survival."

"The old scientific ideal of episteme *– of absolutely certain, demonstrable Knowledge – has proved to be an idol. The demand for scientific objectivity makes it inevitable that every scientific statement must remain* tentative for ever.*"*

In a nutshell

We advance in understanding not by proving theories,
but by attempting to falsify them.

In a similar vein

CHAPTER 39

Karl Popper

When *Logik der Forschung* was published in Vienna in 1934, Karl Popper was only 32 and working as a secondary schoolteacher – slightly surprising given the book's huge influence on twentieth-century thought. *The Logic of Scientific Discovery* (as the title was translated in 1959) put the philosophy of science on a firm footing, and figures such as Imre Lakatos, Paul Feyeraband, and Thomas Kuhn followed in its wake.

The Vienna of Popper's twenties was a place of intellectual and political ferment. Marxism and socialism were popular causes among revolution-minded university students, including Popper, and the "Vienna Circle" of logical positivists were trying to knock down the walls of philosophy with their demarcation between provable statements and metaphysical speculation. This intellectual richness would end with the rise of Nazism, and in 1937 Popper, who was brought up a Lutheran but had Jewish grandparents, fled to New Zealand, where he took up a post teaching philosophy. There he wrote *The Open Society and Its Enemies*, his famous attack on totalitarianism, before moving to Britain, where he reigned at the London School of Economics for 25 years.

The Logic of Scientific Discovery was a reaction against the language-analyzing philosophy spawned by the Vienna Circle and typified by Wittgenstein, who had famously not read Aristotle, believing that all philosophical problems could be solved through looking at language alone. In contrast, Popper believed that the purpose of philosophy was to bring clarity to real-world problems: it must seek to tell us something about our place in the universe. However, unlike engineering or some branch of physical science, in which you know what the problem is and you go to work on solving it, Popper stated that philosophy has no "problem-situation" – there is no groundwork of accepted facts on to which a new question can be placed. Therefore, he said, "whenever we propose a solution to a problem, we ought to try as hard as we can to overthrow our solution, rather than defend it."

In other words, philosophy (and science) could no longer be about finding evidence to prove a theory; this wasn't rigorous enough. A real philosopher or scientist would work to prove *themselves* wrong, attempting to find the holes in any existing theory. Only then might knowledge be worthy of its name.

The problem of induction and its alternative

Popper perceived a giant hole in philosophy and science: inductive thinking.

Inductive statements take a particular, and from it assert something universal. For example, from the observation that all the swans we have seen are white, we assert the probability that swans are white. But we only need one case where this is not true (as for instance when black swans were discovered in Australia) to realize that inductive reasoning is faulty.

He makes the distinction between the psychology of knowledge, which is about collecting, pointing out, or making connections between facts, and the logic of knowledge, which is about testing knowledge itself. If something is said to be true, how do you test it? Indeed, *can* it be tested?

For a theory to be considered genuinely scientific, it must be able to be proven wrong – falsified by anyone, with results that are reproducible. It is totally wrong to believe that your theory is "proven," "verified," or "confirmed" if you can merely collect enough cases that seem to show it is true:

> *"Instead of discussing the 'probability' of a hypothesis we should try to assess what tests, what trials, it has withstood; that is, we should try to assess how far it has been able to prove its fitness to survive by standing up to tests. In brief, we should try to assess how far it has been 'corroborated'."*

A theory is not real if there is no way of testing it to see whether it is false. Furthermore, because he does not believe in induction, Popper says that theories are *never* ultimately and conclusively verifiable, they are only "provisional conjectures" that can find apparent corroboration.

Popper on metaphysics

From these arguments you begin to see how Popper raised the bar on science, separating nice ideas from bona fide theories. Yet he did so only because he believed in the scientific project. He described theories as "nets cast to catch what we call 'the world': to rationalize, to explain, and to master it. We endeavour to make the mesh ever finer and finer."

His demand for rigor did not, however, lead him to denounce metaphysics. The positivists claimed that they had killed off metaphysics because they had shown it to be meaningless: ideas could not be tested by the senses or be made into an unimpeachably logical statement. However, as Popper points out, many laws of natural science cannot be reduced to elementary statements based on sense information alone, and would not have been allowed to be put forward if the senses were our only criterion. "Indeed," he writes, "I am inclined to think that scientific discovery is impossible without faith in ideas which are of a purely speculative kind, and sometimes even quite hazy; a faith which is completely unwarranted from the point of view of science, and which, to that extent, is 'metaphysical.'"

Finally, he does not deny that a person can have a strong conviction about something, and that they may apprehend some truth, only that such a conviction, because its validity cannot be tested by anyone who wishes to, is not science. The "creative intuition" of which Bergson talked, or "intellectual love" as Einstein phrased it, are real enough in Popper's view, but by their nature are not able to be logically analyzed.

Final comments

Late in the book, Popper compares the scientific project to a city on water:

> *"Science does not rest upon solid bedrock. The bold structure of its theories rises, as it were, above a swamp. It is like a building erected on piles ... and if we stop driving the piles deeper, it is not because we have reached firm ground. We simply stop when we are satisfied that the piles are firm enough to carry the structure, at least for the time being."*

Though it may only be a structure "built on piles," and even if it never gives us the certainty we crave, science is still valuable. That Venice is not built on bedrock does not lessen the fact that it is nevertheless a worthwhile place to be. The same goes for philosophy.

Karl Popper

Popper was born in Vienna in 1902. His father was a lawyer, but also took a keen interest in the classics, philosophy, and social and political issues. His mother gave him a passion for music, and he almost followed music as a career.

At the University of Vienna he became heavily involved in left-wing politics and Marxism, but after a student riot abandoned it entirely. He got a primary school teaching diploma in 1925, took a PhD in philosophy in 1928, and qualified to teach mathematics and physics in secondary school the following year.

The growth of Nazism compelled him to leave Austria, and in 1937 he took up a position at the University of Canterbury in New Zealand, where he remained for the duration of the Second World War. In 1946 he moved to England, where he became professor of logic and scientific method at the London School of Economics. He was knighted in 1965, and retired in 1969, though he remained active as a writer, broadcaster, and lecturer until his death in 1994.

A Theory of Justice

"A theory however elegant and economical must be rejected or revised if it is untrue; likewise laws and institutions no matter how efficient and well-arranged must be reformed or abolished if they are unjust."

"Men are to decide in advance how they are to regulate their claims against one another and what is to be the foundation charter of their society. Just as each person must decide by rational reflection what constitutes his good, that is, the system of ends which it is rational for him to pursue, so a group of persons must decide once and for all what is to count among them as just and unjust."

"The general conception of justice imposes no restrictions on what sort of inequalities are permissible; it only requires that everyone's position be improved."

In a nutshell

The best societies are those that do not simply offer personal freedom, but lessen the lottery of life by giving fair chances for all.

In a similar vein

Jeremy Bentham *Principles of Morals and Legislation* (p 50)
John Locke *Essay Concerning Human Understanding* (p 176)
John Stuart Mill *On Liberty* (p 200)
Plato *The Republic* (p 230)
Jean-Jacques Rousseau *The Social Contract* (p 252)
Michael Sandel *The Tyranny of Merit* (p 264)

CHAPTER 40

John Rawls

John Rawls is seen as the most important political philosopher of the twentieth century, and *A Theory of Justice* is a key text in moral and political philosophy because of its brilliant treatment of the "fairness" issue.

Yet because of his primary insistence on personal freedom in the mold of John Stuart Mill, Rawls' book does not advocate a redistribution of wealth and power in any kind of socialist way. Rather, his focus is on equality of opportunity in the first place. The book's famous question is: What would happen if citizens were temporarily robbed of the awareness of their place in society (their wealth, status, etc.) and were then told to go and organize things in the fairest way possible? How would that society be different to what exists now?

This ingenious scenario is the heart of *A Theory of Justice*. First, though, we look at Rawls' basic concept of a just society through his two guiding principles of freedom and equality.

The original position and two guiding principles

As a political philosopher, Rawls was strongly influenced by traditional "social contract" theories expounded by Locke and Rousseau, in which citizens willingly give up some of their freedoms in return for state protection and order. In these theories, the "state of nature" is the original position prior to any system of laws or justice. Rousseau, for instance, compared the costs and benefits of such a state with life in a society based on law, concluding that what is lost is more than made up for in what is gained.

Rawls has a corresponding "original position" in which a group of free people come together to imagine possible principles by which a society could be justly ordered. These include utilitarian principles (the greatest happiness of the greatest number), intuitionist principles (those considered appropriate or acceptable by citizens), and egoistic principles (society is ordered, if at all, for the sole benefit of the individual).

Imagine that you are among this group. Among these alternative sets of principles, you have to make a choice based on uncertainty. If you do not know the future, how can you arrange society in terms of least harm and potentially greatest upside for all? Another way of seeing this is: How would each set of principles turn out if they were taken up by your group's worst enemies? If we choose to base a society on egoistic principles, for example, we can imagine that it would be wonderful for some people (who have access to many resources and advantages) but terrible for others (who lack them).

Rawls proposes his own principles by which a just society could be guided:

❖ There must be basic freedoms (e.g., of speech, association, religion).
❖ The inequalities that inevitably result from freedom are so arranged to bring most benefit to the worst off, including full equality of opportunity.

The first "priority rule" supporting these principles is that freedom can only be restricted when it results in other freedoms. As Rawls puts it, "a less extensive liberty must strengthen the total system of liberty shared by all."

The second priority rule is that justice is always more important than efficiency or utility of outcomes. Specifically, equal *opportunity* is more important than achieving a certain whole-of-society outcome, or what some government may believe is for the good of the people. The individual is more important than the mass, because whatever whole-of-society gain might be obtained (in a utilitarian way), it should occur secondary to, or as a result of, *everyone* having the chance to be lifted up.

The veil of ignorance as a path to justice

The big problem, as Rawls sees it, with existing theories for achieving a just society lies in the biases and prejudices of those charged with running it. To get around this, he makes his famous "veil of ignorance" proposal.

Every member in society agrees to voluntary and temporary amnesia. As the veil of ignorance descends on them, they forget who they are and the place they hold in society, so that fairness to all is their main concern. After all, Rawls notes, if someone knew they were rich, they might want to oppose taxes or welfare policies, not only because it might reduce their fortune, but because they may have conditioned themselves to see welfare as an unjust principle. The veil of ignorance eliminates such prejudices, because each person is blind to their station in life.

Under the veil of ignorance, we know that our chances of ending up in a good position, while attractive, are not great. To protect ourselves against ending up a downtrodden serf, for instance, we would choose a society where there is a reasonable chance at a good life, whatever our station, and plenty of room for upward mobility. This is a rational decision not merely for ourselves, but for our family and future generations, all of whom will be affected.

Justice as fairness

Rawls names his position "justice as fairness." He sees it as heir to the social contract theory, and yet distinct from utilitarian forms of justice.

Social institutions must exist not simply to provide order, or to protect property, but to achieve the most just outcomes. Yet Rawls rejects the utilitarian model with its "algebraic sum of advantages," because it does not give sufficient attention to individual rights and interests. For him, the greater good should never be built atop the loss of freedom for some.

He assumes that any society has a scarcity of resources, and therefore who gets what, and how much, becomes the key issue. While some may see this negatively in terms of "redistribution," Rawls puts it in terms of "social justice," which involves rights as well as responsibilities, or "the appropriate distribution of the benefits and burdens of social cooperation."

While people disagree on what constitutes justice and fairness, they generally agree that a concept of justice should regulate society. For most of us, Rawls suggests, "institutions are just when no arbitrary distinctions are made between persons in the assigning of basic rights and duties and when the rules determine a proper balance between competing claims to the advantages of social life."

The problem with existing institutions is that they tend to be skewed to benefit some people over others, not because of some particular merit, but purely because of an accident of birth or lucky starting place in life. The main task of social justice is therefore removing discrimination against people based on factors or characteristics over which they had no control. Because of his insistence on freedom, never does Rawls suggest that his ideal society would be one of absolute equality, but only that, where there is inequality in status or wealth, it has come about only *after* there having been a totally level playing field in the first place. Hierarchies may be needed to run organizations, but matters would only turn out this way after there had been full and free access to jobs and positions. While a society based on promotion by merit may be an ideal, it only achieves its full expression if there is equality of opportunity to attain the merit.

Creating the just society

In Part Two of *A Theory of Justice*, Rawls imagines his citizens, having decided on their guiding principles for a just society, getting down to work, creating a constitution, and developing laws. Only after this process is the veil of ignorance lifted, and everyone involved can see their position in society.

The chosen emphasis on liberty makes the society an echo of the American constitution; indeed, it ends up looking like a liberal democracy, with bodies of legislators, independent courts, and so on. Other features would include public schools, a minimum social wage, and an open and competitive economy and the prevention of monopolies. By a "just savings" principle, the current generation must put aside some funds for future generations.

In Part Three, Rawls shows how a society based on justice as fairness will also be a good and stable society, because all its members will see how it helps them to grow personally, benefiting their families too. Justice as fairness is a sort of social glue that binds society together. Human psychology comes into it too: if we see how fairness benefits everyone, then breaking laws involves social as well as legal issues, which people will try to avoid. To go along with a just system is to feel just ourselves, so a society based on fairness has personal, selfish benefits as well as public ones. Echoing Rousseau, Rawls notes:

> "[T]he desire to express our nature as a free and equal rational being can be fulfilled only by acting on the principles of right and justice as having first priority."

By acceding to being part of a well-ordered, just society, we paradoxically experience freedom. We are not fighting for survival or for rights, and we can pursue other projects as we desire.

But above all, a society based on justice as fairness sits well with our moral nature. If our heart is in the right place in relation to our fellows, everything else good will follow. The problem with the utilitarian view is that it sees us simply as machines for satisfying our desires. It is not feasible as a long-term model for a good society. Rawls' view, in contrast, takes account of *all* aspects of our nature, the noble and the ignoble.

Final comments

The balancing act that Rawls tries to achieve with his two principles is to preserve freedoms while enhancing opportunity. Where inequality exists, it would be arranged to offer the greatest possible benefit to the worst off in society. Yet, as many have pointed out, a society arranged to reduce inequality inevitably means a stronger government hand, and consequently curtailed freedoms.

Anarchy, State and Utopia (1974), Robert Nozick's libertarian manifesto, pointed out the inherent paradox in Rawls' principles. Nozick wrote:

> "Individuals have rights, and there are things no person or group may do to them (without violating their rights). So strong and far-reaching are these rights that they raise the question of what, if anything, the state and its officials may do. How much room do individual rights leave for the state?"

The room left is only for a minimal state protecting against violence, theft, and fraud and enforcing contracts. Anything more will force people to do things for some greater good with which they may not agree. Even though Rawls' view may put a noble emphasis on freedom, critics says, in reality it provides the rationale for a big welfare state that takes equality of opportunity to extremes. On the other hand, Rawls' philosophy provides a perfect counter to individualistic, Ayn Rand–style political ideals, which many commentators think have corrupted society and citizen alike.

Whatever your view, the good intentions and humanity of *A Theory of Justice* should be admitted. Its scope and imagination make it a modern-day counterpart to Plato's *Republic*: both provide a vision for a just society, one based on fairness for all, the other on the superior knowledge of a class of elites. Despite the differences in content, Rawls' "veil of ignorance" is up there with Plato's allegory of the cave as one of the great images in philosophy.

John Rawls

Rawls was born in 1921. His comfortable upbringing in Baltimore (his father was a prominent lawyer) was marred by the illness and death of his two brothers.

He attended the private Kent School in Connecticut before going to Princeton University. He was a top student, and considered joining an Episcopalian seminary. After graduating with honors in 1943, he joined the army and was stationed in the Pacific. In Japan he witnessed the aftermath of the United States' bombing of Hiroshima.

After earning his PhD in moral philosophy at Princeton, Rawls taught there for a couple of years before taking up a Fulbright Scholarship to Oxford, where he was influenced by the essayist and political philosopher Isaiah Berlin. After teaching stints at Cornell and MIT, he took up a professorship at Harvard, where he would remain for the duration of his career, influencing many emerging philosophers including Martha Nussbaum and Thomas Nagel.

Other key works are Political Liberalism *(1993),* The Law of Peoples *(1999), applying his concepts of justice to international affairs, and* Justice as Fairness: A Restatement *(2001), plus many significant articles.*

In 1999, Bill Clinton presented Rawls with the National Humanities Medal, noting that his ideas had "helped a whole generation of learned Americans revive their faith in democracy." In the same year Rawls won the Schock Prize for Logic and Philosophy.

He died in 2002. An asteroid, "16561 Rawls," is named after him.

The Social Contract

*"To renounce freedom is to renounce one's humanity,
one's rights as a man and equally one's duties."*

*"The social pact, far from destroying natural equality, substitutes,
on the contrary, a moral and lawful equality for whatever physical
inequality that nature may have imposed on mankind; so that however
unequal in strength and intelligence, men become equal by covenant
and by right."*

*"Every man having been born free and master of himself, no one else
may under any pretext whatever subject him without his consent. To
assert that the son of a slave is born a slave is to assert that he is not
born a man."*

In a nutshell

A free society raises up and ennobles its citizens, but also entails
giving up some of our personal liberty for the needs of the whole.

In a similar vein

CHAPTER 41

Jean-Jacques
Rousseau

O ne of the major figures of the French Enlightenment along with Denis Diderot and Voltaire, Jean-Jacques Rousseau was a man of many interests, but it is his writings on political philosophy that have had the greatest impact.

Rousseau followed John Locke and Thomas Hobbes before him in rejecting the idea of the "divine right" or "natural right" of monarchs to rule. Like them, he believed that sovereignty lay with the people. However, whereas Hobbes and Locke accepted that the ruler would be given some assent to rule, Rousseau took matters more literally: if power really was with the people, then it was the people themselves who should do the ruling.

Surveying the political landscape of his day, Geneva-born Rousseau famously writes on the first page of *The Social Contract*:

"Man was born free, and everywhere he is in chains. Those who think themselves the masters of others are indeed greater slaves than they."

It is easy to see why he was eventually hounded out of France and Switzerland for such remarks. They could not have been more of an affront to Europe's *ancien régime*, which had glided along on medieval assumptions of everyone in society having their place.

Rousseau's thinking was a major influence on the French Revolution (after he died he was given France's highest honor and entombed in the Pantheon), yet his message goes beyond particular historical situations. In the fervor for liberty and political participation from the Velvet Revolution to the Arab Spring, the ghost of Rousseau walks in our time too.

The social order and its benefits
Rousseau's social contract or pact works on the basis that "however unequal in strength and intelligence, men become equal by covenant and right." That is,

only through living in a framework of laws can people flourish. While they can be happy (in a brute sort of way) living in a state of nature, they can never reach their fullest potential, because only society provides an environment that can develop human virtues, and it is virtues that elevate man. Political equality and freedom are not natural rights, but rights required for the highest kind of human being or community to come into existence.

Rousseau believed that liberty was not possible unless there were laws. In his *Lettres écrites de la montagne* he wrote,

> *"Liberty consists less in doing one's own will than in not being subject to that of another; it consists further in not subjecting the will of others to our own."*

A caveman would look down on a city from his cave and only see restrictions, unable to appreciate the high development that civilization affords. What man gives up by leaving a state of nature (the freedom to do as he pleases, plundering or stealing without recourse to law) is more than compensated for by what he gains. By giving up his freedoms to the state, a precarious and arbitrary existence is replaced by justice and an inalienable right to property.

In society, man is called on to replace instincts and impulses with duty, reason, and the thinking of others. In nature, man is a "stupid and unimaginative animal," who in joining a community based on law and equal rights becomes "an intelligent being and a man." People only properly exist within the framework of a state, and a good society ennobles its citizens, "for to be governed by appetite alone is slavery, while obedience to a law one prescribes to one's self is freedom."

When are power and force legitimate?

The idea of "might makes right" was accepted without irony in Rousseau's day, and in *The Social Contract* he seeks to reveal its hollowness:

> *"Force is a physical power; I do not see how its effects could produce morality. To yield to force is an act of necessity, not of will; it is at best an act of prudence. In what sense can it be a moral duty?"*

Regarding the principle of "obeying those in power," he notes that as soon as this power weakens, there is no basis for obedience. The only way there can be a duty to be obedient is if those in power have a moral authority that everyone recognizes. He therefore reasons that "Since no man has natural authority over his fellows, and since force alone bestows no right, all legitimate authority among men must be based on covenants." And what of the idea (which still had some credence in the eighteenth century) that rulers gained their authority from God? Rousseau's witty rejoinder to this notion is:

"All power comes from God, I agree; but so does every disease, and no one forbids us to summon a physician."

He raises the idea of a bargain between the people and despots, where what the people seem to get in return is "the assurance of civil tranquillity." However, he observes that despots tend not to rule well, and are just as likely to waste huge sums of public money on wars, or to use the people as cannon fodder. And even if an individual were to make this deal with a despotic state, Rousseau argues, he cannot do it on behalf of his children, for they are born in freedom, and "no one but themselves has the right to dispose of it."

The private will and the general will

The problem with personal fealty to kings, Rousseau believed, was that there was no transparency or certainty in governance. Civil contracts were always at the risk of being undermined by the whim of the sovereign, whereas in a true democracy in which everyone willingly gives up their rights to the people or state as a whole, each person's contractual rights are clear and inalienable. This is the great benefit of the rule of law compared to rule by monarchical dictate.

Yet in giving up one's rights to the state, one may find that one's private will is different to the general will of the assembly. The social pact between individual and state requires that individuals who "refuse to obey the general will shall be constrained to do so by the whole body." Rousseau puts this even more plainly: such an individual will be "forced to be free."

This is where Rousseau the extreme democrat starts to sound authoritarian. However, his intentions were only good, as according to his model, only the sovereignty of the assembly or popular will can ensure the proper working of a democratic society. He makes a distinction between the will of all (or what all individuals want) and the general will: while the will of all is simply the sum of everyone's private interests and desires, the general will is the common interest, or what is really best for everyone. All the individual desires balance each other out, and from this melee emerges the wider public interest. Rousseau warns that we should always be on our guard against some sectional or group interest becoming so powerful that it skews the general will. (Given the power that lobby groups and industry associations wield over present-day governments, on this he was very prescient.) The state, if it is supported by all, should exist for all, and not for one group or person over others.

Rousseau's warning that a society marked by a polarity of views and fractiousness, in which no one is willing to subsume their private opinions in the name of the general good, is unhealthy seems to speak to many of today's mature democracies, which are marked more by partisanship than by a spirit of cooperation. His focus is on assemblies of people having real participation in government, following the Swiss model with which he had grown up, and he did not foresee today's lumbering elected democracies, with their representative party blocs and lack of direct personal participation. Yet every time we hear of a move toward people having a greater say in government, there is an echo of Rousseau.

Final comments

Whereas Hobbes thought that people had to make a choice between being ruled and being free, Rousseau said that it was possible to have both; you could remain free if your "ruler" was yourselves (in the form of an assembly of citizens set up to make laws). Critics have said that while this might have worked in the Swiss cantons with which Rousseau was familiar in his youth, such optimism was less suited to the real world. Nevertheless, his overall vision remains powerful.

Indeed, Rousseau wisely did not try to dictate the ideal form of government, since this would differ according to the people and the country. However, in a section titled "Signs of a Good Government," he does give an indication of what a good democratic state would look like – it would have a large, flourishing population who feel safe and free within its borders. If this is the case, the exact nature of the governing structure is academic.

As long as there are people living under despotic regimes, *The Social Contract* will remain relevant. Monarchs have often felt that if they establish peace they are doing well, but Rousseau notes that "what really makes the species prosper is not peace but freedom." As long as people "remain supine under the yoke" (that is, in an absolute monarchy or dictatorship), they live in a state of decay in which rulers can destroy them at any time. Great wars, famines, and other events come and go, but whether a population is basically free or not, expressed in a sound and long-lasting constitution, is what matters most.

The Social Contract is also an eternal reminder to modern democracies, so many of which have become unrepresentative and overly partisan, to smarten up their act. As Rousseau warned:

> *"The greater the harmony that reigns in the public assemblies, the more ... the general will is dominant; whereas long debates, dissensions and*

disturbances bespeak the ascendance of particular interests and the decline of the state."

Both as an intellectual weapon against despots and as a tonic for sick democracies, Rousseau remains timeless reading.

Jean-Jacques Rousseau

Rousseau was born in 1712 and his mother died only a few days later. His watchmaker father Isaac was learned and instilled in him a love of reading, particularly classical literature.

At 16 Rousseau became an apprentice engraver, but he hated his boss. He found himself over the border in Catholic Savoy, where he befriended a noblewoman, Madame de Warens. In her household he had access to a great library, received music lessons, and became a music teacher; he was also her lover. During his twenties he pursued a musical career and created a new system of musical notation. At 31 he gained experience in politics, working for the French Ambassador to the Venetian Republic, but this was not a proper diplomatic role and Rousseau felt like a servant. Back in Paris, he struck up a relationship with his laundry maid. They would have five children, but all were given up to orphanages.

In 1749 Rousseau entered an essay competition, egged on by his friend Denis Diderot (of the famous Encyclopedia), which he won, and he became a literary sensation. He was also a reasonably successful composer of ballets and operas, and in 1752 had a play performed for France's King Louis XV.

Rousseau was keenly interested in education and his famous Émile (1762) tried to show how children could be brought up so that they would not seek to dominate, but to have an equal feeling with others. In criticizing church practices and dogma, Rousseau was severely attacked by the Church. He was forced to flee Paris and the attacks made him paranoid. After an invitation from his friend David Hume he sought refuge in Britain, but he there fell out with Hume. In his last years in Paris he wrote the Confessions, a classic work of autobiography. It was published a few years after his death in 1778.

The Conquest of Happiness

"Happiness is not, except in very rare cases, something that drops into the mouth, like a ripe fruit, by the mere operation of fortunate circumstances."

"To like many people spontaneously and without effort is perhaps the greatest of all sources of personal happiness."

In a nutshell

Happiness comes from throwing ourselves into life, which generally lessens the preoccupation with the self – a primary cause of unhappiness.

In a similar vein

Aristotle *Nicomachean Ethics* (p 28)

Ludwig Wittgenstein *Philosophical Investigations* (p 312)

CHAPTER 42

Bertrand Russell

Bertrand Russell was one of the most lauded philosophers and mathematicians of the modern era. He wrote the monumental *Principia Mathematica* (with Alfred North Whitehead), many significant scholarly articles and books on logic, and bestsellers such as *A History of Western Philosophy*. At Cambridge he was the mentor of Wittgenstein, and was a public intellectual who energetically supported causes including communism (before he met Lenin and Trotsky) and nuclear disarmament.

Russell succeeded to an earldom in his sixties, married four times, and was a noted atheist. Living to the age of 98, he had ample time to test the validity of his philosophical and political ideas and apply them to his own life.

This is the significance of *The Conquest of Happiness*. There has been a rash of books on happiness in the last few years, many of them based on empirical research. Russell had none of this data, yet his philosophy carries the ring of truth. He led an extremely full, productive, and largely happy life himself, and perhaps this fact is the best advertisement for the book.

How to grow happier

At the beginning of *The Conquest of Happiness*, Russell admits that he was not a happy child. His favorite hymn was "Weary of earth and laden with my sin." In adolescence, he writes, "I hated life and was continually on the verge of suicide, from which, however, I was restrained by the desire to know more mathematics."

However, with each passing year his happiness increased, both from doing more of the things he enjoyed and eliminating wishes that were unattainable. But the main cause of his happiness, he says, was "a diminishing preoccupation with myself":

> *"Interest in oneself ... leads to no activity of a progressive kind. It may lead to the keeping of a diary, to getting psycho-analysed, or perhaps to becoming a monk. But the monk will not be happy until the routine of the monastery has made him forget his own soul."*

Happiness is held back by introspection, which rests on the belief that we are separate from others. It is gained by identifying ourselves with causes, passions, and interests, and by making the welfare of others more important than our own. Russell learned this not through philosophy, but through experience.

His life was in part a reaction to Victorian morality and the idea of sin. Like Freud, he believed that repression of sex and love is much more damaging to the person than the act itself. Repression of natural feelings creates a discord between the unconscious and conscious minds, which manifests in various unhealthy ways. A sense of sin makes us feel inferior and alone and so deprives us of happiness; haunted and hampered by inner conflicts, we will not be able to achieve any external purpose. Of course, unhappiness can also arise when people fail to regulate their conduct because there is no rational ethic on which to base their behavior. The solution, Russell felt, lay in adopting a "modern outlook" in which superstitions have no place, and in which we act only when we know that our actions will cause no harm to others.

The mistake of unhappiness

Unhappiness is a condition not based only on things that happen to you. It is, rather, the result of mistakes in thinking and outlook, Russell says:

> "[M]istaken views of the world, mistaken ethics, mistaken habits of life, leading to destruction of that natural zest and appetite for possible things upon which all happiness, whether of men or animals, ultimately depends."

The psychological causes of unhappiness are many and varied, but a common reason seems to be the deprivation of some normal satisfaction while young. Since that satisfaction is valued above all else, emphasis is directed to achieving that one thing, and other activities are sidelined.

Some people feel that the state of the world gives them no reason to be happy. However, Russell notes, "The truth is that they are unhappy for some reason of which they are not aware, and this unhappiness leads them to dwell upon the less agreeable characteristics of the world in which they live."

The balanced life

There is no struggle for life for most people – it is more a struggle for success. A businessman will call it a struggle for life in order to give dignity to something essentially trivial, Russell observes:

> "What people fear when they engage in the struggle is not that they will fail to get their breakfast next morning, but that they will fail to outshine their neighbours."

For the achievement of happiness, a sense of perspective and a balanced life are everything. Not only does the pursuit of money alone not bring happiness, it results in boredom. We must have intellectual interests if we are to grow and fulfill our potential.

Even more than actual success, Russell says, effort is an essential ingredient of happiness; a person who is able to gratify all whims without effort comes to see that attainment of desires does not make them happy. "To be without some of the things you want," he concludes, "is an indispensable part of happiness."

On boredom

The desire for excitement and adventure is innate in human beings, Russell notes, particularly in males. In the hunting stage of civilization this was gratified naturally, but with the advent of agriculture boredom set in. The machine age has lessened that lassitude somewhat, but not the fear of being bored. "Boredom is therefore a vital problem for the moralist, since at least half the sins of mankind are caused by the fear of it." Russell's bold contention is that most wars, pogroms, and persecutions are a result of the desire to flee from tedium. "A certain power of enduring boredom is therefore essential to a happy life," he argues. Childhood pleasures should include activities that require effort and inventiveness, and therefore passive enjoyments like going to the theater or films should be limited. It is useful to cultivate "fruitful monotony" in a child rather than giving them constant exposure to new stimuli.

Among adults, pleasures such as gambling that are removed from nature result in no lasting joy, whereas those that bring a person into contact with the earth are profoundly satisfying. Urban populations suffer ennui only because they are separated from nature.

Other insights

❖ It is difficult for us to accept that others do not share the high opinion we have of ourselves, says Russell. We know that others have faults, but expect them to think that we have none. Overestimating our merits, love of power, and vanity lead to unhappiness.

❖ The feeling of love is what gives us happiness, rather than the object of that feeling. Love is "in itself a source of delight" and, what is more, it "enhances all the best pleasures, such as music, and sunrise in mountains, and the sea under the full moon."

❖ Our happiness comes primarily from those close to us: "Very few people can be happy unless on the whole their way of life and their outlook on the world is approved by those with whom they have social relations, and more especially by those with whom they live."

❖ The conceited are unpleasantly surprised by failure, while those who are modest are pleasantly surprised by success. Therefore, it is best to have low expectations.

❖ Disenchantment is a malady, and even if it is caused by particular circumstances, it is wise to overcome it as soon as possible. The more things a person is interested in, the greater their chances of happiness.

❖ Those who forgo parenthood relinquish a great happiness, and are likely to feel dissatisfaction without knowing why. Our offspring bring continuity and togetherness, which make you "feel you are part of the stream of life flowing on from the first germ" and continuing into an unknown future. Russell had several children.

❖ Another essential for happiness, continuity of purpose, stems from work: "Without self-respect genuine happiness is scarcely possible. And the man who is ashamed of his work can hardly achieve self-respect."

❖ All areas of a person's life, whether it is work, marriage, or raising children, require outward effort, and it is the effort itself that brings about happiness.

Final comments

Russell's prescription for happiness involves a number of elements, important among which is what he calls a "golden mean" between effort and resignation. Seeking perfection in everything inevitably causes unhappiness, whereas (to use his quaint example) the wise person will overlook the dust the maid has not dusted, or the fact that the cook has not cooked dinner properly, until such time as he is free to deal with it unemotionally. If we resign ourselves to many things, we can focus on what matters and where we can really make a difference. Indeed, the person who is able to cope with multifarious causes of *un*happiness will be the one who remains happy.

Russell concludes (somewhat obviously) that happiness depends "partly upon external circumstances and partly upon oneself." It is derived from food, shelter, love, work, family, and a hundred other things. Given that the sources of happiness are all around us, he observes, only someone who is psychologically maladjusted will fail to become happy.

Going a little deeper, he notes that unhappiness is the result of a lack of integration between the conscious and the unconscious mind, or between the self and society: "The happy man is the man who does not suffer from either of these failures of unity, whose personality is neither divided against itself nor pitted against the world."

Above all, happiness can be gleaned from directing our interests *outward*, being less self-centered and avoiding envy, self-pity, fear, self-admiration, and a sense of sin. Looking at these passions consciously, studying why they are present, and then facing them will help in overcoming them.

Though in terms of academic philosophy *The Conquest of Happiness* is not one of Russell's major works, it is a bridge between Russell the philosopher and Russell the man, and for that reason it is fascinating. He subscribed to "neutral monism," the metaphysical notion that everything in the universe is of the same "stuff," whether it is matter or consciousness. We are therefore less separate from other people than we think, and a belief that we are a truly separate entity is a mistake that will cause unhappiness, because all disturbing thoughts arise from a feeling of unwanted separation and a focus on the self as something real. When this illusion of separation is seen for what it is, it is difficult not to be joyful.

Bertrand Russell

Russell was born in 1872 in Trellech, Wales, into an influential, liberal, and aristocratic family. His parents were Viscount Amberley and Katherine, daughter of the 2nd Baron Stanley of Alderley. At only 3 he was left an orphan and was taught by governesses and tutors.

In 1890 he went into residence at Trinity College, University of Cambridge, and his brilliance was soon noticed. While still in his teens he published a book on German social democracy, and during his time at Trinity he discovered "Russell's paradox," which challenged the foundations of mathematical set theory.

In 1903 he published his first important book on mathematical logic, The Principles of Mathematics, *and in 1905 wrote the essay* On Denoting. *The first of three volumes of* Principia Mathematica, *coauthored with Alfred North Whitehead, was published in 1910. The work made Russell famous in the fields of logic and mathematics.*

Russell was noted for his many antiwar and antinuclear protests, which led to time in jail and dismissals from both Trinity College and City College, New York. He was awarded the Nobel Prize for Literature in 1950.

He gave away much of his inherited wealth, but in 1931 he acceded to, and kept, his earldom, though he claimed that its only benefit was getting seats in restaurants. He died in 1970.

The Tyranny of Merit

"Meritocratic hubris reflects the tendency of winners to inhale too deeply of their success, to forget the luck and good fortune that helped them on their way. It is the smug conviction of those who land on the top that they deserve their fate, and that those on the bottom deserve theirs, too."

"The ethic of fortune appreciates the dimensions of life that exceed human understanding and control. It sees that the cosmos does not necessarily match merit with reward. It leaves room for mystery, tragedy, and humility."

In a nutshell

Equality of opportunity or meritocracy is not enough to create a good society.

In a similar vein

Aristotle *Nicomachean Ethics* (p 28)
Plato *The Republic* (p 230)
John Rawls *A Theory of Justice* (p 246)

CHAPTER 43

Michael Sandel

The college admissions scandal of 2019, in which wealthier families could apparently pay their way into top American universities, seemed to go against everything we hold dear about living in a meritocratic society. College entry should be based on brains and ability alone; there must be no "back door" for the privileged.

Yet the bulk of Ivy League and Oxbridge admissions still come from the top 20 per cent of the income scale. Wealthy parents pay for admissions counsellors and extra tutoring. Richer students are directed to sports that give them a higher chance of getting sporting scholarships.

Traditionally, entry into a top university has been seen as a ticket to material security and status, so it makes sense that places are highly coveted, and the process very competitive. Yet many of the parents involved in the college admissions scandal were well off or celebrities; top college entry for their kids was not an economic necessity. So why were they so intent on securing places?

"In an unequal society" says Harvard philosopher Michael Sandel, "those who land at the top want to believe their success is morally justified." Getting somewhere thanks to money alone is shameful, whereas achievement via merit is honored.

Meritocracy is equated with the American Dream. Few would dare to question it, but in *The Tyranny of Merit: What's Become of the Common Good?*, Sandel provides a compelling case for the corrosive effect of the meritocratic principle itself.

What's wrong with meritocracy?

Surprisingly, the word "meritocracy" was only coined in the 1950s by Michael Young, a British sociologist. As he was writing *The Rise of the Meritocracy* (1958), Britain was changing. Its old class-based system was being shaken up, and working class people were getting more chances to rise. But Young looked back from an imagined future in the year 2033, and saw the dark side of meritocracy: that it gave rise to feelings that one's subordinate status was a personal failure. In the class-based system, a person could know they were intelligent but be resigned to not being able to ascend, because the best jobs were given to the hereditary class. In the new meritocracy, if you had a chance to rise but didn't, all you'd feel is humiliation.

Young foresaw that in a meritocracy, inequality would actually increase. Those with higher intellect and credentials would hardly bother to speak to those without credentials, indeed they would be strongly prejudiced against them. This meritocratic hubris would be contrasted with a social stigma felt by those with limited education. The combination would be explosive, Young said. He predicted a populist revolt in the year 2034. But it happened 18 years ahead of schedule, Sandel notes – in 2016, with Brexit, Trump, and the rise of other populists such as Marine Le Pen. It would lead to Hillary Clinton dismissing some less-educated, mostly white Trump supporters as "deplorables."

Sandel has two big questions about meritocracy as the basis of a society:

1. Given the lottery of birth, in which some people are born with more abilities than others, is a perfect meritocracy actually just or fair?
2. Even if it were considered fair, would it be a "good" society? With a class of smart, successful, self-made people looking down on everyone else, it's hard to see how this would lead to human flourishing across the board. Any idea of the common good would go out the window.

The "rhetoric of rising" is now a part of the politician's toolkit. Barack Obama constantly spoke of an America which allowed people to "go as far as their talents will take them." But this emphasis made us forget other, older qualities of a good society such as citizenship and service.

If you get into a prestigious university, you assume that it was all your own doing, when in fact you had many helping hands. Conversely, if you fail to get in, it feels like you only have yourself to blame. In both cases, the student puts too much emphasis on their own striving, and not enough on environmental factors. This way of thinking, says Sandel, is "corrosive to civic sensibilities," because "the more we think of ourselves as self-made and self-sufficient, the harder it is to learn gratitude and humility."

Minus gratitude and humility, we tend to be less thankful for the society and milieu which produced us. We care less about the "common good." Governments now equate the common good with GDP. The value of individuals is based on the value of goods and services they can produce. Yet market capitalism has failed to deliver public goods like it did in the post-war period, when all of society was lifted up. Now it's more of a competition to see who can extract the most gains. You can't outsource moral and political judgement to markets, Sandel says. When you do, the vacuum is inevitably filled by populism, fundamentalism or nationalism.

When the successful become the good

The culture of meritocracy has its roots in early Protestant theology – whether or not you would go to heaven was up to the grace of God, and you could not know during your lifetime whether you were one of the "elect." All you could do was devoutly follow your vocation – not to advance yourself, but to glorify God. This led to the combination of extreme hard work (the famous "Protestant work ethic"), yet conspicuously not wanting to enjoy the fruits of it. Protestant merchants started to amass wealth precisely because their commercial success was teamed with low consumption.

Over time, this outlook changed. Instead of believing they were helpless before God's grace, people started believing in their own merit. If you had worldly success, it was a sign that you were good. If poor, you were morally weak. The effect of this, Sandel writes, is that it "heightens the moral stakes of economic competition. It sanctifies the winners and denigrates the losers." Today we see it in the form of the American prosperity gospel, which emphasizes hard work, striving, positive thinking, upward mobility, and attaining wealth. God wants us to be rich, and prosperity is a sign of virtue.

Yet there is a problem with this ethic of mastery compared with the ancient outlook of fortune, argues Sandel: "The ethic of fortune appreciates the dimensions of life that exceed human understanding and control. It sees that the cosmos does not necessarily match merit with reward. It leaves room for mystery, tragedy, and humility."

A greater appreciation of this by successful or fortunate people might lead to a more generous view of others. Instead, they have a belief that people basically get what they deserve. This is the dark side of an ethic that fuelled the rise of capitalism, and that alleviates many of conscience.

Credentialism

The traditional route to a better life is gaining a college degree. More people have had the opportunity to gain one, but it has created a divide that Sandel calls "credentialism." Highly-educated meritocratic elites, experts and professionals have been the winners of market-driven globalization, and have more in common with elites in other countries than their fellow citizens. Meanwhile, their working class compatriots are left to compete with workers in other countries.

In the 1970s, you could have a job that paid enough to raise a family, and not have a college degree. That's much harder now – the "college premium" has doubled. Workers not only have less pay, but lower social esteem because they have not gone through the college sorting process which deems them "smart." In 1971, 93 per cent of Americans with only a high school diploma were working full time. By 2017, it was only 69 per cent. It's as if, Sandel says, this group of people could not deal with the indignities of doing work that was not socially valued, so dropped out altogether. "Deaths of despair" (via drugs, alcohol, suicide) are overwhelmingly associated with those without a college degree. The deaths cannot be blamed on poverty alone. The more likely cause is the crushing feeling of living in a society where you do not possess credentials that are honored and rewarded.

Credentialism is "the last acceptable prejudice," says Sandel. Donald Trump threatened to sue colleges he had attended if they revealed his (poor) college and SAT scores. Joe Biden has inflated his college credentials. Among Obama's cabinet members, most had gone to Ivy League universities and had higher degrees. Like Plato's caste of philosopher-kings in *The Republic*, they believed that brains alone could solve America's problems. In fact, their credentials arguably made them arrogant and separated from most people's lives. Obama's administration bailed out the banks in the financial crisis of 2008, which permanently lowered the estimation of the Democratic Party in the eyes of working class people. Obama's cabinet respected and even idolized Wall Street, because it is a bastion of meritocratic rising.

Studies indicate that the prejudice of well-educated people against the less educated is even stronger than that against poor people or people of color or immigrants. The "smart" educated class apparently believe that low education is a result of lack of effort. Today, the proportion of people getting elected for office who do not have a college degree is tiny (3 or 4 per cent), which means that politicians often have little in common with the people they represent. They fail to fix inequality because they themselves are "winners" in the system and don't see a big problem. The result? Alienated, working- and middle-class voters turn to populists like Trump and Le Pen.

It's a myth that "the best and brightest" in terms of degrees make the best leaders. Sandel points out that George Washington, Abraham Lincoln, and Harry Truman, three of the greatest US presidents, did not go to college. Just because you are highly educated does not mean you possess civic virtue in the Aristotleian sense, or that you live to serve the country. The Attlee post-war government in Britain, for example, was full of working class people. It helped shape the post-war world and created the National Health Service.

In the 1990s, Bill Clinton and Tony Blair emphasized education. As Clinton put it: "What you can earn depends on what you can learn." But the more you emphasize higher education as the means of rising, the more it stigmatizes those who don't have it. If the "smart" people, the technocratic elites, seem to be running the world, doesn't that make me "dumb"?

Citizens not consumers

If modern capitalism has created a "global market for talent," then massive gains will go to a few. This could not be more different to a society in which every citizen is valued for who they are, and not what they can produce or consume. It's important, says Sandel, that states give out honors and offices which reflect justice and service, not just market measurements of wealth or fame. Another remedy for the marketization of life is to turn the emphasis away from universities and to career and vocational and technical education. Being a plumber or electrician is important for the common good, and should not be seen as a consolation prize for not getting into university. Beyond this, Sandel favours a return to civic education – via community colleges, job sites, union halls. Everyone has a right to think and learn about morality and politics, not just the educated.

The phrase "the American dream" was coined by James Truslow Adams in 1931 in *The Epic of America*. It was a dream in which every American could fulfil themselves "and be recognized by others for what they are, regardless of the fortunate circumstances of birth or position." Adams mentions the Library of Congress as an example of an institution dedicated to equality of condition; anyone from any walk of life could come there and read and study and better themselves. It was provided by democracy, paid for by the people's taxes, to benefit all people.

Sandel bemoans the fact that today, public spaces where people gather from all walks of society and income, class and race, are few. Huge inequality of incomes means people lead separate lives, living, working and shopping in different places, with their children in different schools. So "it is little wonder we have lost the ability to reason together about large public questions, or even listen to one another."

Democracy does not require perfect equality, but it does require more than just maximizing the welfare of consumers. It means healthy civic common spaces (real world and online) where all citizens come together as equals. In his travels to America, de Tocqueville noted how engaged the populace was in civic matters. There was a sense of ownership. This sense of "we're in this together" now seems quaint. Globalization and financialization (because of the inequality they have created) have made us less appreciative of our fellow citizens, and less open to the idea of solidarity and shared vision. We're less inclined to feel that we owe everything to the society (family, laws, institutions, culture) that created us, and more inclined to believe that "I did it my way." The self-interest of the consumer has replaced the pride of the citizen.

Final comments
Sandel's reasoning is powerful, but not without issues.

In a section of *The Tyranny of Merit* on "success ethics," Sandel argues that as mega-successful people like Steve Jobs and J.K. Rowling were born with their talents, they have simply won the lottery of life. Obviously they worked hard, but can we say that they *deserve* their talents? If not, then a society based on this birth happenstance cannot be a fair one. You have simply replaced a hereditary aristocracy with one of the super smart or creative.

In saying this, Sandel reveals an academic's misunderstanding of success. Jobs and Rowling may have been born with more intellect or imagination than the average, but what they achieved was *built*. Jobs made people's day-to-day lives more productive and interesting, and through superb design, more beautiful. Rowling dramatically increased the rate of reading in the population and opened up whole literary worlds, and her work led to the employment of millions thanks to the movies created and the book stores that sold her work. Sandel may have fallen into the trap of giving too much weight to environment and not enough to risk, work, and ingenuity – things people are not born with, but which they develop, and which can have exponential benefits over time. In this respect, perhaps people fully deserve their success.

Sandel's points about globalization, individualism, and the decimation of civic life are all true, but he assumes that it is the state's role to fix things. He advocates a return to an Aristotleian philosophy of society that celebrates civic contribution over success, and criticizes Friedrich Hayek for conflating the market value of a person's output with their actual contribution to society. In Hayek's logic, it's fine that a casino operator earns much more than a school teacher, even if the teacher's contribution to society is arguably greater. The Hayekian contention that the market ultimately decides what is valuable goes against every classical idea of the *polis* and a values-based society that Sandel holds dear. For him, that does not seem like a place worth living in.

Despite its faults, *The Tyranny of Merit* is deeply compassionate, and makes us think again about whether we want to live in a mere economy, or be part of a society. Would you be a consumer in a minimal state that has a high level of freedom, or a citizen in a nation where provision is made for all to flourish?

Michael Sandel

Born in Minneapolis in 1953, Sandel's family moved to Los Angeles when he was 13. He excelled at school and at Brandeis University before winning a Rhodes Scholarship to Balliol College, Oxford.

He has taught at Harvard since 1980, and holds the position of Anne T. and Robert M. Bass Professor of Government. In 2002, he was elected a Fellow of the American Academy of Arts and Sciences, and from 2002 to 2005 he served on the President's Council on Bioethics. In 2005, his 'Justice' lectures were filmed and became a 12-episode television series. In 2009 Sandel delivered the BBC Reith Lectures; his theme was citizenship and prospects for "a politics of the common good."

Other books include Liberalism and the Limits of Justice *(1982),* Democracy's Discontent: America in Search of a Public Philosophy *(1996),* The Case Against Perfection: Ethics in an Age of Genetic Engineering *(2007) and* What Money Can't Buy: The Moral Limits of Markets *(2012).*

Being and Nothingness

"Man is condemned to be free; because once thrown into the world, he is responsible for everything he does."

"I am responsible for everything … except for my very responsibility, for I am not the foundation of my being. Therefore everything takes place as if I were compelled to be responsible. I am abandoned in the world … in the sense that I find myself suddenly alone and without help, engaged in a world for which I bear the whole responsibility without being able, whatever I do, to tear myself away from this responsibility for an instant."

"[H]uman reality does not exist first in order to act later; but for human reality, to be is to act."

In a nutshell

There is no essential nature at the heart of our being. We are free to invent a self and create a life as we wish.

In a similar vein

Hannah Arendt *The Human Condition* (p 22)
Simone de Beauvoir *The Second Sex* (p 44)
Martin Heidegger *Being and Time* (p 130)
Immanuel Kant *Critique of Pure Reason* (p 148)

CHAPTER 44

Jean-Paul Sartre

Existentialism often attracts a "life is meaningless" caricature, but in fact its best-known exponent, Jean-Paul Sartre, was actually one of the greatest philosophers of human freedom. It is not easy to arrive at this realization, however, because of the sheer difficulty and weightiness of his most significant work, *Being and Nothingness*.

In the introduction, for instance, Sartre defines consciousness as "a being such that in its being, its being is in question in so far as this being implies a being other than itself." Heidegger's influence is apparent in such impenetrability; what could it actually mean?

To understand, we should start with Sartre's basic division of the world into two: things that have consciousness of self (beings "for themselves"); and things that do not (things "in themselves," the objects around us that make up the world). Consciousness exists for itself because it can comprehend itself. Most of the book is devoted to this kind of consciousness, and what it means to those who truly have it: human beings.

Central to Sartre's thinking is the view that people have no essential "essence." In fact, when humans analyze their own being, what they find at the heart of it is nothing. Yet this nothingness is something great, since it means that we are totally free to create the self or the life we want. We are free in a negative way, since there is nothing to *stop* us being free. Sartre remarks, "man being condemned to be free carries the whole weight of the world on his shoulders; he is responsible for the world and for himself as a way of being."

Being and Nothingness caught the mood of postwar France in which all the old certainties had crumbled away. If France's existing value system had got it into such a mess in the war, was it worth anything? Sartre represented a new way of seeing and being. People could *choose* their future, and it was this apparently new philosophy that excited a generation.

Freedom and responsibility

Not simply are we responsible for what we do, Sartre says, we are responsible for our world. Each of us is living out a certain "project" with our life, so whatever happens to us must be accepted as part of that. Sartre goes so far as to say that "there are no *accidents* in life."

He gives the example of being called up to fight in a war. It is wrong to think of the war as something external that comes from outside and suddenly takes over our life. In fact, the war must become *my* war. I could always get out of it by killing myself or deserting, but for one reason or another (cowardice, inertia, or not wanting to let down my family or my country), I stay in the war and "For lack of getting out of it, I have *chosen* it." A war depends on its soldiers for its existence, and I have "decided that it does exist." There is no point in seeing it as a block of time removed from my life, taking me away from what I really want to do (pursue a career, have a family, and so on); by being in the war I must take full responsibility for it and for my time in it. "I choose myself from day to day," as Sartre puts it. Humanity's state of being is a constant choosing of one's self. People may wish that they lived in another time to avoid being in the war, but the fact is that they are part of the epoch that led to war, and to be in any other time would contradict that. "Thus, I *am* this war" – my life is an expression of the era in which I live, so to wish for some other life is a meaningless, illogical fantasy.

We are "abandoned" in the universe, Sartre says. Anguish comes from the realization that we are not "the foundation of our own being" (i.e., we did not invent ourselves, or choose our own birth) and neither can we be the foundation of being for other people. All we can do is to choose the meaning of our being, seeing everything in the world as an *opportunity* (whether used, not used, or lacking in the first place). Those who realize that they choose the meaning of their own being, even if it is a frightening thought, are absolutely free. They can live without excuses, regrets, or remorse, and take absolute responsibility for their actions.

The human goal is to realize and appreciate our own being and our freedom. Other goals that we create as substitutes for this indicate a "spirit of seriousness," which mistakenly suggests that what I am *doing* is all-important. As Sartre notes, "Success is not important to freedom." To be free, we do not have to attain what we wish, we simply have to be free to make a choice.

Living as if our actions are all-important, or spending our life trying to live up to some kind of universal moral value system, is a kind of bad faith. Only by truly choosing for ourselves what we will be every minute, creating our life like it is a work of art arising from this total freedom, do we realize our potential as a human being.

Sartre's statement that "Man is what he is not and is not what he is" means that we cannot escape our "facticity," the concrete facts of our existence like our gender, nationality, class, or race. All of these provide a "coefficient of adversity" that makes any kind of achievement in life an uphill battle. And yet, neither are we simply the sum of our facticity. The problem is that we shrink back from doing totally new things, things that are out of character, because we value consistency in ourselves. Consistency, or character, is both a form of security and the lens through which we view and make sense of our world, but it is largely an illusion. Despite all the limiting factors of our existence, we are freer than we imagine, Sartre says.

Bad faith

Sartre's famous concept of "bad faith" (*mauvaise foi*) rests on a distinction between two types of lying: the regular lie, which implies "that the liar actually is in complete possession of the truth which he is hiding," whose lie relates to something in the world of objects, expressing the view that I and others are separate; and the lie to oneself, a lie of consciousness that does not involve a separation between deceiver and deceived. This second lie is less black-and- white but more serious, since it involves a flight from our freedom. As Sartre puts it:

> *"Bad faith then has in appearance the structure of lying. Only what changes everything is the fact that in bad faith it is from myself that I am hiding the truth."*

Bad faith requires a person to accept matters on face value, and rests on a resistance to the idea of uncovering things completely to find the truth. If not an outright lie, it is persuading oneself not to look too closely, in case something is found that one does not like.

Sartre spends several pages rebutting Freud. Freud believed that people's choices and actions are constantly hijacked by their unconscious mind, but when Sartre sat down to read Freud's cases for himself, he found that the people on the Viennese doctor's couch were simply examples of pathological bad faith. Another Viennese psychiatrist, Stekel, agreed with Sartre, and wrote, "Every time that I have been able to carry my investigations far enough, I have established that the crux of the psychosis was conscious." Indeed, Sartre would have welcomed the revolution in cognitive therapy of the last 40 years, which dismisses the idea that we are sabotaged by subterranean urges and stresses that we can in fact condition our thinking.

Nevertheless, freedom is a burden, which is why so many people escape into bad faith. Sartre notes that bad faith may be a normal way of life, with only occasional, brief awakenings to good faith. Those of bad faith can see quite clearly what they are doing, but choose to deceive themselves as to its meaning. He gives the example of a woman who has agreed to go on a first date with a man. Though she does not try to prevent his acts of flirtation and pronouncements of love or affection for her, at the same time she does not wish to make any kind of decision about the relationship. So what does she do? To keep enjoying the charm of the evening, she reduces the man's statements to their literal meaning only. When he says to her "I find you so attractive," she is careful not to accept any other meaning (such as I want to sleep with you, or I want to get serious with the relationship). When he takes her hand, she does not want to destroy the evening by withdrawing it, so pretends to herself that she has not noticed her hand is in his. Seeing her own body as a mere object has the effect of preserving her freedom. She has made no commitment; or at least, this is how she chooses to see it. However, in separating her body, or the "facts" of the situation, from her transcendent self (her true "I," if you like) she is creating a lie to serve a particular purpose: maintaining a sense of freedom or noncommitment.

Everyone operates between bad faith and good faith all the time, but Sartre says that it is possible through "self-recovery" to achieve authenticity, which simply means a person "being what they are." For such a person, candor "ceases to be his ideal and becomes instead his being." This does not happen naturally; a person becomes sincere, or what they are, only as a conscious act.

Freedom and relationships

It may seem an obvious question, but why are human beings obsessed with relationships? Sartre's answer is that, although each of us is an individually conscious being, we also need others to see us and "make us real." The problem in relationships is that we try to turn other free consciousnesses (people) into objects, which is never possible.

The implication of Sartre's views is that our best chance for happiness or success in relationships is to recognize and allow the other's freedom, despite our natural wish to "own" them. We need to see the person as a free being, not simply the sum of their facticity. We can try to make others dependent on us emotionally or materially, but we can never possess their consciousness. "If Tristan and Isolde [the mythical love pair] fall madly in love because of a love potion," Sartre writes, "they are less interesting" – because a potion would cancel out their consciousness.

It is not solely the person we want to possess, as an object, but their conscious freedom to *want us*. Not even a pledge or a vow measures up to this; in fact, these are nothing compared to the full giving of a person to another in spirit. As Sartre puts it, "the Lover wants to be 'the whole World' for the beloved." To the other person, "I must be the one whose function is to make the trees and water exist." We must represent to them the final limit of their freedom, where they voluntarily choose to see no further. For ourselves, we want to be seen by the other not as an object, but as something limitlessness:

"I must no longer be seen on the ground of the world as a 'this' among other 'thises', but the world must be revealed in terms of me."

Romantic relationships are so potent, Sartre says, because they join together one person's state of Nothingness to another's Being. In plain terms, when we fall in love with someone they seem to fill a hole. We rely on the Other to make us exist (otherwise, we are the state of Nothing). Yet we are perpetually insecure in love because at any moment we can become, instead of the center of the lover's world, merely one thing among many. Thus, for Sartre this push and pull between objectivity and subjectivity are at the heart of all conflicts and unresolved issues in love. Relationships are a perpetual dance between lovers wanting to perceive each other's freedom and wanting to see each other as an object. Without the other being free, they are not attractive, yet if they are in not some way an object, we cannot have them. It is only in recognizing the other's total freedom that we can ever be said to possess them in any way. Perhaps, reducing ourselves to an object to be used by the other, but voluntarily, is in a strange way the height of being human, since it is a kind of giving that goes against the very nature of humans to be free – a gift like no other.

Sex and desire

Sartre sees sexual desire as having much less to do with the sexual organs than with states of being. We are sexual beings from birth to death, yet the sex organs do not explain our feelings of desire.

We do not desire someone merely for pleasure, or simply because they are a vessel for the pleasurable act of ejaculation; as noted above, we desire a *consciousness*. There is a big gap between normal desire and sexual desire, he points out. We can desire to drink a glass of water, and once we have drunk we are satisfied. It is that simple. But sexual desire *compromises* us, Sartre notes. Consciousness becomes "clogged" by desire; to put it another way, it invades us. We can let this happen or try to prevent it, but either way the sexual appetite is not the same as others, since it involves the mind, not only the body. We say that desire "takes hold of us" or "overwhelms us," phrases that we do not tend to use in relation to hunger or thirst, for instance.

Sartre likens sexual desire to being overcome by sleep, which is why we seem to have little power over it. Consciousness gives way to merely being a body, or in his words, "The being which desires is *making itself body.*" At the same time, during sex we wish to make the other person only flesh (thus also revealing ourselves as only flesh). Not only do we want the other person rid of all clothes and adornments, we want that body to be an *object*, no longer moving:

> *"Nothing is less 'in the flesh' than a dancer even though she is nude. Desire is an attempt to strip the body of its movements as of its clothing and to make it exist as pure flesh; it is an attempt to incarnate the Other's body."*

The caress, Sartre says, "causes the Other's flesh to be born," awakens desire in them, and at the same time makes us realize ourselves as a body, one that belongs to the world. The interplay between mind and body he describes in this way: "consciousness is engulfed in a body which is engulfed in the world."

Final comments
For a person who said that appreciating one's freedom and state of being was more important than "bourgeois" achievements (he refused the Nobel prize, for instance), Sartre's achievements were great. Notwithstanding his remark that "Success is not important to freedom," could it be said that he left us with a recipe for success?

Clearly, yes. Apart from the broader ethic of individual freedom, the recipe is to "insert my action into the network of determinism." By this he meant that we must accept the milieu into which we have been born, yet be willing to transcend it. We must accept the grain of our particular universe, and yet be creative in our pursuit of a meaningful life. The whole of *Being and Nothingness* is a warning not to let the apparent facts of our existence dictate its style or nature. Who we are is always a project of our own making. Sartre himself lived out this philosophy. The death of his father when he was quite young meant that there was no pressure to model himself on his parent, and he felt free to invent himself as whatever person he wished.

Consistent with their refutation of all bourgeois or middle-class values, he and fellow philosopher Simone de Beauvoir never married or had children, but their union of minds made them one of the great couples of the twentieth century. For most of their lives they lived in apartments within a stone's throw of each other and would spend several hours a day together; they admitted that it was difficult to know which ideas in their writing originated with one or the other. Their thoughts on being, love, and relationships remain some of the most penetrating ever written.

Jean-Paul Sartre

Sartre was born in Paris in 1905. His father was a naval officer who died when his son was only a year old. Sartre was raised by his mother, a first cousin of philosopher and missionary Albert Schweitzer, and his grandfather, a doctor who provided him with a knowledge of the classics.

He attended the prestigious École Normale Supérieure, where his reading of Henri Bergson's Time and Free Will sparked his love of philosophy. He became deeply influenced by Hegel, Kant, Kierkegaard, and Heidegger, and was well known at the École for his practical joking. In 1929 he met Simone de Beauvoir, who was at the Sorbonne. Their relationship would include affairs on both sides and the sharing of lovers of both sexes.

Sartre was conscripted during the Second World War, serving as a meteorologist. He became a prisoner of war and was later discharged from military service due to ill health. Being and Nothingness *was a product of this rich period, as were* The Flies *(1943),* No Exit *(1944), and* Anti-Semite and Jew *(1944). He collaborated with existentialist Albert Camus briefly before working on* The Roads to Freedom *(1945), a trilogy of novels about the philosophical and political viewpoints on the war. Another landmark title is the* Critique of Dialectical Reason *(1960).*

Sartre traveled widely, visiting Cuba to meet Fidel Castro and Ernesto "Che" Guevara. In 1964 he refused the Nobel Prize for literature, but it was awarded to him in any case. His constant smoking and amphetamine use made his health deteriorate; he died in 1980 and is buried in Paris's Montparnasse Cemetery.

The World as Will and Representation

"The world is my representation: this is a truth valid with reference to every living and knowing being, although man alone can bring it into reflective, abstract consciousness. If he really does so, philosophical discernment has dawned on him. It then becomes clear and certain to him that he does not know a sun and an earth, but only an eye that sees a sun, a hand that feels an earth; that the world around him is there only as representation ... If any truth can be expressed a priori, it is this."

"[T]he objective world, the world as representation, is not the only side of the world, but merely its external side, so to speak, and ... the world has an entirely different side which is its innermost being, its kernel, the thing-in-itself."

In a nutshell

The advanced person tries to live less according to the blind urges of their will (or ego) and more in attunement with whatever is eternal and beyond the self.

In a similar vein

CHAPTER 45

Arthur Schopenhauer

At the start of the second volume of *The World as Will and Representation*, Arthur Schopenhauer includes a quote from Seneca: "Paucis natus est, qui populum aetatis suae cogitat." (Whoever in his thinking takes note of his own age will influence only a few.) Though he later had a large influence on Richard Wagner, Nietzsche, Freud, Einstein, and Wittgenstein, for most of his life Schopenhauer was an independent scholar who received little recognition. The big-name German philosopher of his day was Hegel, and the cantankerous Schopenhauer despised him and his ideas. The message of the quote above is: "Don't be led by philosophies such as Hegel's which may seem right now, but will be discredited in time. Instead, I give you a worldview that is both correct and timeless."

Remarkably, Schopenhauer wrote *The World as Will and Representation* while still in his twenties. In 1844 he published an extended version of it, twice the length of the original, and continued to tinker with it for the rest of his life, though his basic ideas remained the same. Ever forthright, he told readers to go through the work twice, noting, "What is to be imparted by it is a single thought. Yet in spite of all my efforts, I have not been able to find a shorter way of imparting that thought than the whole of this book."

Though heavily influenced by Plato and Kant, what set Schopenhauer apart among Western philosophers was his deep knowledge of the ancient Hindu and Buddhist texts, and his thinking provides an early, valuable bridge between East and West. He was a brilliant writer who made his ideas intelligible to the nonacademic reader, and almost 200 years after publication the book remains both accessible and richly rewarding, mixing academic rigor with very personal thoughts on the world.

Representation and reality

To understand Schopenhauer we must first go back to Kant, who believed that there is the phenomenal world, which we can perceive with our senses, and then there are "things in themselves," which have an eternal reality existing separate to our perception. Given that we are restricted to our senses, we can never actually know this "world in itself." Schopenhauer accepted this, but thought that through reason we could work out the true reality (the "nouemenon").

In contrast to our multifarious world of many things and many percep-tions, the nouemenon had to have a unity and be beyond space and time. What we take to be so real, Schopenhauer argues, is in fact merely a representation or projection of the mind. In a total inversion of common sense, the world that we barely intimate does have a permanent reality and, logically, the phenomenal, conditional, or representational world (the "real" world) lacks any permanent reality or substance, for everything in it either dies or changes form.

However, Schopenhauer says that the phenomenal world is not chaos but operates according to "sufficient reason," or the laws of cause and effect. As long as we admit that we live in a world of causality, it makes perfect sense, even if it is one that has been projected by our minds. Indeed, the principle of sufficient reason is what stops a world of representation from being a hopeless illusion. Even the laws of time and space are part of the conditional world, he notes, and have no eternal verity themselves – they are not things-in-them-selves, but simply a good way of explaining the phenomena of time and space. Time does not really exist, but it seems to do so to us observers, who must construct a world of representation along the dimensions of time and space. For Schopenhauer, Kant's notion of "things-in-themselves" was strongly similar to Plato's "Forms," expressed in the allegory of the cave.

Everything in time and space is relative. That is, one moment in time only has reality in relation to the moment coming just after or before it. In space, one object only has reality in relation to another one. From the Western tradition, Schopenhauer invokes Heraclitus' observation that things are in eternal flux and have no fixed reality, and from the East he refers to the Hindu concept of "Maya," that the world is simply a projection or a dream, very open to misinterpretation by the observer. Not only is space, or the world of objects, a representation of who views it, but so is time. Taking an indirect dig at his nemesis Hegel, Schopenhauer argues that history is not an objective account of what happened, or some process leading to a particular goal or aim, but is simply a story told in the eye of the perceiver: "Past and future are as empty and unreal as any dream."

Schopenhauer's will

For Schopenhauer, "will" is the innermost being of the phenomenal world, and expresses itself as a sort of blind and purposeless striving of all kinds – a will to life. Rather than the traditional meaning of the term as conscious willing, will is best seen as a kind of energy constantly looking for an outlet. It explains not only the striving of humans, but the life force in animals, plants, and even the inanimate world.

In the prize-winning *Parerga and Paralipomena*, Schopenhauer examined the question of free will, writing:

"Subjectively ... everyone feels that he only does what he wills. But this means merely that his actions are the pure manifestation of his very own essence."

What we will is merely the expression of what we are, our character, and we cannot have any actions that are not consistent with that character. Our motives are not freely chosen, and therefore we cannot be said to have free will. Indeed, many of our actions are taken without really knowing why. For the average person, "consciousness keeps him always working steadfastly and actively in accordance with the aim of his willing ... This is the life of almost all men."

It is easy to see how Sigmund Freud, who depicted humans as creatures driven by subconscious urges, was influenced by Schopenhauer. Freud's conception of "ego" clearly resembles Schopenhauer's will.

Can the will be transcended?

Whereas most philosophers would see such a life force or will in neutral or positive terms, Schopenhauer envisages it as a negative power that must be transcended if we are to get anywhere. He notes that "great intensity of willing" inevitably causes suffering, because all willing comes from want. Whereas the good and wise person identifies with the formless and the true, viewing themselves as simply a corporeal expression of timeless spiritual substance, the uncultured or wicked person identifies totally with their body and their will. Such a person believes fully in their sovereignty as an individual; by contrast, everyone and everything else is less important. Yet individual will is of less import than the general will that drives everyone and everything, so too much belief in oneself entails a life of illusion, never perceiving that the phenomenal world is merely a big construction, behind which lies something real: ·

"In this form he sees not the inner nature of things, which is one, but its phenomena as separated, detached, innumerable, very different, and indeed opposed."

Such a person tends to see things in opposites, makes strong judgments all the time, and seeks pleasure to avoid pain, without realizing that its pursuit in fact causes pain. Eventually they may come to see that the *principium individuationis* by which they live is the source of their dread.

Those who perceive the world in a less separate way find a path toward freedom. We comprehend that what we do to others, we do to ourselves. Only at the point where we see that there is no "I," and our actions reflect this, do we free ourselves from the cycle of birth, old age, sickness, and death, as well as from imprisonment within the bounds of time, space, and causality. The wise person sees good and bad, pleasure and pain as mere phenomena, various expressions of Oneness. They know that the denial of their personal will (or ego), and the realization that they are not separate from others, leads to peace.

Means of transcendence

Moving beyond the "I" was for Schopenhauer the key to transcending the will, and the obvious way to this was through the ascetic or monastic life, which enabled a person to turn away from the brute forces of will, desire, and the body. Thankfully, though, there was another route through the experience of nature or art.

The normal human state of mind is constant analyzing, reasoning, or evaluating, but it is possible to give our whole mind to the present moment. When looking at a landscape, for instance, we can lose ourselves in the object, such that "we forget our individuality, our will, and continue to exist as a pure subject, as clear mirror of the object ... and thus we are no longer able to separate the perceiver from the perception, but the two have become one."

What is left, Schopenhauer notes, is not simply an object existing in relation to other objects, but the very "Idea" of the thing, its eternal form. Lost in seeing it, the viewer is no longer an individual, but is one with the idea. The world suddenly seems clearer and more meaningful, because we have penetrated beyond obvious appearances to the essence. Art can isolate one crucial idea or thing and by presenting it in a certain way illuminate the Whole, which lies beyond reason or causality. Science, on the other hand, being only concerned with the phenomenal world, is a never-ending quest that cannot ever give us complete satisfaction.

Schopenhauer defines genius as "the capacity to remain in a state of pure perception," forgetting the individual self and existing for a time in state of imagination only, seeing the timeless Ideas of the universe. When, inevitably, we come back to the experience of being an individual self, we will have compassionate sympathy for all living things. This feeling for others is a means for us to remain beyond the grasp of the will or ego, because in living a compassionate life we hardly have time to worry about ourselves.

Final comments

Writing at a time when European missionaries were fanning out across Asia to convert people to Christianity, *The World as Will and Representation* offered Schopenhauer's well-known prophecy that such efforts would be as effective as firing "a bullet at a cliff." Rather, he believed, Eastern wisdom would flow back to Europe to "produce a fundamental change in our knowledge and thought."

He was right. Though Christianity has had more success on the subcontinent than he expected, Eastern religion and mysticism have had a big, and growing, impact in the West, particularly concepts of the Whole compared to the atomizing, categorizing outlook of the Western mind.

The conventional view of Schopenhauer is that he was the "supreme pessimist." Because the will had no positive goal, obviously the human experience had to be one of constant challenge, at its best, or meaningless pain, at its worst. He did not try to pretend that the world and people's motivations were something they were not, and this impressed pessimistic writers like Joseph Conrad and Ivan Turgenev, as well as the existentialists. And yet, Schopenhauer's conclusion is not actually dark at all, but rather uplifting: it is only our dependence on the world of phenomena (the "real world") as the source of truth that always proves to be such a painful dead end. Though we are beings who exist in time and space, paradoxically it is only in moving beyond these constructs that we are liberated.

Arthur Schopenhauer

Schopenhauer was born in 1788 in what is now the Polish city of Gdansk. When he was 5 the family left for Hamburg, because Gdansk was about to be taken over by Prussia. It was expected that he would follow in his father's merchant footsteps, taking over the family firm. Between 1797 and 1799 he spent a long period living in France with his father, and he also lived in England, the Netherlands, Switzerland, and Austria. But in 1805 his father committed suicide, which opened the way for his son to follow his own wishes and attend university.

At Gottingen Schopenhauer enrolled in medicine, but also attended philosophy lectures and studied Plato and Kant. He spent two years in Berlin, where he went to lectures by Fichte, and his dissertation for the University of Jena was "On the Fourfold Root of the Principle of Sufficient Reason." After writing The World as Will and Representation, *Schopenhauer returned to Berlin, where he became a freelance lecturer. Hegel was also at the university and Schopenhauer scheduled his lectures to coincide precisely with Hegel's, expecting to draw students away, but in fact they deserted Schopenhauer and his academic career stalled. He was only able to survive thanks to an inheritance from his father.*

His mother Johanna was a novelist and a socialite, and for most of his life she was more famous than him. Though his relations with her were rocky, her literary circle allowed him to meet Goethe (with whom he corresponded) and other writers and thinkers.

Fleeing the cholera epidemic that claimed Hegel, in 1831 Schopenhauer fled Berlin and settled in Frankfurt. The prize-winning Parerga and Paralipomena *(1851) finally brought him the fame he craved. He died in 1860.*

The Life You Can Save

"Most of us are absolutely certain that we wouldn't hesitate to save a drowning child, and that we would do it at considerable cost to ourselves. Yet while thousands of children die each day, we spend money on things we take for granted and would hardly miss if they were not there. Is that wrong? If so, how far does our obligation to the poor go?"

"Giving to strangers, especially those beyond one's community, may be good, but we don't think of it as something we have to do. But if the basic argument presented above is right, then what many of us consider acceptable behaviour must be viewed in a new, more ominous light. When we spend our surplus on concerts or fashionable shoes, on fine dining and good wines, or on holidays in faraway places, we are doing something wrong."

In a nutshell

Giving to those in need on a systematic basis is an important part of living a good life.

In a similar vein

Aristotle *Nicomachean Ethics* (p 28)
Jeremy Bentham *Principles of Morals and Legislation* (p 50)
John Rawls *A Theory of Justice* (p 246)
Michael Sandel *The Tyranny of Merit* (p 264)

CHAPTER 46

Peter Singer

Every day you pass a pond in a park on your way to work, where children like to play when the weather is hot. One morning you see a child flailing about in the water, apparently drowning. If you wade into the water to get to the child you will ruin the new shoes you have just bought, muddy your suit, and be late for work.

In Peter Singer's classes on practical ethics, his students unanimously say that you should get into the water to save the child; the other things simply don't matter. Yet if our normal reaction to such things is that *of course* you would act to save the child's life, why do we spend so much on unnecessary things (more pairs of shoes, dinners out, a house renovation) when that money could easily save children's lives? Or, as Singer bluntly puts it: "Is it possible that by choosing to spend your money on such things rather than contributing to an aid agency, you are leaving a child to die, a child that you could have saved?"

Such conundrums are the meat of Singer's utilitarian philosophy. The Australian-born Princeton professor came to prominence with *Animal Liberation* (1973). His supremely rational approach has led him to controversial stances, such as a rejection of the sanctity of human life and elevating the rights of primates, so when he began looking at the question of world poverty the results were always going to be interesting. *The Life You Can Save* is a very accessible book that also manages to encapsulate Singer's broader philosophical positions, so is a great entry point to his thinking.

Look at the facts

Singer is not blind to the massive increase in prosperity in the last 50 years, which has lifted hundreds of millions out of poverty. In 1981, four in ten people around the world lived in extreme need; by 2008, it was one in four. Nevertheless, over 1.4 billion people still live on less than $1.25 a day, the World Bank's poverty threshold, and despite rapid increases in standards of living in East Asia, the number of people who are extremely poor in Sub-Saharan Africa (50 percent of the population) has not changed in 30 years.

Moreover, Singer points out, what "poor" means in developed countries is different from "poor" in the rest of the world. Most people in this category in rich countries still have running water, electricity, and access to basic healthcare, and their children can get free education; most have televisions and cars; even if their diet is not good, hardly any actually go hungry. For poor people in developing countries, poverty means not having enough food to eat for at least some of the year, difficulties in finding clean water, and little or no healthcare provision. Even if they do have enough food, their diet may well lack essential nutrients, which can leave their children permanently brain damaged.

One in five children in poor countries dies before they are 5; in rich countries it is one in a hundred. Thousands die of measles, an easily treatable disease, because of the simple fact that their parents cannot afford to take them to hospital. What must it feel like, Singer asks, for parents to watch a child slowly weaken and die, knowing that this could have been prevented?

Through various examples Singer describes how, though "most of us consider it obligatory to lessen the serious suffering of innocent others, even at some cost (or even a high cost) to ourselves," we only seem to do this when confronted with situations right in front of us. Yet if we are to live in line with that statement, intuition must be replaced with logic:

1. If people are dying from not enough food or water or medical care, and you can prevent this without sacrificing anything big, you should do so.
2. By giving money to aid agencies, you can be directly responsible for saving lives, without much cost to you.
3. Therefore, it is wrong *not* to give to aid agencies.

Our duty to act

To build his case, Singer draws on a surprising source: religion. He notes that there are 3,000 references in the Bible to alleviating poverty. Aquinas said that whatever we have beyond natural provision for ourselves and our family "is owed, of natural right, to the poor for their sustenance." The Hebrew word for charity, *tzedakah*, means "justice," a term that rests on the assumption that giving is an essential part of living a good life. Moreover, the Talmud states that charity equals all the other commandments combined, and that Jews should give at least 10 percent of their income as *tzedakah*. In the Islamic concepts of *zakat* and *sadaqa* we also find ideas of systematic giving; in the Chinese tradition there are similar messages. Singer suggests: "There is nothing new about the idea that we have a strong moral obligation to help those in need." Giving, he says, is not a matter of charity but of "our duty and their rights."

In response to the argument that "giving money or food breeds dependency," Singer agrees, noting that we should give money or food only for emergencies like drought or floods. It is much better to help communities build sustainable sources of wealth or grow their own food. And in response to the view that we should give to our own before thinking of the wider world ("charity begins at home"), Singer accepts that it may be more natural for us to want to give to our families, friends, and local communities, but that does not make it more ethically justified.

He also addresses the view that people should make decisions on giving for themselves and there is no absolute right or wrong on the matter. Singer dismisses this as weak moral relativism. Surely, if we can save a child's life this is a matter of obligation: if an adult watching a child drowning did nothing on the basis of "freedom of choice," we would think them mad or evil.

Why don't we give more?

Singer points out the various psychological factors accounting for a lack of giving. He notes the fact that people give more when presented with a picture of a starving child, compared to being given statistics on poverty. He recalls Mother Teresa's remark: "If I look at the mass I will never act. If I look at the one, I will." We are less disturbed by natural disasters that happen in some far country, because we have no emotional connection to them. For instance, Americans gave $1.5 billion to the victims of the Asian tsunami, but the following year donated $6.5 billion to help those affected by Hurricane Katrina in New Orleans. A desire to help those in our family or tribal group is part of our evolution, so this more immediate focus for giving is understandable. However, in this day of instant communication such parochialism is no longer justified. We can see devastation on the news one evening, and within a few days our money can be having a real effect on people's lives on the other side of the planet.

Singer also considers the fact that we are less likely to act if our giving seems like "drops in the ocean." This "futility factor" means that we are much more likely to donate when our contribution means that 50 people in a group of 100 will be saved, than if it means that 200 out of a group of 1,000 will be saved. It is not the total number of lives saved that affects us, but the power that we think our giving will have. And yet, the lives of the people we do help can be transformed.

While psychological studies demonstrate that humans prefer to look after their own rather than strangers, Singer says that this should never be a justification for not giving to those we do not know or will never meet. The key question must be what we *ought* to do – our giving should not rest on emotional reactions. While some traditions have emphasized anonymity as the highest form of giving, Singer instead suggests "getting it into the open"; that is, creating a new cult of giving that makes it ever more socially acceptable and expected.

Your child or mine?

Given how many lives the money could save, Singer wonders whether we can justify sending our child to an expensive private school or a top university. We can, but only if there is the intention that the child will benefit many people as a result of that education (whether it is through direct work for the worse off or in giving money earned), instead of solely themselves. This question is part of the larger issue of how we weigh up the worth of our own children's lives in relation to other children. If, for instance, we spend 400 or 4,000 times more on our own kids than a desperately poor child somewhere else, does that mean that their life is 4,000 times more valuable? He concludes that we will never get around human nature in thinking that we can love and care for other children as much as we do our own; but neither can we really justify giving our children luxuries when it means that we cannot help out in providing basic needs to other children.

Singer is not a communist or an extreme socialist. He does not, for instance, advocate higher taxes, and he takes his hat off to entrepreneurs for making the world richer. He also admits that sometimes it is better to give less now if you are building a business that could generate much more wealth later on; on the other hand, by giving now you can reduce poverty, which will reduce the later effects of that poverty.

How much to give

How much should we give? Singer notes that there are around 855 million rich people in the world; that is, with an income higher than the average earnings of an adult in Portugal. If each gave only $200 a year, that would *halve* global poverty (not short-term aid fixes, but money going toward making poor communities genuinely sustainable). And $200 is hardly a lot of money: a couple of nice meals out, or less than $20 a month.

Singer takes aim at the ridiculous profligacy of the world's billionaires. Apart from the tens of millions laid out on huge yachts and private planes, he mentions the telecoms entrepreneur Anousheh Ansari, who gave a reported $20 million merely to spend 11 days in space. Microsoft co-founder Paul Allen's yacht cost $200 million and has a permanent staff of 60, as well as huge carbon emissions. "It's time we stopped thinking of these ways of spending money as silly but harmless displays of vanity," Singer comments, "and started thinking of them as evidence of a grievous lack of concern for others."

He tells the story of Chris Ellinger and his wife Anne, who set up an organization called The 50% League, whose members commit to giving away at least half of their wealth. Not only for millionaires, the organization's website mentions a couple who have committed to living on less than the US median income of $46,000, giving away whatever they earn on top of this. The donor remarks: "I could easily have lived a life that was boring and inconsequential. Now I am graced with a life of service and meaning."

Final comments

Singer ends the book by mentioning his friend Henry Spira, a campaigner for animal rights and social justice, who on his deathbed said:

> *"I guess basically one wants to feel that one's life has amounted to more than just consuming products and generating garbage. I think that one likes to look back and say that one's done the best one can to make this a better place for others. You can look at it from this point of view: what greater motivation can there be than doing whatever one possibly can to reduce pain and suffering?"*

A survey of 30,000 Americans found that those who made giving a part of their life were on average 43 percent more likely to say that they were "very happy" compared to those who did not. The figure was similar for those who did voluntary work for charities. This seems to prove Buddha's statement: "Set your heart on doing good. Do it over and over again, and you will be filled with joy." Yet part of the point of *The Life You Can Save* is that we should go beyond the emotional benefits of giving and see its unassailable ethics.

Singer reminds us that the good life is not about good health, property, new cars, and holidays, but about recognizing what we can do to make the world a more just place. His wish to reach beyond the walls of academic philosophy has put him on lists of the world's top public intellectuals. *The Life You Can Save* is a reminder of how powerful philosophy can be in the real world.

Peter Singer

Singer was born in 1946. His parents emigrated to Australia to escape Nazi persecution in their native Austria. He studied law, history, and philosophy at the University of Melbourne, and then won a scholarship to Oxford, where he focused on moral philosophy. After stints teaching at Oxford and at New York University, he spent two decades back in Australia at Melbourne and Monash Universities. In 1999 he took up his current post as Ira W. De Camp Professor of Bioethics at Princeton University.

Other books include Practical Ethics *(1979),* The Expanding Circle: Ethics and Sociobiology *(1981),* Hegel *(1982),* Should the Baby Live? The Problem of Handicapped Infants *(1985),* Rethinking Life and Death: The Collapse of Our Traditional Ethics *(1994),* A Darwinian Left *(2000), and* The Ethics of What We Eat *(2007, with Jim Mason).*

You Must Change Your Life

"Modern 'culture' came about when the appreciation of miracles gave way to an appreciation of the miraculous."

"Whoever who has not been seized by the oversized does not belong to the species of Homo sapiens.*"*

"Wherever one encounters human beings, they are embedded in achievement fields and status classes."

In a nutshell

The human wish to be better or rise higher occurs through "practices" athletic, artistic, or religious; it's what makes us different to other animals.

In a similar vein

Hannah Arendt *The Human Condition* (p 22)
Martin Heidegger *Being and Time* (p 130)
Friedrich Nietzsche *Beyond Good and Evil* (p 218)

CHAPTER 47

Peter Sloterdijk

Why did religion return as a force in modern life, just when secularism and scientific Enlightenment values seemed to have won?

The question is misleading, says German philosopher Peter Sloterdijk, because "religions" are not what they seem. They are only on the surface spiritual institutions; what they in fact are, is "psychological immune systems."

If you see religions as a set of practices that offer mental immunity from the vicissitudes of life, the difference between "true religion" and superstition is meaningless. All that matters is how effective a religion is at propagating itself, and the main distinction is between the trained and untrained. Religions, ethical traditions such as Stoicism, and all self-help/personal development ideas, are just points on a spectrum of human practice that: a) provide protection from suffering; and b) offer a means to improve ourselves.

Sloterdijk takes a very wide, macro view of humanity, almost as if he is an alien come to examine planet Earth. *You Must Change Your Life* provides a philosophical foundation for understanding human striving through the ages.

Planet of the practising

All humans: 1) seek immunity from suffering, and 2) seek to realize their potential. What differs is the specific practices and outlooks (that differ in time and place) we adopt to achieve this. We seek immunity to life's physical and biological threats, but we also seek to avoid the shadow of death and chaos through skills, rituals, languages, etiquette, training, exercises, education, habits, and custom.

"Anthropotechnics" is a word Sloterdijk coins for the study of the way humans work on themselves and use technology to aid their progress. *Homo repetitivus* or *Homo artista* ("the human in training") is constantly involved in self-forming or self-enhancing behaviour in pursuit of goals. We possess the belief that, "Small human forces can achieve the impossible if they are multiplied by the longer distance of practice."

Most self-development practices grew out of religion – then became secularized. Today, most people are engaged in activities to enhance and improve life. The loser from this trend, Sloterdijk argues, will be religion. If religions are revealed as simply bodies of practice, they somewhat lose their aura.

Humans are acrobats

"Wherever one encounters human beings," Sloterdijk says, "they are embedded in achievement fields and status classes." Humans are an "upward-tending animal …Whoever goes in search of humans will find acrobats."

The title of Sloterdijk's book is taken from Rilke's sonnet 'Archaic Torso of Apollo' at the start of his *New Poems: The Other Part* (1908). The sonnet is about the stone sculpture of a headless torso of Apollo in the Louvre museum. Rilke writes:

> … *for there is no place*
>
> *That does not see you*
>
> *You must change your life*

The last lines are a shock, because until this point the poem has been a description of a statue. Now, having taken in its power, the effect of it is to electrify the viewer, Rilke, into doing something, to make *his* life great. It's the same experience we get after walking out of the cinema with a head full of inspiration – an imperative to act.

Every teaching of every religion, every programme of every sect and philosophy, Sloterdijk says, if they could all be distilled into a single idea, would be Rilke's command *You must change your life*. That is, "I am already living, but something is telling me with unchallengeable authority: you are not living properly." This "vertical tension" is the gap between what we are now and what we wish to be.

The ancient Greeks often made victorious sportsmen into gods of sorts. The athlete's body, therefore, is one of the earliest symbols of authority, and is expressed today in the form of the personal trainer. When they command, "You must get in shape!" even billionaires listen obediently, because they know that comfort is the enemy of greatness.

If you were an alien looking down on earth, Nietzsche says in *The Genealogy of Morals*, you would see it as the ascetic planet, its humans disgusted with themselves and with life. He sees a crucial difference between the Christian ascetics, who tried to outdo each other in suffering and self-denial, and who believed that they were setting the standard and must be followed by others – and athletes, warriors, artists, and philosophers, who work on themselves only to optimize their performance and achieve their own goals, not at the expense of anyone else.

Sloterdijk's own distinction is between the "God-referential" (people engaged in practices all about losing or lessening the self) and the self-referential (people whose practices are to improve and expand the self). History reveals a "despiritualization" of ascetic practices (sporting achievement is the best example) on one hand, and on the other an "informalization" of spirituality (popular music gives a spiritual rush and sense of devotion). Thus the nature of humans as practising beings can be seen as a wide spectrum.

At the end of *Genealogy of the Morals*, Nietzsche anxiously asks how humans will manage after the "twilight of the gods." He shouldn't have been worried, Sloterdijk says. The main thing is that there is always a vertical dynamic in humans (with or without God); we are always moving towards something higher or better.

In earlier epochs in which everything was seen as coming from God, it seemed very wrong for people to make much of themselves, to stand out. The heroic move was losing the self to gain transcendence. Today, humans are seen to have responsibility for their own life – *not* making much of ourselves is the crime.

Self-striving and self-shaping

Wittgenstein wrote in one of his notebooks: "Culture is a monastic rule. Or at least it presupposes a monastic rule." He meant that cultures form on the basis of a group of people wanting to live by a certain standard. Religious motifs and the quest for ethical perfection ran through Wittgenstein's life. In response to a question from an acquaintance, he reputedly said, "Of course I want to be perfect!" He was one of the few modern philosophers who wanted to bring philosophy back from being an academic subject, to a discipline for life. For Wittgenstein, language either reflected an attempt to live consciously according to a chosen set of rules, or it reflected unconscious absorption and acceptance of culture, or what he called "swinishness."

The other philosopher who was interested in human "exercise" – or practice – is Foucault. Towards the end of his life, this archetypal Parish intellectual moved away from his earlier revolutionary stance to a more positive view of humankind. From the wish to destroy, to observations of how people build. He became interested in "self-work" and "self-shaping," and the possibility of transcending the self. Foucault studied the ascetic practices of the early Stoics, which he thought were an example of "technologies of the self." He was moving away from "pure" philosophy to the history of human practice. This "General Disciplinics" as Sloterdijk terms it, was simply about the fulfilment of human potential.

Self-improving society: fate vs action

Gautama Buddha strived to set his teachings apart from the *niyati* philosophy of his contemporary, Makkhali Gosala, which emphasized the inability of humans to direct their fate. Gosala said that beings were condemned to a cycle of 84,000 incarnations, and there was nothing they could do to get outside it. Buddha disagreed: we are not condemned to anything. We can accelerate our awakening through wisdom and methods.

It was no accident that Buddha attracted the better off people in society, Sloterdijk says, because advanced civilizations generate people who want to move ahead quicker. "They look for proof that they are moving themselves, not simply being carried along by the course of things like the rock on the imperceptibly flowing glacier." They are no longer content to accept "fate." Buddhism was very similar to Greek sophism, which saw fatalism as "an assault on *areté*, the willingness to self-help."

You can view history as "General Immunology," Sloterdijk says, whereby the societal body builds an immune system to ward off the diseases of entropy and fate. But groups within society may start to believe that it is no longer providing these spiritual or moral goods. They create what Foucault called a "heterotopia" where they can work on themselves or pursue a direction without distraction, heading off vulnerability to fate, death and chaos through rituals, habits, and exercises. A utopia is a perfect place, but a heterotopia is simply a place of personal practice. Examples include the early Christian desert communities, and the Buddhist sangha – anywhere people can pursue self-technologies and self-making.

The anthropotechnic view is based on the belief, Sloterdijk writes, that "small human forces can achieve the impossible if they are multiplied by the longer distance of practice." He identifies five kinds of life trainers:

- ❖ The guru of Hindu tradition
- ❖ The Buddhist master of the doctrine of liberation
- ❖ The apostle who shows the way to the imitation of Christ
- ❖ The philosopher who is witness to the search for truth
- ❖ The sophist who is an expert on the ways of life

At a lesser level, there are athletic trainers, masters of a craft or virtuosity, academic professors, regular teachers, and the Enlightenment author. Today's key trainer is of course the motivational coach or personal physical trainer.

The philosophical anthropologist Dieter Heinrich points out that the modern person is not meant to simply live their life, they have to "lead" it. In a self-improving society, trainers are accorded some reverence because they hold they keys to our acrobatic success.

Final comments

To sum up: the self-improvement project, which began as a religious one involving small spiritual communities, became secular and scientific. We now live in a virtuoso society, a culture of striving. Modernity is a "global fitness exercise," Sloterdijk says, inspired by the possibility of an elevated life. It aims to immunize us against fate or inertia.

The only problem with *Homo artista*, Sloterdijk points out, is that people don't quite know whether they should be working on themselves, or working to improve the world. Is it naïve to believe you can change the world before working on yourself? Foucault was a Left Bank revolutionary before becoming interested in self-technologies. In contrast, Buddhism teaches that decades of practice are the basis of any positive impact; any action taken by an enlightened person is automatically beneficial.

Sloterdijk never makes a moral judgement about Rilke's command, *You must change your life*. Yet by creating an archaeology of striving and self-improvement, he shows just how fundamental this urge is to human life. All government, culture, religion and technology is an attempt to head off the deadening hand of fate and confusion, and to create hope and order. All personal practice, from religious to sporting to work, is for the fulfilment of potential – for our own glory, and for the glory of our species. Look what we can do.

Peter Sloterdijk

Born in 1947 in Karlsruhe, Germany, Sloterdijk had a German mother and Dutch father. In the late 1960s and early 1970s he studied at the Universities of Munich and Hamburg, and gained his PhD in philosophy and the history of modern autobiographic literature in 1975.

He became an independent intellectual and writer. In 1983 he published the two-volume Critique of Cynical Reason, *a bestseller in Germany. In 1989 he was appointed Director of the Institute for Cultural Philosophy at Vienna's Academy of Fine Arts, and in 1992 became Professor of Philosophy and Media Theory at the Karlsruhe University of Arts and Design. From 2002 to 2012 he co-hosted a television show,* In the Glasshouse: The Philosophical Quartet, *on Germany's ZDF channel.*

Sloterdijk's magnum opus is the Spheres *trilogy (1998–2004). Other books include* Nietzsche Apostle *(2013),* Rage and Time *(2010),* In the World Interior of Capital: Towards a Philosophical Theory of Globalization *(2013),* What Happened in the Twentieth Century? *(2018) and* After God *(2020) – dates are English translations.*

Sloterdijk's honours include the Austrian Decoration for Science and Art (2005), France's Commander of the Ordre des Arts des Lettres (2006), and Germany's literary Ludwig-Börne-Prize 2013.

Ethics

"Particular things are nothing but affections of God's attributes, or modes by which God's attributes are expressed in a certain and determinate way."

"As for the terms good and bad, they indicate no positive quality in things regarded in themselves, but are merely modes of thinking, or notions which we form from the comparison of things one with another. Thus one and the same thing can be at the same time good, bad, and indifferent. For instance, music is good for him that is melancholy, bad for him that mourns; for him that is deaf, it is neither good nor bad."

"Human infirmity in moderating and checking the emotions I name bondage: for, when a man is a prey to his emotions, he is not his own master, but lies at the mercy of fortune."

In a nutshell

Free will is an illusion, but by mastering our emotions and appreciating the perfection of universal laws we can lead a good life.

In a similar vein

Gottfried Leibniz *Theodicy* (p 170)
Arthur Schopenhauer *The World as Will and Representation* (p 280)

CHAPTER 48

Baruch Spinoza

Baruch Spinoza's *Ethics* was a path-breaking work in Western philosophy because, in a time when theology was everything, it provided a naturalistic or scientific view of the universe. It also became a guide for approaching life in a rational rather than a religious way. Consistent with his desire to be the voice of reason, the book adopts an almost mathematical style, copying the form of treatises on geometry with every term clearly defined and "proofs" offered for each statement made. This way of doing philosophy has been much copied, by Wittgenstein among others.

Spinoza sees the world as running according to strict physical laws that allow for no miracles, without an end or goal in mind – a notion that would later support Darwin's concept of evolution through directionless natural selection. With such ideas, we see why Spinoza is often considered the first truly modern philosopher, attempting to throw off dogma and superstition to embrace a naturalistic cosmology. He also offers some answers as to how, amid the universe's impersonal workings that seem to have no place for free will, a person might live and raise themselves higher.

When Spinoza had finished writing the *Ethics*, rumors spread; theologians on one side, and followers of Descartes on the other, were "ready to pounce" if the book was published. In this climate, Spinoza, who had been famously expelled from his Dutch synagogue in his twenties for "atheist" views and whose other works had been given a hostile reception, decided not to have it printed.

It is hard now to see what the fuss was all about, for Spinoza's aim was simply to provide a more grounded treatment of religion, the human passions, and nature. In the process he does in fact argue at some length for the existence of a deity, and ends with a call for the "intellectual love of God." However, the problem lay in the nature of Spinoza's God, who was not the personal savior of the New Testament, but rather an impersonal "Substance" that runs the universe according to strict, immutable laws that make no allowances for the specialness of humans; we are merely an impermanent expression of the life force that runs through the universe. This "pantheist" view (God expressed through nature) went against Christian dogma of a clear separation between the creator and creation.

Here we look at what Spinoza actually said and why he has been so influential.

The universe operates via causes, and we are no special case

Spinoza posits that everything that exists has a cause, and everything that does not exist also has a reason why it does not. At any one time, it is either necessary that something exists, or it is impossible for it to exist ("if, in nature, a certain number of individuals exists, there must be a cause why those individuals, and why neither more nor fewer, exist"). However, this cause usually cannot be discerned by humans themselves.

Spinoza writes that "a man is the cause of another man [on a simple biological level], but not of his essence, for the latter is an eternal truth." God is therefore the cause of our coming into being, but He also gives us our desire to persevere in being – our life force, as it were. This should not be confused with freedom of the will. Human beings are simply "modes by which God's attributes are expressed in a certain and determinate way," and there is nothing a person can do to reverse this determination. Naturally, when an entity creates something, it has an intention in mind for it. This intention is the essence of the thing. Accordingly, Spinoza observes,

"In nature there is nothing contingent, but all things have been determined from the necessity of the divine nature to exist and produce an effect in a certain way."

People think that they are free because they seem to have volition and appetites and desires, yet we go through life being largely ignorant of the real causes of things; indeed, we will never know them. For Spinoza, the will is just like the intellect in being simply a "certain mode of thinking." Our will cannot exist on its own: "God does not produce any effect by freedom of the will."

Our will is related to God in the same way that the laws of physics are; that is, the will is set in motion in the first place, and it causes other things to happen in turn. "Things could have been produced by God in no other way," Spinoza notes, "and in no other order than they have been produced." If nature was different to what it was, it would have required God's nature to be different to what it is. That would mean that two or more gods would have needed to exist, which would be absurd.

Humans are able to perceive that things can go either way "only because of a defect of our knowledge," Spinoza writes. Because the "order of causes is hidden from us," we cannot perceive that something is in fact either necessary or impossible. So we believe, mistakenly, that it is contingent.

However, none of this is to say that God organizes all things "for the Good," as Leibniz claimed. This is a prejudice of humans, Spinoza says, who like to believe that God has organized the universe for them. Superstition and religion developed in order that people could feel they were able to read into God's mind the final causes of things, and so that they could stay in God's favor. But this pursuit is a waste of time; it is better to search for truths that we can actually grasp. Through mathematics, for instance, humankind has "another standard of truth" to make sense of its world.

The nature of God

Spinoza was not content simply to agree or disagree that God exists. He brings his great powers of analysis to the question, and concludes the following.

He equates God with "substance," defined as that which is the cause of itself, not needing to be brought into being by anything else. Only God is therefore totally free, because he is uncaused; everything else is not free, because it is caused or determined. God is "absolutely infinite," expressed in an infinity of "attributes" or forms, most of which humans can perceive. We cannot see the substance of something, only its attributes – this is the means by which we must perceive it. The attributes of God are endless and infinite, while the attributes of a person are much more limited.

If God does not exist, Spinoza notes, there would have to be a very good reason why he does not; there would also need to be another substance that could give or take away God's existence. And yet, that other substance would have nothing in common with God (and therefore no power over Him) and so could not give or take away God's existence. The only power to give or take away God's existence lies in God himself; and even if God chose to nullify His existence, this act would still show that he exists. Moreover, such a contradiction would not be possible "of a Being absolutely infinite and supremely perfect." God must therefore exist.

Those things that exist have power, and those that do not lack power. If the only things that exist are finite beings, then these would be more powerful than an infinite Being. However this, Spinoza notes, would be absurd. Therefore, he reasons, "either nothing exists or an absolutely infinite Being also exists." From this, he concludes:

"For since being able to exist is power, it follows that the more reality belongs to the nature of a thing, the more powers it has, of itself, to exist. Therefore, an absolutely infinite Being, or God, has, of himself, an absolutely infinite power of existing. For that reason, he exists absolutely."

Perfection asserts something's identity, while imperfection takes it away. Given this, the perfection of God makes it supremely clear that God exists. (In contrast, the extent of imperfection of everyday things should indicate that they have no real existence.) The more an entity causes other things to exist, the greater its reality. Thus, God being the creator of everything is the most real thing in the universe.

No end in mind for the universe, and it does not exist for us

One of the radical notions in the *Ethics* is that "Nature has no end set before it." By this, Spinoza means that the universe, although it exists according to specific laws ("all things proceed by a certain eternal necessity of nature, and with the greatest perfection"), at the same time has no particular goal toward which it is moving.

How does Spinoza reconcile his belief in the perfection of God with the notion that he has no end in mind for his universe? Surely, if God has total power, he would want it to achieve some goal? Spinoza here comes up with some ingenious reasoning, observing that "if God acts for the sake of an end, he necessarily wants something which he lacks." Because he is perfect and perfectly self-sufficient, this cannot be so.

Spinoza also tries to destroy the idea that the universe was built for humankind. This prejudice means that we have to label everything in terms of good or bad, order or chaos, warm or cold, beautiful or ugly. In fact, if everything has been generated by divine substance, it all has to be intrinsically good. We do not define the world by our reactions or judgments – these define us. Even the perception of order is an affectation, for surely all that exists *is* in order.

Again, Spinoza is creating a platform for the modern scientific worldview, suggesting that we need to study the universe as objectively as we can, discarding our anthropomorphism.

Scientist of human nature

In part three of the book, "On the origin and nature of the emotions," Spinoza sets himself up as a scientist of human nature, with every emotion defined in detail. He notes that if the laws and rules of nature are uniform, then they have to apply to everything. With his characteristic precision, he says:

"The emotions, therefore, of hate, anger, envy etc., considered in themselves, follow from the same necessity and force of nature as the other singular things … I shall consider human actions and appetites just as if it were a Question of lines, planes and bodies."

All emotional states come from three primary emotions: desire, pleasure, and pain, he notes. Yet cutting through the thousands of emotional states that "exceed all computation," he sees them as serving a single, clear purpose: to confirm the existence of one's body, and so to confirm that "I" exist; body and mind are not separate in Descartes' sense. In this, Spinoza foreshadows psychology in its view that emotional states are firmly the product of the brain, nervous system, and bodily feeling rather than the "soul."

Spinoza laments that in day-to-day life most of us are blown about by external events and our emotional reactions to them. However, in the last part of the book he notes that if everything happens according to prior causes, or necessity, then we should not get too emotional about anything, because everything is unfolding as it should. Instead, we should create a framework to deal with emotions, based on the knowledge that an emotion is only overcome by another one with similar power. Thus, hatred must be overcome "with love or high-mindedness, and not ... hatred in return."

An emotion is only bad or hurtful insofar as it prevents the mind from being able to think. What is most important is that we are able to choose our reactions. In part four, Spinoza describes as "bondage" the state in which we are spun about by emotions, unable to discipline ourselves into a state of reason.

Becoming free

Spinoza does not talk of "morality," only of things that are done according to reason. Good and evil, he remarks, are nothing more than feelings of pleasure or pain. Something is good if it preserves or enhances our being, and bad if it diminishes it. "Sin" does not exist naturally, but only in a community or society; what constitutes good or evil is "pronounced by common consent." In other words, sin is simply disobedience of the laws that have been agreed. His understanding of "virtue" is also decidedly modern. Virtue is simply acting according to our own nature, or "on the basis of seeking what is useful to us."

Here, Spinoza's concept of "conatus" is important. Conatus is something's desire to persist in being; not a struggle for existence or the "will to power," but a simple urge to retain its momentum. "From all this, then," he notes, "it is clear that we neither strive for, nor will, neither want, nor desire anything because we judge it to be good; on the contrary, we judge something to be good because we strive for it, will it, want it, and desire it."

Happiness also arises not from desire or pleasure, but from reason. Reason includes knowledge of ourselves, and of the world around us as far as our intelligence allows. Whatever hinders the growth of our intelligence is not good. On a character level, people should dwell only on "human virtue or power, and the way whereby it may be perfected." We should not live according to what we fear or want to avoid, but according to the joy that we seek in living according to reason.

Spinoza makes a distinction between "adequate" ideas, those truths about life that we have generated by ourselves, through insight or reason, which lead to genuine action; and "inadequate" ideas, those ideas that cause us to act. Living according to inadequate ideas leads to a passive state in which one is always at the mercy of emotions and events. This is not a free existence. He gives some examples: a child believes that it freely wants milk; an angry child seeks revenge; a drunk speaks in what seems to be a free way, but later regrets what he said. Madmen, drunks, chatterboxes, and children all do the same; they cannot stop their impulses. In most cases, what people believe to be their decisions are in fact their appetites speaking, and these, of course, "vary as the disposition of the Body varies." However, through self-discipline and reason our emotions are put into context and seen for what they are: passing things that have no elemental truth. Through "intellectual love of God" (or keeping our mind focused on a realm of perfection beyond our mortal self), we are able to separate fact from fiction, truth from reality.

Our purpose in life is to make a transition from inadequate ideas to adequate ideas, so that we see the universe the way God sees it, instead of being subject to emotions and attachments. Presaging cognitive psychology, and echoing Buddhism, Spinoza notes that when we subject a strong emotion to analysis, its effect disappears.

The wise person moves beyond their passions and attachments to what Seneca called the *vita beata*, the blessed life. Spinoza draws a contrast between the wise person – conscious of himself, with his emotions in check, and at one with God's natural laws – and the ignorant person, driven by lust and distracted, never achieving self-knowledge, who "as soon as he ceases to suffer, ceases also to be." In sum, people who live according to reason are much more useful to others than those who live only according to their passions.

The path of the wise is not easy and is much less trodden, but "all things excellent," Spinoza famously remarks in the last line of the *Ethics*, "are as difficult as they rare."

Final comments

Einstein was once asked whether he believed in God and he replied, "I believe in Spinoza's God." By this he meant a universe run not by some personal or meddling spirit, but by impersonal natural laws.

What does it mean to be human in such a world? One clear implication, as Spinoza saw it, was the need for government that was liberal, open, and democratic, allowing for a great variety of interests and beliefs, and his *Tractatus Theologico-Politicus*, published in 1670, provides a rationale for religious liberty. The Holland of his time was one of the most liberal places in the world, but even there Spinoza's free thinking caused him trouble.

Hegel among many others believed Spinoza's work to mark the beginning of philosophy in its modern form, and one can make a good case for Spinoza being the Isaac Newton of his discipline. Such was his naturalistic bent that, were he reborn today, we can be pretty sure that he would not even use the word "God" in his writings, but rather focus on the unerring perfection of the laws on which the universe runs.

Baruch de Spinoza

Spinoza's Jewish ancestors had fled the Portuguese Inquisition and settled in prosperous Holland. He was born in Amsterdam in 1622 and his father Michael was a successful trader.

Spinoza received a good education at a local Jewish school that focused on learning Hebrew and memorizing the scriptures and grammar. He was set to become a rabbi, but when the family fortunes waned, and within a relatively short space of time his older sister, stepmother, and father died, the responsibility of continuing the family business fell to him. He carried out his duties, but also pursued a program of self-education, teaching himself Latin and studying Descartes. He began expressing doubts about his biblical education and the belief in souls and immortality, and when word got out about his views an attempt was made on his life. At 24 he was excommunicated, and even his family were not allowed to speak to him. Despite the social and emotional pressure, he did not recant.

Although somewhat of a recluse, Spinoza was said to be obliging and open, and became popular in Holland's intellectual circles. He lived in a rented room above a painter and family on one of Amsterdam's canals, and earned an income through grinding lenses. He died in 1677, at only 44 and a few months after his famous meeting with Leibniz. The Ethics was published soon after.

The Black Swan

"Linear relationships are truly the exception; we only focus on them in classrooms and textbooks because they are easier to understand. Yesterday afternoon I tried to take a fresh look around me to catalog what I could see during my day that was linear. I could not find anything, any more than someone hunting for squares or triangles could find them in the rainforest."

"We, members of the human variety of primates, have a hunger for rules because we need to reduce the dimension of matters so they can get into our heads. Or, rather sadly, so we can squeeze them into our heads. The more random information is, the greater the dimensionality, and thus the more difficult to summarize. The more you summarize, the more order you put in, the less randomness. Hence the same condition that makes us simplify pushes us to think that the world is less random than it actually is."

In a nutshell

We want to make the world seem an orderly place, but the frequency of truly unexpected events should tell us that we do not really know what causes things.

In a similar vein

David Hume *An Enquiry Concerning Human Understanding* (p 136)
Karl Popper *The Logic of Scientific Discovery* (p 242)
Baruch Spinoza *Ethics* (p 298)

CHAPTER 49

Nassim Nicholas Taleb

U ntil a black swan was sighted in Western Australia by early explorers, people assumed that swans were white; it was part of the definition of swans that they were white. However, as Nassim Nicholas Taleb points out in this sprawling, brilliant work, all you need is one variation to show up the falsity of your assumptions.

From this simple observation, derived from Hume, Taleb creates an entire theory of events and causality. His definition of a "black swan" event is one that happens against all expectations and has an extreme impact. Most intriguingly, human nature after the fact tries to explain it away, as if it had been predictable.

Our history has become the story of big events that no one expected. No one, for instance, foresaw the severity of the First World War, the rise of Hitler, the sudden collapse of the Soviet bloc, the spread of the internet, or the terrorist attacks on 9/11. No one foresees particular ideas, fashions, or art genres coming into vogue. And yet, Taleb points out,

"A small number of Black Swans explain almost everything in our world, from the success of ideas and religions, to the dynamics of historical events, to elements of our own personal lives."

Moreover, the effect of black swans is increasing because the world is becoming more complicated. The combination of low predictability and large impact causes a problem for the human mind, because our brain is built to focus on the known and visible.

Taleb imagines two places to express our ways of seeing the world. "Mediocristan" is a state in which there is an equal relation between effort and result, where the future can be predicted, and where most things fall into a wide band of averages. "Extremistan" is an inherently unstable, unpredictable, winner-takes-all kind of place. It is the latter in which we actually live, and accepting that fact is the first step to thriving in it.

As a "skeptical empiricist," Taleb's heroes are David Hume, Sextus Empiricus, and Karl Popper. He is very critical of the kind of philosophy focused on language that fills academia. While interesting, it has nothing to do with the real world, he says, a world in which people have to live with uncertainty.

What we do not know...

The black swan effect has made a mockery of attempts to curb uncertainty, whether in the form of fancy financial algorithms that purport to eliminate risk, or the predictions of social scientists. Think about your own life: how many things, from meeting your spouse to the profession you entered, came according to plan or on schedule? Who expected that you would be fired, exiled, enriched, or impoverished? Taleb observes that "Black Swan logic makes *what you don't know* far more relevant than what you do know," because it is the unexpected that shapes our lives. And if that is so, why do we keep believing that things will go as they have done in the past? Our mind, he says, suffers from a "triplet of opacity":

❖ False understanding – we believe that we understand more of what is going on in the world than we actually do.

❖ Retrospective distortion – we ascribe meaning to events after they have happened, creating a story. This is what we call "history."

❖ Overvaluing facts, statistics, and categories – we should not fool ourselves that they can predict the future, or even give us an accurate picture of reality.

We live according to rules for what we consider normal, but normality is rarely the test of anything. When something major happens out of the blue, we are keen to discount its rarity and unexpectedness. We want to be able to explain it away. Yet we do not really know a person until we see how they act in an extreme situation, and neither can we assess the danger of a criminal based on what he does on a regular day. It is the rare or unusual event that often defines a situation, not whatever is "normal."

It is not merely that the average person does not see what is going on, the so-called experts and people in charge do not either. Taleb's grandfather was a minister in the Lebanese government during its civil war, but claims that he knew no more about what was happening than his driver. He does not hold back from pointing out the "epistemic arrogance of the human race," including CEOs who believe that their company's success is down to them and not a million other factors, including blind luck. Such fantasies are encouraged in business schools, he notes.

Taleb comments that no one expected the rise of the world religions. Christian scholars are baffled by the lack of mention of their faith in its early days by Roman chronicles; equally, who could have foreseen the rapid diffusion of Islam? The historian Paul Veyne noted that religions spread "like bestsellers." Nevertheless, in our mind they quickly become part of the scenery – we normalize them. The same trait means that we will be shocked by the sudden rise of the next new religion.

To illustrate his point about extreme events, Taleb asks us to consider a farm turkey. The turkey will look on the farmer in very kindly terms, since every day he provides an abundance of food, plus shelter. But its experience thus far is totally misleading, because one day, totally unexpectedly, it is slaughtered. The moral is that, despite what we have been told, the past generally tells us nothing about the future; the apparent "normalness" of today is "viciously misleading." E.J. Smith, a ship's captain, said in 1907: "I never saw a wreck and have never been wrecked nor was I ever in any predicament that threatened to end in disaster of any sort." Five years later, the vessel under his helm was the *Titanic*.

The human brain is wired to make general assumptions from experience. The problem is that in real life, a black swan can come along after a whole existence of seeing only white ones. It is better to rest in the fact of how little we know, and also be aware of the faults in our reasoning; the point is not to be able to predict black swan events, only to be a little more mentally prepared. It is human nature to react to big, unforeseen events with small, focused adaptations that either try to prevent an event happening again (if it was bad) or to make it happen it again (if it was good). But what we should be doing is peering into what we do not know and why we do not know it. Humans think much less than we believe we do, Taleb says; most of our action is instinctive. This makes us less likely to understand black swan events, because we are always lost in the details, only reacting. Everything comes from unknown factors, while "all the while we spend our time engaged in small talk, focusing on the known, and the repeated."

...and how to get around it

We like certainty, but the wise see that certainty is elusive, that "understanding how to act under conditions of incomplete information is the highest and most urgent human pursuit."

Taleb notes that a "successions of anecdotes selected to fit a story do not constitute evidence." Instead of trying to confirm our existing ideas, we should, as Popper taught, be trying to falsify them. Only then might we get a semiaccurate sense of the truth. When making a financial bet, the best investors, like George Soros, try to find instances where their assumption is wrong. Taleb sees this "ability to look at the world without the need to find signs that stroke one's ego" as genuine self-confidence. He admits:

> "It takes considerable effort to see facts ... while withholding judgment and resisting explanations. And this theorizing disease is rarely under our control: it is largely anatomical, part of our biology, so fighting it requires fighting one's own self."

That we are like this is understandable. We have to make rules and oversimplify in order to put endless information into some order in our heads. Myths and stories enable us to make sense of our world. Science is meant to be different, but instead we use science to organize things for our own benefit. Seen in this context, knowledge is *therapy*, doing little more than making us feel better. Scientists and academics of all stripes are guilty of this, and of course we see examples in the media every day. If a candidate loses an election, "causes" will be trotted out. Whether or not they are correct is of little import; what does matter is that a narrative is quickly put in place for why an event happened. It would be shocking for the newsreader to say, "Smith lost the election, but we actually have no idea why."

Not only do we not know stuff, we totally overestimate the extent of our knowledge, and how efficient and effective we are. This overconfidence seems to be hardwired. Taleb mentions experiments with students who have to estimate the time needed to complete their assignment. Broken into two groups, the optimistic ones thought they could deliver in 26 days; the pessimists promised that they would deliver in 47 days. What was the actual average time for completion? 56 days. (Taleb's own manuscript was delivered to his publisher 15 months late.)

We are like this because we "tunnel" mentally, not taking account of the "unexpected" things that take us off course, while of course the unexpected should be incorporated into calculations for the achievement of anything.

Final comments

Taleb's assertion that "almost no discovery, no technologies of note, came from design and planning – they were just Black Swans" is easily argued against. For example, DuPont spent years developing Nylon, knowing how valuable the material would be; and most successful medicines, though they often stem from chance discoveries, need years of development and planning before being brought to market. Yet Taleb is right that organizations and individuals need to focus more on tinkering than on planning, in the probability that, through constant trial and error, the chances are increased of creating a *positive* black swan – an idea that sweeps all before it, a product that becomes the market leader. The other tip Taleb offers is to have patience:

> *"[E]arthquakes last minutes, 9/11 lasted hours, but historical changes and technological implementations are Black Swans that can take decades. In general, positive Black Swans take time to show their effect while negative ones happen very quickly."*

Building a great enterprise will occupy many years, and though we can never know what the future holds, the long view allows us to take obstacles and reversals in our stride.

The Black Swan itself is a microcosm of Taleb's argument about complexity: it has almost too much information, too many startling challenges to our thinking, to be susceptible to a neat summary. It is best to read it yourself, if only for the many entertaining digressions and examples that there is no room for here. Summarization takes out the possibility of random discovery, and it is such discoveries that make all the difference in our life and career.

Taleb is famed for having predicted, in the original edition of the book, the 2008 financial crisis, when he wrote about the fragility of the large banks, suggesting that if one collapsed they could all go, as they were so entwined with each other. In the second edition (2010) he elaborates on this concept of fragility, noting that few lessons have been learned. His critique of mega-sized companies and institutions is that they can get away with much more than smaller ones, and so their risks tend to be hidden. This makes them more, not less, vulnerable to black swan events.

Nassim Nicholas Taleb

Taleb was born in Amioun, Lebanon, in 1960. His parents had French citizenship and he attended a French school. During the Lebanese Civil War, which began in 1975, he studied for several years in the basement of his home.

A former derivatives trader turned mathematical analyst specializing in problems of probability and uncertainty, he held positions with major banks such as Credit Suisse First Boston, UBS, and BNP-Paribas. Taleb is currently Distinguished Professor of Risk Engineering at New York University's Polytechnic Institute and is also a consultant to Universa, a hedge fund, and the IMF. His degrees include an MBA from the Wharton School, University of Pennsylvania, and a PhD from the University of Paris.

Other books include Fooled by Randomness *(2001),* Dynamic Hedging *(1997),* The Bed of Procrustes *(2010), and* Antifragile: Things That Gain from Disorder *(2012).*

Philosophical Investigations

"For naming and describing do not stand on the same level: naming is a preparation for description. Naming is so far not a move in the language-game – any more than putting a piece in its place on the board is a move in chess."

"Does one say, for example: 'I didn't really mean my pain just now; my mind wasn't on it enough for that?' Do I ask myself, say: 'What did I mean by this word just now? My attention was divided between my pain and the noise –'?"

"Philosophy is the struggle against the bewitchment of our minds by means of language."

In a nutshell

Language is about meaning, not words. Yet language cannot express every kind of meaning.

In a similar vein

A.J. Ayer *Language, Truth and Logic* (p 34)
Saul Kripke *Naming and Necessity* (p 158)
Bertrand Russell *The Conquest of Happiness* (p 258)

CHAPTER 50

Ludwig Wittgenstein

When his sister Hermine visited Ludwig Wittgenstein at Cambridge University in 1912, Bertrand Russell said to her, "We expect the next big step in philosophy to be taken by your brother," who was only 23.

Ten years later, Wittgenstein's *Tractatus Logico-Philosophicus* was published in a parallel German–English edition, with an introduction by Russell. Written in seclusion in a log cabin in Norway, its key sentence is: "The limits of my language means the limits of my world." Language should simply try to express pictures of facts; everything else, including talk of abstract concepts, values, philosophy, and so on, is meaningless. The *Tractatus* described Wittgenstein's doctrinaire phase, and is famously summed up in the statement "what we cannot speak about we must be silent about."

With the completion of the *Tractatus*, Wittgenstein believed that he had brought an end to philosophy and he left the academic world. He gave away all his money to his siblings (he was the eighth child in a wealthy Viennese family), worked as a primary schoolteacher in a mountain village, gardened in a monastery, and designed a house for his sister (to incredibly exacting measurements). In 1929, though, he returned to Cambridge University as a research fellow, later becoming professor of philosophy.

Philosophical Investigations was published after his death. As he notes in a preface, it is made up of remarks, statements, and thoughts that often seem to jump from one matter to another. He had wanted to weave it into a more flowing work, but decided that giving the book a direction would make it artificial. Consisting mostly of thought experiments and word games, it is an easier read than the *Tractatus*, and does not attempt the earlier book's exactitude. But with both, it is what Wittgenstein leaves unsaid (purposely) that is almost more important than the text itself.

What is language?

Simple language is not about explanation, Wittgenstein says, it is solely a pointer to things. Thus, when a toddler is beginning to speak, it is a matter of training her to know the names of objects. No explanation of language itself is required. "Uttering a word is like striking a note on the keyboard of the imagination," he writes, in which each "note" or word conjures up a picture.

Since the meaning of words in relation to things differs according to the context, time, and place in which they are spoken, Wittgenstein does not describe language in terms of a set of abstract rules. Rather, it is a "game." As children we move from words almost literally "being" things (e.g., the word chair comes to mean chair in our minds) to an understanding that words signify things, with use of more abstract words like "this" and "there." Then, we start to think in terms of categories. In this way, Wittgenstein says, language grows:

"Our language can be seen as an ancient city: a maze of little streets and squares, of old and new houses, and of houses with additions from various periods; and this surrounded by a multitude of new boroughs with straight regular streets and uniform houses."

Wittgenstein attempts to show the sheer variety of language games. These include giving and obeying orders; describing the appearance of an object or giving its measurements; reporting or speculating about an event; forming and testing a hypothesis; presenting the results of an experiment in tables; making up a story and reading it; play acting; singing catches; guessing riddles; making and telling jokes; solving a problem in arithmetic; translating from one language into another; and "asking, thanking, cursing, greeting, praying." He observes:

"It is interesting to compare the multiplicity of the tools in language and of the ways they are used, the multiplicity of kinds of word and sentence, with what logicians have said about the structure of language. (Including the author of the Tractatus Logico-Philosophicus.)"

Here Wittgenstein is admitting that he was wrong about language as a means of describing the world; it is much more. Words do not simply name things, they often convey elaborate meaning, and many different meanings from the same word. He mentions exclamations like Water! Ow! Help! Fine! and No! and asks: Can you really say that these words are simply "names of objects"?

Language, then, is not a formal logic that marks the limits of our world, as he had once said; it is a free-flowing, creative means for *making* our world. The depth and variety of our language making are what separate us from other animals; "Commanding, questioning, recounting, chatting, are as much a part of our natural history as walking, eating, drinking, playing."

The actual words spoken often mean less than the *way* they are spoken and the line of speech as a whole. When we ask someone to bring us a broom, we do not phrase it in terms of "Please bring me a stick with a brush attached to it." Language does not break things into logical pieces, but, if anything, works to make the representation of actual objects unimportant next to their intended use. If we ask someone to bring us a broom, it can be another way of saying that we are about to do some sweeping, and the other person may instantly understand this. A word does not exist on its own, but is part of a "family of meanings." Wittgenstein goes to great lengths, for instance, to identify what we mean when we say the word "game." He exhausts all the possible kinds of games (board games, sports, a child playing, and so on) and is unable to say exactly what a game is and what it is not. And yet we all *know* what a game is. Again, this should tell us that definitions do not matter next to meaning; to put it another way, language does *not* dictate the limits of our world. It has no hard-and-fast rules, no objective logic, as philosophers had hoped to identify. Language is a social construction, a game where the order of play is loose and evolves as we go along.

Naming things, Wittgenstein says, is an "occult process" that philosophers take to extremes. They make connections between names and objects just by willing the connection to exist. Philosophical problems arise when philosophers see the naming of some idea or concept as a "baptism," an important moment, when in fact contextual meaning is what matters, not names. Genuine philosophy, he famously says, is a constant battle against the "bewitchment" of the discipline by language itself.

Private language

Wittgenstein raises the question of "private language," or the words or meanings that we give to ourselves to describe certain inner states or sensations. These private meanings are not really a language, because a language requires some external, social setting in which its meaning can be confirmed. He imagines several people each of whom has a box, inside which they have something that everyone is going to call a "beetle." But what if what is in the boxes is totally different in each case? This shows us that the names of things, if they are made privately, are not really names at all, since names require common assent as to their meaning. By implication, thoughts only have validity if they can be expressed and understood. "An 'inner process,'" he remarks, "stands in need of outward criteria."

Another famous line in the book is: "If a lion could talk, we could not understand him." Language depends on common assent to its meaning, and animals naturally have a wholly different order of meaning. A lion, for instance, sees someone walking through the savannah not as a "person," but as a potential source of food. Without agreeing on what things mean, how could we have a conversation with a lion, even assuming it could talk? Wittgenstein applies the idea to entering a foreign country. Aside from any language barriers, we may feel no kinship with the people simply because their way of seeing the world is totally different to ours. We feel that they do not "speak our language" – that is, our language of meaning, not actual words.

Imponderable evidence

The problem with psychology as a discipline, Wittgenstein says, is that it is trying to study humans in terms of evidence, yet so much of our knowledge of what makes people tick is based on "imponderable" information. We are able to perceive the subtleties of others' inner states, but we cannot say exactly how we come to have this knowledge:

> *"Imponderable evidence includes subtleties of glance, of gesture, of tone.*
>
> *I may recognize a genuine loving look, distinguish it from a pretended one (and here there can, of course, be a 'ponderable' confirmation of my judgment). But I may be quite incapable of describing the difference. And this not because the languages I know have no words for it.*
>
> *Ask yourself: How does a man learn to get a 'nose' for something? And how can this nose be used?"*

Knowing what moves someone else is not a matter of hooking them up to a machine and testing their physiological or brain states; it involves a *judgment*, and it is possible to learn such knowledge, Wittgenstein says, only through life experience, not by "taking a course in it." If psychology has rules, they are not part of a system that can be studied, because we cannot put such indefiniteness into words.

Final comments

Wittgenstein did not try to deny that we have inner lives, only that they could not be spoken of sensibly. Even though the "language game" is of extraordinary depth and complexity, there are areas of experience that can never be expressed properly in language, and it is wrong to try to do so.

Wittgenstein was strongly influenced by William James's *The Varieties of Religious Experience*, the philosophical Christianity of Kierkegaard, and the writings of Augustine; despite his largely Jewish ancestry, he was brought up a Catholic and during his war years could not be separated from his Bible.

He loved visiting churches and cathedrals, and told his Cambridge friend M. O'C. Drury that "all religions are wonderful." But was he actually a believer, or did he simply like the trappings of spirituality? If we follow Wittgenstein's own thinking it does not matter either way, or at least a discussion of it has no meaning, since one cannot pinpoint a person's inner states. What does matter is how one expresses oneself. In a memoir, Drury reported him as saying: "If you and I are to live religious lives it must not just be that we talk a lot about religion, but that in some way our lives are different."

In an account of her brother, Hermine fully admitted his extreme prickliness, social awkwardness, and sensitivity, but also spoke of his "big heart." His Russian teacher, Fania Pascal, described him in similar terms, but also noted his unusual "wholeness" and certainty about his views; someone good to have around in a crisis, but not forgiving of everyday human worries and foibles.

Such memoirs draw a picture of a man largely uninterested in himself, or *the* self, and instead suggest a focus on being *of use*, in a world where things might "work well." When Drury had doubts about his training as a doctor, Wittgenstein told him not to think of himself, only of the good he could do. What a privilege, he pointed out, to be the last one to say goodnight to patients at the end of the day! Though important to him, Wittgenstein saw his work as just another "game"; language and philosophizing were nothing next to life itself.

Ludwig Wittgenstein

Born in 1889 into an illustrious and cultured Viennese family (his sister Margaret was painted by Gustav Klimt), Wittgenstein was educated at home, only attending school for the final three years. In his teens he went to Berlin to study mechanical engineering, then to Manchester where he did research into aeronautics. While in England he read Bertrand Russell's The Principles of Mathematics, *which changed his course toward logic and philosophy.*

He moved to Cambridge in 1911 and when war broke out enlisted in the Austrian army; by choice he made his way to the front line, receiving medals for bravery, but became a prisoner of war in Italy. In the prison camp he wrote the Tractatus, *but it was not published in English until 1922.*

Between 1920 and 1926 Wittgenstein had no university affiliation. The school where he taught was in Trattenbach, a tiny Austrian mountain village. The house he designed in the Kundmanngasse, Vienna, is now a museum.

He returned to Cambridge in 1929 as a research fellow, and was later awarded a professorship at Trinity College despite lacking a higher degree. He died in Cambridge in 1951.

50 More Philosophy Classics

1. **Jane Addams** *Democracy and Social Ethics* **(1902)**
    Addams' work with America's down-and-out expressed the pragmatism of William James and John Dewey in practice. Her philosophy, particularly "sympathetic knowledge" (which helps to bridge social barriers), is now seen as valuable in its own right.

2. **Theodore Adorno** *Minima Moralia: Reflections from Damaged Life* **(1951)**
    A dense critique of modern capitalism and the possibilities for freedom by a leading light of the Frankfurt School of critical theory, inspired by Hegel, Marx, Kierkegaard, Nietzsche, and Freud.

3. **Elizabeth Anscombe** *Intention* **(1957)**
    Wittgenstein's student and translator famously demolished C.S. Lewis's proofs for the existence of God, but in her masterwork Anscombe laid the foundations for "action theory." To what extent are our actions the product of desires or beliefs, or both?

4. **Augustine** *City of God* **(426)**
    A big influence on the West through the Middle Ages, this draws a distinction between the ideal heavenly city, on which humanity must set their eyes, and earthly preoccupations, which can only end badly. Written not long after the sack of Rome by the Visigoths.

5. **Marcus Aurelius** *Meditations* **(2nd century AD)**
    The Roman Emperor's timeless expression of Stoic philosophy, still widely read and enjoyed.

6. **Averroes** *The Incoherence of the Incoherence* **(12th century AD)**
    This Arabian philosopher's justification of the use of Aristotlean thought in Islamic philosophy; the title is a rejoinder to Al-Ghazali's *The Incoherence of the Philosophers*.

7. **Francis Bacon** *Essays* **(1597)**
    Originally written as a diversion from Bacon's main scientific and theological works, the *Essays* are his most-read work today. Fascinating thoughts from the founder of empiricism and the scientific method.

8. **Alain Badiou** *Being and Event* (1987)
   "Multiplicity," not individuality, explains the nature of our being. An important text of French poststructuralism.

9. **Henri Bergson** *Creative Evolution* (1911)
   In contrast to the pessimism and determinist outlook of most twentieth century philosophers, Bergson emphasized creativity, free will, and joy in existence. We want to see the universe in mechanistic and determined terms, but in reality (because it involves life and time), the universe is in fact fluid and constantly open to possibility.

10. **Roland Barthes** *Writing Degree Zero* (1953)
    The way something is written is as important as the content. A major work of the structuralist school.

11. **George Berkeley** *Treatise Concerning the Principles of Human Knowledge* (1710)
    Containing the Anglo-Irish bishop's remarkable contention that the world is essentially made up of ideas, not things. While we can never be sure what the "real" world is like (matter is an abstraction), the world of ideas in our mind is certainly real enough, and things only have reality to the extent that they are perceived ("To be is to be perceived"). We should trust that the pattern of our experience makes sense, since it is divinely ordered.

12. **Boethius** *The Consolation of Philosophy* (6th century AD)
    After the Bible, the most influential work of the Christian Middle Ages, written while Boethius was on death row. Provides an elegant rationale for the goodness of God in a turbulent and often evil world.

13. **Martin Buber** *I and Thou* (1923)
    Buber left his orthodox Jewish upbringing to study Western philosophy. This famous essay made the distinction between two modes of being: "I-It" (our experience of objects experienced through the senses) and "I-Thou" (experience of being through relationships). The meaning of life is found in our relationships.

14. **Gaytri Chakravorty Spivak** *Can The Subaltern Speak?* (1988)
    This classic essay in postcolonial studies by the Indian scholar and Derrida translator argues that the poorest people in developing countries have, in addition to their lack of economic agency, no voice or platform. Eurocentric intellectuals cannot speak for them.

15. **Gilles Deleuze & Felix Guitarri** *Anti-Oedipus* (1972)
    How private desires come into conflict with social frameworks, drawing on psychoanalysis and Marxist thought.

16. **Jacques Derrida** *Of Grammatology* (1967)
Outlining the famously difficult theory of "traces" in linguistics; also Derrida's most accessible work.

17. **John Dewey** *How We Think* (1910)
The great American pragmatist and educational theorist addresses more effective thinking. After 100 years, still many great insights.

18. **Jacques Ellul** *Propaganda: The Formation of Men's Attitudes* (1973)
Never more relevant, French Christian anarchist Ellul explains how propaganda goes beyond politics to be about making the individual serve and conform. One of his insights is that those people who consume the most media are the most propagandized.

19. **Paul Feyerabend** *Against Method* (1975)
The work that made Feyerabend almost as influential as Popper and Kuhn in the philosophy of science. Makes the case for an "anarchist" approach to science that does not privilege it with a rationality outside of culture or society. Science is, rather, an ideology like any other.

20. **J.G. Fichte** *Foundations of Natural Right* (1797)
The philosophy of personal freedom and its implications for political organization and rights.

21. **Gottlob Frege** *The Foundations of Arithmetic* (1894)
A fascinating foray into the concept of "number" in civilization, which was dismissed while Frege was alive but has grown in importance. Rather than being a boring treatise on mathematics, it shows how the number is a way in to philosophical truth and meaning.

22. **Antonio Gramsci** *The Prison Notebooks* (1929–35)
One of the leading twentieth-century Marxist thinkers, Gramsci's big insight was into "hegemony," or how states maintain themselves. A group does not take but *becomes* the state, he said.

23. **Jurgen Habermas** *The Structural Transformation of the Public Sphere* (1962)
During the eighteenth century in Europe a new "public sphere" emerged from the need of civil society for information. According to Habermas it led to the flourishing of reason, but was later corrupted by commerciality and consumerization.

24. **Heraclitus** *Fragments* (Sixth century BC)
Although this collection of sayings and statements covers the nature of the physical universe, ethics, and politics, it is Heraclitus' metaphysical ideas that still resonate. Specifically, that everything changes all the time, yet there is a hidden harmony to the universe.

25. **Thomas Hobbes** *Leviathan* **(1651)**
Arguably the first book of modern political philosophy, set against the fading out of medieval Christendom. Advocates a secular state with absolute power exercised by a sovereign. Within such a system, the common person had the best chance of stability and security.

26. **Edmund Husserl** *Logical Investigations* **(1900–01)**
Major work of the mentor to Heidegger and founder of phenomenology.

27. **Julia Kristeva** *Desire in Language: A Semiotic Approach to Literature and Art* **(1980)**
A key work in cultural theory, with striking analyses of nineteenth-century French fiction.

28. **Jacques Lacan** *Ecrits: A Selection* **(2002)**
An excellent introduction to Lacan's psychoanalytical philosophy, very influential for contemporary thinkers such as Žižek.

29. **David Lewis** *On the Plurality of Worlds* **(1982)**
An original and influential work of "modal logic," laying out the theory that many worlds can exist simultaneously.

30. **Jean-François Lyotard** *The Postmodern Condition* **(1979)**
Perhaps the major statement on postmodernism, which Lyotard describes as "incredulity towards meta-narratives" such as the concept of "Progress."

31. **Maimonides** *Guide for the Perplexed* **(1190)**
A masterful attempt to bridge Judaism and Greek philosophy, influential in both East and West throughout the Middle Ages.

32. **Nicolas Malebranche** *Search after Truth* **(1674–75)**
Inspired by Descartes, the first and most comprehensive work of a key rationalist philosopher.

33. **Herbert Marcuse** *Eros and Civilisation* **(1955)**
A synthesis of Freud and Marx, providing a vision of a society free from repression.

34. **Karl Marx** *Capital* **(1867)**
The work of political philosophy that has arguably had the greatest impact on history.

35. **Maurice Merleau-Ponty** *Phenomenology of Perception* **(1945)**
We experience the world not along the lines of Descartes' *cogito*, but through the body.

36. **Montesquieu** *The Spirit of the Laws* **(1748)**
A major work of liberal political philosophy that influenced the French Revolution, advocating constitutional government, the separation of powers, and an end to slavery.

37. **G.E. Moore** *Principia Ethica* **(1903)**
Revolutionized the philosophy of ethics and introduced the famous concept of the "naturalistic fallacy," which says that it is impossible to determine in a technical sense what is "The Good" – something intuitively felt and known. Moore was also an advocate of "commonsense" philosophy that does not negate the beliefs of ordinary people.

38. **Robert Nozick** *Anarchy, State and Utopia* **(1974)**
A well-reasoned defense of a limited state, "limited to the narrow functions of protection against force, theft, fraud, enforcement of contracts, and so on." Every person has the right to pursue their own "projects," and such rights are violated when states reach into all aspects of life.

39. **Derek Parfit** *Reasons and Persons* **(1984)**
Oxford moral philosopher's compelling foray into the meaning of personal identity across a lifetime, and its implications for action, ethics, and justice. A seminal work in the "philosophy of the self," which has been invigorated by recent findings in neuroscience.

40. **Parmenides** *On Nature* **(early 5th century AD)**
Behind apparent change, the universe has an unchanging unified order. When you feel disoriented by the whirl of events in your life, take a break and seek solace by grounding yourself in this central source.

41. **Hilary Putnam** *The Collapse of the Fact/Value Dichotomy and Other Essays* **(2002)**
The separation between empirical facts and human values has been the foundation of much of philosophy, but Putnam argues that it is ill conceived; philosophy should be looked at anew.

42. **Willard van Orman Quine** *Word and Object* **(1960)**
Lays out the Harvard philosopher's idea of "indeterminacy of translation," by which a language translation can fulfill certain requirements without necessarily reflecting what is actually meant; no unique meaning can be given to words and sentences.

43. **Richard Rorty** *Philosophy and the Mirror of Nature* **(1979)**
An American philosopher who became disillusioned with analytical philosophy's relentless and often pointless search for objective truth,

instead gravitating toward the pragmatism of William James and Dewey. This stance led to considerable attack from academic philosophers.

44. **Bertrand Russell & Alfred North Whitehead** *Principia Mathematica* **(1910–13)**
A major twentieth-century work in any field, its three volumes sought to formalize mathematical logic.

45. **Gilbert Ryle** *The Concept of Mind* **(1949)**
Oxford professor's destruction of Descartes' mind/matter dichotomy, dismissing it as a "category mistake" and "the dogma of the ghost in the machine."

46. **George Santayana** *The Life of Reason, or the Phases of Human Progress* **(1905–06)**
A popular five-volume work of moral philosophy by the Spanish-born American, containing the famous line, "Those who cannot remember the past are condemned to repeat it."

47. **Seneca** *Letters* **(1st century AD)**
Only in the twentieth century was Seneca "rediscovered," and his letters are a treasure trove expressing his Stoic philosophy through the events of a busy political life.

48. **Sextus Empiricus** *Outlines of Pyrrhonism* **(3rd century AD)**
Foundational work of skeptical empiricism; most of what was later put forward on the subject of doubt by the existentialists and phenomenologists had already been uttered by Sextus.

49. **Xenephon** *Conversations of Socrates* **(4th century BC)**
Xenephon was a friend and follower of Socrates. This work is one of the best introductions to his thinking.

50. **Slavoj Žižek** *Living In The End Times* **(2010)**
A "sort of communist" who loves the writings of Ayn Rand, Slovenian philosopher Žižek argues that capitalism has become an ideology that allows no alternatives. Yet it's ill-equipped to face major environmental and social problems.

Glossary

Analytical philosophy A philosophical school based around precision in language, statements, and concepts.

Behaviorism A psychological theory stating that organisms are the product of their conditioning or their environment.

Continental philosophy The array of European philosophical traditions including German idealism, phenomenology, existentialism, structuralism, postmodernism, and cultural theory, as distinguished from the Anglo-Saxon tradition of analytical and empirical philosophy.

Deductive reasoning A movement of thought that begins with general observations and proceeds toward specific truths, e.g., a theory leads to a hypothesis, which is then tested or observed, then confirmed.

Empiricism A way of finding what is true or correct based on data that anyone can refute or validate using their own senses.

Enlightenment An intellectual movement in eighteenth-century Europe that emphasized reason and science in the advancement of knowledge instead of faith, revelation, and tradition.

Epicureanism A philosophical school based on the teachings of Epicurus, including the belief that life's highest good is pleasure (or being free from disturbance and pain); the word later came to mean leading a life of sensual pleasure and luxury.

Epistemology The theory and philosophy of knowledge; what we can know, and what we can validate as true.

Existentialism A philosophical outlook or spirit that centers on the question of living. Emphasizing freedom and choice, it is often associated with the view that a person's existence has no preordained reason or purpose, but must be created over a lifetime.

Idealism Any philosophy concerned with abstract or spiritual truth, as opposed to knowledge gained only through the senses.

Inductive reasoning Thinking that proceeds from data or observations toward principles or hypotheses. The opposite of deductive reasoning.

Materialism Existence or reality can be explained solely in material terms. There is no role for spirit or consciousness.

GLOSSARY

Metaphysics Philosophies concerned with the essential property or nature of things, whether physical or nonphysical, material or spiritual.

Naturalism The belief that the universe runs according to physical laws and that there is no reality beyond the physical universe.

Ontology The philosophy of being, including its various aspects and levels.

Paradigm A particular mindset, outlook, or pattern of thinking, which exists for a time to solve a problem of its users.

Phenomenal (world) The world as it appears through the five senses, the "real" world.

Phenomenology Developed by Edmund Husserl, the study of things being made manifest or appearing, usually consciousness.

Postmodernism An outlook arising in the late twentieth century based on awareness of "metanarratives," or the unarticulated assumptions that shape culture and society (e.g., the idea of "progress").

Poststructuralism A twentieth-century movement that refutes the idea of the authority of the text, instead emphasizing multiple interpretations of cultural material. What matters is not the author's intended message, but how it is used. The concept of objective truth becomes irrelevant.

Pragmatism An approach to philosophy that focuses on the end value of statements or theories; that is, whether they "work" in terms of providing actual benefit to the users, believers, or practitioners.

Rationalism Truth or knowledge arrived at through reason or thought, as opposed to direct observation of nature or things.

Stoicism A school of ancient Greek philosophy that emphasized equanimity in the face of life's ups and downs, virtue, and aligning one's actions with fate or universal will.

Structuralism Originating in France, the view that human beings can only be understood in the context of social structures and institutions.

Teleology Any kind of philosophy or theory that posits a purpose, design, or "final cause" to the world's workings.

Utilitarianism A philosophy and path of action that is aimed at achieving the greatest happiness or welfare of the greatest number of people.

Credits

Most of the great works of philosophy have had multiple translations and/or publishers. The list below is therefore not definitive, but is rather a guide to the versions used in researching this book. Many of the works are now in the public domain and are freely available online.

Aquinas, T. (2000) *Summa Theologica*, Notre Dame, Indiana: Ave Maria Press.

Arendt, H. (1998) *The Human Condition*, Chicago, IL: University of Chicago Press.

Aristotle (2002) "Nicomachean Ethics," in S.N. Cahn (ed.), *Classics of Western Philosophy*, 6th edn, Indianapolis, IN: Hackett.

Ayer, A.J. (1982) *Language, Truth and Logic*, London: Pelican.

Baudrillard, J. (1995) *Simulacra and Simulation*, trans. Sheila Faria Glaser, Ann Arbor, MI: University of Michigan Press.

de Beauvoir, S. (1989) *The Second Sex*, trans. H.M. Parshley, New York: Vintage.

Bentham, J. (1879) *An Introduction to the Principles of Morals and Legislation*, Oxford: Oxford University Press.

Berlin, I. (1957) *The Hedgehog and the Fox: An Essay on Tolstoy's View of History*, New York: New American Library.

Bohm, D. (1980) *Wholeness and the Implicate Order*, London: Routledge.

Butler, J. (1990) *Gender Trouble: Feminism and the Subversion of Identity*, New York & London: Routledge.

Chomsky, N. (2002) *Understanding Power: The Indispensable Chomsky*, ed. Peter Rounds Mitchell & John Schoeffel, New York: New Press.

Cicero, M.T. (1913) *De Officiis* (Loeb edition), trans. Walter Miller, Cambridge, MA: Harvard University Press. http://www.constitution.org/ rom/de_officiis.htm

Confucius (n.d.) *Analects*. http://classics.mit.edu/Confucius/analects.html

Descartes, R. (1985) *Discourse on Method and the Meditations*, trans. F.E. Sutcliffe, London: Penguin.

Emerson, R.W. (n.d.) "Fate," in *The Online Works of Ralph Waldo Emerson*. http://user. xmission.com/~seldom74/emerson/fate.html

Epicurus (1993) *Essential Epicurus: Letters, Principle Doctrines, Vatican Sayings and Fragments*, trans. and intro. Eugene O'Connor, Amherst, NY: Prometheus.

Foucault, M. (2005) *The Order of Things: Archaeology of the Human Sciences*, London: Routledge.

Frankfurt, H. (2005) *On Bullshit*, Princeton, NJ: Princeton University Press.

Hegel, G.W.F. (1977) *Phenomenology of Spirit*, trans. A.V. Miller, Oxford: Oxford University Press.

Heidegger, M. (1962) *Being and Time*, trans. John Macquarie & Edward Robinson, London: SCM Press.

Hume, D. (1993) *An Enquiry Concerning Human Understanding*, Indianapolis, IN: Hackett.

James, W. (2004) *Pragmatism: A New Name for Some Old Ways of Thinking*, Project Gutenberg, http://www.gutenberg.org/ebooks/5116

Kant, I. (1998) *Critique of Pure Reason*, trans. Paul Guyer & Allen W. Wood, Cambridge: Cambridge University Press.

Kierkegaard, S. (2005) *Fear and Trembling*, trans. Alastair Hannay, London: Penguin.

Kripke, S. (1980) *Naming and Necessity*, Cambridge, MA: Harvard University Press.

Kuhn, T. (1962) *The Structure of Scientific Revolutions*, Chicago, IL: University of Chicago Press.

Leibniz, G. (2005) *Theodicy: Essays on the Goodness of God, the Freedom of Man and the Origin of Evil*, trans. E.M. Huggard, Project Gutenberg, http://www.gutenberg.org/ebooks/17147

Locke, J. (2004) *An Essay Concerning Human Understanding*, Project Gutenberg, http://www.gutenberg.org/ebooks/10615

Machiavelli, N. (1910) *The Prince*, trans. Ninian Hill Thomson, WikiSource, http://en.wikisource.org/wiki/The_Prince_%28Hill_Thomson%29

McLuhan, M. & Fiore, Q. (1967) *The Medium Is the Massage*, coordinated by Jerome Agel, London: Bantam.

Midgley, M. (2004) *The Myths We Live By*, New York & London: Routledge.

Mill, J.S. (1909) *On Liberty*, University of Adelaide e-books, http://ebooks.adelaide.edu.au/m/mill/john_stuart/m645o/

Montaigne, M. (1967) *Essays*, trans. J.M. Cohen, London: Penguin.

Murdoch, I. (1970) *The Sovereignty of Good*, London: Routledge.

Nietzsche, F. (1997) *Beyond Good and Evil: Prelude to a Philosophy of the Future*, trans. Helen Zimmern, New York: Dover.

Pascal, B. (2005) *Pensées*, ed. and trans. Roger Ariew, Indianapolis, IN: Hackett.

Plato (2008) *The Republic*, trans. Benjamin Jowett, Project Gutenberg, http://www.gutenberg.org/files/1497/1497-h/1497-h.htm

Plotinus, (1991) *Enneads*, trans. by Stephen MacKenna, London: Penguin.

Popper, K. (2002) *The Logic of Scientific Discovery*, London: Routledge.

Rawls, J. (1973) *A Theory of Justice*, Oxford: Oxford University Press.

Rousseau, J.-J. (1979) *The Social Contract*, trans. Maurice Cranston, London: Penguin.

Russell, B. (1993) *The Conquest of Happiness*, London: Routledge.

Sandel, M. (2020) *The Tyranny of Merit: What's Become of the Common Good?*, London: Penguin.

Sartre, J.-P. (1957) *Being and Nothingness: An Essay on Phenomenological Ontology*, trans. Hazel E. Barnes, London: Methuen.

Schopenhauer, A. (1958) *The World as Will and Representation*, vols. 1 & 2, trans. E.F.J. Payne, Indian Hills, CO: Falcon's Wing Press.

Singer, P. (2009) *The Life You Can Save: Acting Now to End World Poverty*, Melbourne: Text.

Sloterdijk, P. (2013) *You Must Change Your Life: On Anthropotechnics*, trans. Weiland Hoban, Cambridge: Polity Press.

Spinoza, B. (2012) *The Ethics*, trans. R.H.M. Elwes, University of Adelaide e-books, http://ebooks.adelaide.edu.au/s/spinoza/benedict/ethics/

Taleb, N.N. (2007) *The Black Swan: The Impact of the Highly Improbable*, London: Penguin.

Wittgenstein, L. (1992) *Philosophical Investigations*, trans. G.E.M. Anscombe, Oxford: Blackwell.

Acknowledgments

50 Philosophy Classics is dedicated to my mother, Marion Butler-Bowdon, who died in November 2012. Her great love and knowledge of literature were a real influence on me and my siblings. She was looking forward to this book being published, and we had quite a few chats about the philosophers I was covering. It is general readers like her for whom the book is written.

Thanks also to:

Nicholas Brealey, who was keen on the book from the start. I baulked because of the size of the project, but am very glad we persevered.

Sally Lansdell, for editing and incorporating my many changes to get it right; and agent Sally Holloway for sorting out the terms of publication.

The Bodleian Library in Oxford. Most of the philosophy classics are on open shelves, and I was lucky to spend many days working there.

The living philosophers included in the book, for their great contributions.

All who gave advice on what should be included in the list of 50, and the researchers who helped on a handful of the biographies and commentaries.

Cherry, Tamara, and Beatrice. Your love and support provided the necessary peace of mind and time for the book to be written – thank you.

Finally, deep gratitude to the many loyal readers of the 50 Classics series over the years. This volume may take you in directions you never intended, but I hope you enjoy it anyway.

50 ECONOMICS CLASSICS

*Your shortcut to the most
important ideas on capital,
finance, and the global economy*

Tom Butler-Bowdon

Economics drives the modern world and shapes our lives, but few of us feel we have time to engage with the breadth of ideas in the subject. *50 Economics Classics* is the smart person's guide to two centuries of discussion of finance, capitalism and the global economy. From Adam Smith's *Wealth of Nations* to Thomas Piketty's bestseller *Capital in the Twenty-First Century*, here are the great reads, seminal ideas and famous texts - clarified and illuminated for all.

"The synopses in this book are fair, balanced, and about as good an introduction to the broad range of modern economic writing, along with a few classics, as one is likely to find."

Professor James K Galbraith, University of Texas, author of *Inequality: What Everyone Needs to Know*

"A good starting point for someone new to economics wanting a general overview. Capturing the essence of a book in 3 pages is a difficult task. Tom Butler-Bowdon is a very well-read person with this rare skill."

Diane Coyle, author of *GDP: A brief but affectionate history*

Trade paperback 978-1-39980-099-0 (2022)
336pp 216x135mm

50 PSYCHOLOGY CLASSICS
SECOND EDITION

Your shortcut to the most important ideas on the mind, personality, and human nature

Tom Butler-Bowdon

In a journey spanning 50 books, hundreds of ideas and over a century, *50 Psychology Classics* looks at some of the most intriguing questions relating to what motivates us, what makes us feel and act in certain ways, how our brains work, and how we create a sense of self. This brand new edition includes new classics like *Thinking, Fast and Slow; Quiet* and *The Marshmallow Test*.

50 Psychology Classics explores writings from some iconic figures such as Freud, Adler, Jung, Skinner, James, Piaget and Pavlov, but also highlights the work of contemporary thinkers such as Gardner, Gilbert, Goleman and Seligman. *50 Psychology Classics* will further your understanding of human nature and yourself.

> "At long last a chance for those outside the profession to discover that there is so much more to psychology than just Freud and Jung. *50 Psychology Classics* offers a unique opportunity to become acquainted with a dazzling array of the key works in psychological literature almost overnight."

Dr Raj Persaud, Gresham Professor
for Public Understanding of Psychiatry

> "This delightful book provides thoughtful and entertaining summaries of 50 of the most influential books in psychology. It's a 'must-read' for students contemplating a career in psychology."

VS Ramachandran, Director, Center for Brain and Cognition,
University of California, San Diego

Trade paperback 978-1-85788-674-0
320pp 216x135mm

50 POLITICS CLASSICS

Your shortcut to the most important ideas on freedom, equality, and power

Tom Butler-Bowdon

From Abraham Lincoln to Nelson Mandela, and from Aristotle to George Orwell, *50 Politics Classics* distills the essence of the books, pamphlets, and speeches of the major leaders and great thinkers that drive real-world change.

Spanning 2,500 years, left and right, thinkers and doers, Tom Butler-Bowdon covers activists, war strategists, visionary leaders, economists, philosophers of freedom, feminists, conservatives and environmentalists, right up to contemporary classics such as *A Promised Land* and *Caste*. Whether you consider yourself to be conservative, liberal, socialist, or Marxist, this book gives you greater understanding of the key ideas that matter in our politically charged times.

"A refreshing tour of political thought unmoored by traditional chronological organization."

Library Journal

Trade paperback 978-1-39980-098-3 (2022)
336pp 216x135mm

WWW.BUTLER-BOWDON.COM